Praise for *Global Class*

Top Global Executives

"Aaron and Klaus have literally written the book on international go-to-market. Their observations and rubrics are very powerful for our business. This is the book I wish I had fifteen years ago!"
—Abe Smith, Head of International, Zoom

"Trust is the number-one value when expanding your business internationally. It goes hand in hand with customer success. *Global Class* is a blueprint for how to achieve both and have YOUR business be a platform (catalyst) for change in every market and community you enter and embrace."
—Polly Sumner, Chief Adoption Officer, Salesforce

"Aaron and Klaus provide structure, process, and clarity where there once was only mystery and complexity—*Global Class* is the perfect guidebook for navigating the challenges of global expansion."
—John Brandon, former Vice President of International, Apple

"*Global Class* helps solve the puzzle for how to globalize and expand internationally in today's competitive and dynamic business environment."
—Elise Rubin, Global Head of Program Management,
Internationalization & Product Launch, Google Nest

"*Global Class* has built a vocabulary for business leaders like myself to effectively get organizational alignment around international growth initiatives."
—Troy Malone, Vice President of International Operations, Drata
(former GM of International Expansion, Evernote)

"Localizing a business is challenging. Through *Global Class*, Aaron and Klaus cracked the code on how to do it by showcasing some of the world's best success stories and focusing on important factors like language and culture, something that, as a computational linguist, I have seen is crucial to success at global scale."
—Kathryn Hymes, former Head of International Product Expansion, Slack

"Building a global business takes focus and hard work. Insights from *Global Class* will help you with the goals and strategies to expand internationally."
—Scott Coleman, former Head of Growth & International Product, Pinterest

"People are the backbone of every organization and the Interpreneur concept perfectly captures the type of talent we look for at Patreon. *Global Class* offers practical frameworks and a new way to look at building an international business that can help any type of company build a best-in-class global team."
—Tiffany Stevenson, Chief People Officer, Patreon

"At Euromonitor, we are in the business of shaping the world of tomorrow for our clients. The ideas and frameworks in *Global Class* reconfirmed some of our best practices and allowed us to challenge ourselves in areas we're still striving to improve as a business."
—Tim Kitchin, CEO, Euromonitor International

"To succeed as a global business in today's ultracompetitive environment, you have to act fast and hyperscale. In *Global Class*, Aaron and Klaus show you how to create the speed and momentum needed to succeed in that environment."
—Emil Michael, former Chief Business Officer, Uber

"*Global Class* not only shares valuable tools necessary for global business success but also highlights the often overlooked and underappreciated elements of expanding a business to new countries."
—Chris Murphy, CEO, ThoughtWorks, North America

Start-up Founders

"The way Aaron and Klaus describe a Global Class Company is the exact model we aspire to at Flexport—culturally curious, localized, and strong in our core company values."
—Ryan Petersen, founder and CEO, Flexport

"Until adopting a beginner's mindset of the *Global Class*, learning from local customers and employees alike, Rakuten's early strategy was to standardize and centralize company culture, prioritizing uniformity over localization. This can lead to overlooking how local culture differs from their home market. While there are many aspects of a business that can be controlled, the local culture isn't one of them."
—Seichu Masatada Kobayashi, co-founder and Chief Well-Being Officer, Rakuten

"Curious about how the world's most successful companies scaled their businesses globally? Aaron and Klaus show you how these companies did it, and how yours can, too."
—Heini Zachariassen, founder and former CEO, Vivino

"I had to learn everything Aaron and Klaus outlined the hard way, in the field. As I built BlaBlaCar, I coordinated with the teams my own 'field trips' to top companies in order to gather the international expansion best practices you can read about in *Global Class*. This book will save lots of time for global company builders."
—Frédéric Mazzella, founder and CEO, BlaBlaCar

"*Global Class* understands how to convey the alignment of a company's role in society with our own mission to be a catalyst for economic growth by preparing the next generation of high-impact entrepreneurs around the world. Get a copy of *Global Class* and save yourself the wasted time and money of attempting to expand your business globally without it."
—Freddy Vega, founder and CEO, Platzi

"*Global Class* offers a great tool kit, helping many business owners answer the tough questions about expanding into new markets. It brings into focus the often overlooked and underappreciated elements that can make or break a business."
—Chang Wen Lai, co-founder and CEO, Ninja Van

"*Global Class* offers an ideal combination of case studies, relevant insights, relatable anecdotes, and powerful frameworks to paint the picture for how to expand any business globally."
—Mikkel Brun, co-founder and SVP of APAC, Tradeshift

"We partnered with the *Global Class* team to implement the Localization Premium Analysis to support our international expansion efforts in Europe. Their support really helped us build momentum and manage complexity while localizing our business for new markets."
—Jivko Bojinov, co-founder, ShipBob

"Companies today are thinking global day one and *Global Class* is an essential tool to turn these thoughts into action. The *Global Class* mindset described in this book helps companies like us to build a successful distributed company."
—Gabriel Engel, co-founder and CEO, Rocket.Chat

Bestselling Authors

"Achieving global scale takes iteration while managing complexity. In *Global Class*, Aaron and Klaus provide the playbook you need to navigate these changes and reach global scale."
—Eric Ries, Author of *The Lean Startup*

"This book should be required reading for any business leader with an eye on international markets."
—Steve Blank, The Father of Modern Entrepreneurship and author of *The Startup Owner's Manual*

"Entering new global markets is hard. *Global Class* helps you bridge the chasm between local market success and global-market fit."
—Alex Osterwalder, CEO, Strategyzer, and inventor of the Business Model Canvas

"*Global Class* is a crash course in effective international business growth. Through the lens of more than two hundred of the top global companies, Aaron and Klaus uncover how you can expand any business internationally."
—Patrick Vlaskovits, *New York Times* bestselling author of *The Lean Entrepreneur* and *Hustle*

"Excellent! Learning to become a global company that stays agile through changing markets, cultures, and legislations can feel like an overwhelming task. *Global Class* will focus your priorities and walk you step-by-step through the methodology to take your company to the next level."
—Dr. Marshall Goldsmith, *Thinkers50* #1 Executive Coach and *New York Times* bestselling author of *Triggers*, *Mojo*, and *What Got You Here Won't Get You There*

Top Investors

"Just like agile unlocked innovation, the strategies and tactics captured in *Global Class* unlock the secrets to successful global expansion . . . the companies that leverage this book will be the top global companies of tomorrow."
—Whitney Bouck, Managing Director, Insight Partners

"I've seen hundreds of start-ups go through the pain of international growth. Now I will ask every founder to read *Global Class*! I personally wish I had this book when I did global expansion at Yahoo! Inc. It would have saved me a lot of time and pain."
—Marvin Liao, former Partner, 500 Startups

"As an investor in fast-growing start-ups, I always look for ways to provide outside resources and counsel to our start-ups. The team behind *Global Class* has built an incredible platform that powers start-ups to become successful on a global scale."
—Batara Eto, founder and Managing Partner, East Ventures

GLOBAL
CLASS

GLOBAL CLASS

How the World's Fastest-Growing
Companies Scale Globally
by Focusing Locally

AARON McDANIEL and KLAUS WEHAGE

Matt Holt Books
An Imprint of BenBella Books, Inc.
Dallas, TX

Matt Holt is an imprint of BenBella Books, Inc.
10440 N. Central Expressway
Suite 800
Dallas, TX 75231
benbellabooks.com
Send feedback to feedback@benbellabooks.com.

BenBella and *Matt Holt* are federally registered trademarks.

Printed in the United States of America
10 9 8 7 6 5 4 3 2 1

Library of Congress Control Number: 2022934968
ISBN 9781637742181 (hardcover)
ISBN 9781637742198 (electronic)

Copyediting by Judy Myers
Proofreading by Michael Fedison and Jenny Bridges
Indexing by WordCo Indexing Services, Inc.
Text design and composition by PerfecType, Nashville, TN
Cover design by Brigid Pearson
Cover image © Shutterstock / Liu zishan
Printed by Lake Book Manufacturing

• CONTENTS •

PART 3: EMPOWER
The Three Pillars for Achieving Global Scale

· INTRODUCTION ·

The Genesis of *Global Class*

L ee had a problem.

There he stood, with sweaty palms, having just begun sharing an update on the company's international expansion initiative to a room full of board members and most of his company's C-level executives. It was not going well. His goal of aligning company leadership around providing necessary funding to enter three new markets and fixing some of the problems with the company's existing international footprint seemed to be slipping through his fingers.

Lee joined a rapidly growing direct-to-consumer health and wellness product company as one of the leaders on the international team after the company was already in a few international markets and had set its sights on expanding to more. Success in the company's home market had already led to rapid expansion into three global markets. Company leadership insisted the first international markets be the UK and Australia (I mean, they already spoke English, so website translation should be easy), followed by Spain (one of the company executives had studied abroad there). All the pre-launch research was conducted from headquarters (HQ), and subsequently some mid-level managers moved to these markets to lead market entry efforts.

Unfortunately, entering these markets led to a plethora of obstacles, from trouble getting approval to sell the products from local regulators, to supply chain and distribution issues affecting product quality. The general managers in the local markets were spending their time scrambling to figure out how to change product packaging to meet local requirements instead of building much-needed partnerships and hiring a local marketing team. Since the company used the same speed-at-all-costs strategy as in their initial market, it's no surprise that the company had yet to achieve product-market fit in any of these global markets.

Lee knew this meeting would be tough since company leadership didn't give the international initiatives the attention necessary and weren't keen on changing the business to fit the needs of local markets. They saw the existing business model as a main reason for the company's success thus far and wanted to continue adhering to the current way of doing things, rather than give local teams much-needed latitude to localize the business to gain traction in these new markets.

To add to the pressure, the company recently secured a round of funding, much of which was earmarked for global growth. This kick-started board and executive engagement, but Lee knew that blindly throwing more money at additional expansion efforts without a more cohesive strategy would waste time and money.

He made a case for resetting the company's global strategy: giving the local teams more autonomy, creating processes to support scale in multiple markets, and operating in a way that fit with the realities of the local market instead of insisting on the company way. The response from company leadership? Skepticism. They tasked Lee to report back in a few weeks with a better plan for the company's global expansion going forward.

As Lee left the boardroom, the gap between the expansion strategy company leadership preferred and what he knew would be effective felt like a chasm. *What should Lee do next?*

Problem: Growth stage company already in some markets (and a mandate to expand to more) has created operational complexities, lacks leadership alignment on a cohesive international expansion strategy, and prioritizes the company way while avoiding localization needed to fit product-market fit in global markets.

Solution: *Global Class* can help Lee navigate these challenges by providing him with:

- A comprehensive playbook that puts structure around how to gain traction and scale in multiple global markets simultaneously

- A strategy to align company leadership around granting local teams autonomy to localize the business model (*Four Commitments for Successful Global Growth*)
- An agile process for finding product-market fit in new international markets (*Business Model Localization Canvas*)
- A unified format for explaining the strategy for further penetrating existing markets and launching in new ones (*Global Growth Pitch Deck*)
- An analysis tool that tracks all the business model changes needed to achieve scale in current and new markets, helping company leadership prioritize which markets to target and the localizations that could be scaled to multiple countries (*Localization Premium Analysis*)

• • •

Isabel was ready for a change.

She had worked in the marketing department of a domestic financial services company for a couple years but was itching for something new. She had previously been a management consultant for a few years, working across a number of industries and practice areas. She particularly enjoyed a long-term project she had for an energy sector customer in Indonesia and, while there, recognized the opportunity in the emerging economy that came from a combination of a fast-growing population and economic growth happening across multiple sectors.

This, however, wasn't her first international experience. She studied political economy with a minor in French and did a post-college trek through Latin America, where—although she came from an immigrant family—she first began to understand a world vastly different from the suburban upbringing of her childhood.

Isabel recently recalled a course she took back in college on the developing economies in West Africa and, after doing some research, was becoming more passionate about how technology could help accelerate the growth of the local economies in the region.

Isabel had long dreamed of an international career and finally found a specific area to be excited about, but she didn't know how to make the professional pivot.

After looking at some job postings for companies expanding in Nigeria and Ghana, she finally found the perfect job with a fintech company that had a vision of improving the financial systems in developing countries. But, with limited experience in applying to international roles, let alone doing interviews, Isabel felt uncertain as to whether it would be worthwhile to apply at all. She simply felt that she didn't have the "common vocabulary" of international business and needed guidance.

Isabel definitely wants to apply, but what will she say if she gets an interview, and what will she do if she gets the job?

Problem: Globally minded professional looking to build a career in international business but not quite sure how to describe the role she is looking for or identify the skills she would need to build in order to succeed.

Solution: *Global Class* can help Isabel make this career change by:

- Highlighting the skills and mindset she needs to call upon and further polish to be successful in international roles (*the Interpreneur*)
- Formalizing a framework that details what she should look for when filtering through job opportunities to find companies with the right mindset to succeed at reaching global scale (*the Global Class Mindset*)
- Equipping her with ideas to share during the interview process so she stands out among the other candidates
- Providing her with the playbook to follow to influence the organization and guide it to success in global markets once on the job

---

• • •

This was the fifth time Samantha had pleaded her case to her peers from marketing and sales, but they still didn't get it. Their myopic view around how to improve the stagnating international market performance didn't consider some of the biggest problems Samantha saw clearly.

Samantha led a product organization for an enterprise software company with multiple product lines in the productivity and sales enablement space. The company had operated in over a dozen countries for more than a decade, kicking off expansion efforts in some of the stronger business markets at the time: Japan and Germany.

Her past experience in these markets had been helpful in understanding how to adapt the go-to-market strategy to get deeper market penetration outside of the existing enterprise customer base, but she had met resistance at every turn. The company saw organic international growth before entering these markets (mainly from existing customers who had international employees in these markets) and used that as the chief indicator for market entry.

The company hadn't localized the business much, and because of budget constraints, Samantha had found it difficult to get engineering to prioritize features that she knew were needed to meet the local market requirements for the fast-growing mid-market business segment (an untapped opportunity in existing markets).

Moreover, the command and control management style HQ maintained meant that innovation could only come from the home country, leaving local market teams ill equipped to find the right model for further growth. HQ kept sending over people with little local market knowledge to lead operations in these countries. There was also a low retention rate among the local team, as HQ had tended to lose focus on global markets, shifting to the next big initiative to bolster the stock price and quarterly earnings.

Her peer in sales insisted on selling direct in the Japanese market, but Samantha knew that local system integrators were essential, while her peer in marketing pushed back on any changes to value proposition or local market messaging for the German market since the whole marketing function was centralized at HQ. Her appeals rang on deaf ears. It was clear that international didn't have a home on the company's organizational chart.

Samantha, undeterred, thought of her next steps and how to put some structure behind her insights to gain a coalition of support among company leadership.

How can Samantha rally all the teams touching international operations around a more collaborative and structured plan to improve on the current ineffective strategies and to prioritize the markets she knows have the best opportunity?

Problem: Functional leader in a mature company that has an established international presence but low local market penetration, struggling to get resources and cross-functional alignment to scale in existing markets and solve lingering problems with international operations.

Solution: *Global Class* can help Samantha with building a strategy that includes:

- A holistic way of visualizing and managing the complexities that come from changing the go-to-market and operating models in global markets (*Localization Premium Analysis*)
- Guidelines on how to build a distributed team that has strong local and company knowledge (*Global Class Team Building Framework*)
- A dynamic management model to foster two-way innovation and capture those best practices working in smaller markets through feedback loops and communication structures (*Global Class Management Model*)
- Effective processes and structures to generate momentum around expansion efforts (*Localization Resource Team*)
- A clear picture of the resources needed for localizing the business to secure both funding and focus from HQ (*Total Cost of Entry Formula*)

● ● ●

For anyone experiencing challenges similar to what Lee, Isabel, or Samantha face, this book will provide a treasure trove of real-life examples, frameworks, case studies, and overlooked aspects of how to build a global business while helping you apply the concepts herein to enhance your international career journey and assist your company on the road to global growth and scale.

The issues Lee, Isabel, and Samantha encounter are drawn from the interviews we conducted with more than three hundred business leaders across over fifty countries from more than two hundred companies in varying stages of scaling globally. We aggregated and analyzed the insights, success stories, and failures shared by these leaders to develop the content for this book.

In speaking to all these business leaders, we found that companies encountered a number of problems when building a global organization, many intensified by the trends that the pandemic accelerated, like distributed work.

We found that almost everyone reinvented the wheel when scaling globally. Expanding to international markets is hard, and there was no playbook outlining what to do. Eric Ries, author of *The Lean Startup*, shared with us that, in his experience, most international growth decisions are not guided by any frameworks at all, or they rely on a command and control strategy. Through this book, we strive to provide the playbook that companies can call on to reach global scale more quickly while better utilizing resources, saving time and money.

Scaling a business globally is a complex process. Complex to measure, complex to track, complex to get right. As Eric explains, the truth about international business growth is this: "Finding product-market fit is different in international expansion than in an initial market. With an initial market, if you fail, the company has other options (pivot, persevere, or perish). Generally speaking, when you commit to expanding internationally, the expansion *will* happen. The variable is the opportunity cost of doing it badly—the time and money wasted in the process." Many mistakes are made, and most companies spend way more of these precious resources in the process than necessary.

We learned that it is difficult to get internal alignment around a global growth initiative. A common language, set of frameworks, and principles can be extremely valuable in getting people on the same page.

The research process also led us to a simple conclusion: *Global is the new agile*. What does this mean? It means that some of the core tenets of agile methodology apply to scaling a business globally. Just like with agile, company leaders must be involved in the international expansion process (it should not be outsourced) and the whole organization must buy into the methodology and mindset for it to work (in the case of international growth, this is the Global Class mindset). Agile methodology (a modified version we discuss in the book to fit the global use case) can also be pretty effective at helping companies reach product-market fit in new global markets.

Moreover, most companies have come to understand agile principles (at different levels of application and success), and many are looking for the next big thing to stay ahead of the competition.

We also see this book as an evolution of the foundational and important work Steve Blank, Alexander Osterwalder, and Eric Ries have done with agile methodology. We hope that in developing a global layer for agile, it will help businesses use the concepts and tools these three (and others) have created for a new purpose.

In reading *Global Class*, you will learn the mindset of companies that are successful in scaling globally, what to look for when building a team, how to localize your business for new markets while managing complexity, how to build the right structures and processes to enable global growth, the commitments all companies must make to succeed, and the core organizational pillars supporting a global footprint—all with frameworks to help you apply these concepts to your business.

THE GENESIS OF *GLOBAL CLASS*

A Silicon Valley native, Aaron felt a connection to the tech community while growing up, from his dad being a chauffeur for industry executives (including driving the Chiat/Day team to and from their weekly meeting with Steve Jobs) to attending UC Berkeley and presenting strategies to executives at companies like Cisco in business case competitions. He was always aware of the world outside of the Bay Area with a travel agent mother who taught cultural geography and tourism at local junior colleges (and had ten-year-old Aaron grade student assignments, gleefully sharing this fact with her students when the class didn't score well). He had a number of formative international experiences, none better than the gap half-year he took after college that sparked his cultural curiosity and has led him to explore nearly forty countries, as of this writing.

Professionally, Aaron first built his intrapreneurial muscles by joining AT&T as part of its flagship Leadership Development Program. Over nearly a decade, he managed large teams and worked across multiple departments, including in partnership with AT&T's Foundry innovation centers and with an AT&T joint venture partner in China. Through the experience, he saw firsthand the complexities and frustrations that come along with operating a business at scale.

But almost from day one, Aaron had a secret. Entrepreneurial seeds from childhood had germinated as he ran an eclectic mix of side businesses while working at AT&T: a business selling custom wedding invitations, another selling portable beer pong tables, a taxi app that launched around the same time as Uber, a speaking business that led to the publishing of his first two books, and a passion for teaching others. This then blossomed into a career as a serial entrepreneur post-AT&T, with three of his ventures being acquired.

Now Aaron passionately helps students build the right foundation for success in their careers through teaching entrepreneurship at UC Berkeley's Haas School of Business. On campus, he pursues his personal mission to develop the next generation of globally minded business leaders.

• • •

As Klaus zig-zagged his way through the urban streets of Santiago, Chile, in 2006, he was confronted with the harsh realities of emerging economies. Seeing a helpless homeless man with one leg and a patched eye begging for money struck him right to his core. This was a world very different from his comfortable home in Denmark with its comprehensive social welfare system. It was then that his passion for economic development and poverty alleviation awoke within. In the wake of this experience, his career took a complete 180-degree turn at the age of twenty-five as he resigned from his job and returned to school to pursue this mission.

After years of studying international business, Klaus was nearing the end of his schooling and wanted to get experience working in international markets. Through months of courting prominent Danish corporates, he was able to secure an international project for himself and a team of his peers. In this project, he spent time in-market developing a new product launch strategy for Carlsberg in Vietnam, receiving high praise from the regional CEO.

Upon returning from Vietnam, Klaus felt different and out of place (a case of reverse culture shock). There was a pit in his stomach that wouldn't go away. He realized that he didn't feel at home in Denmark anymore and that his true roots were out there in the world somewhere, his experiences leading him to feel like more of a global citizen than a Danish citizen. International business and expansion became his calling. Knowing that the Silicon Valley was one of the best places to explore the intersection of innovation and entrepreneurship, he moved to San Francisco to get an MBA at Hult International Business School. It was there he found his foundation and the love of his life, Jessica, a Taiwanese-American born and raised in Boston. They set down roots in San Francisco and now have two boys who they affectionately call their "dumplings."

After graduating from Hult, Klaus landed a role leading international at Silicon Valley Forum, one of the most prestigious organizations promoting innovation and entrepreneurship. This opportunity provided him the platform to pursue his true calling, forging partnerships and driving impact for the organization globally—a role that took him to all corners of the world, advising ministry officials, governors, and policy makers on how to drive economic impact through entrepreneurship. To partners, Klaus was often jokingly referred to as the "Silicon Valley Ambassador."

• • •

The idea of 10X Innovation Lab came to Klaus as he realized there was a better way to support and build global entrepreneurial and innovation ecosystems, and he was ready to embark on an entrepreneurial journey of his own. As 10X was born, Klaus looked to a friend for some guidance. Klaus and Aaron met each other the same way all successful business founders meet: through their mothers-in-law, who are best friends. At first, Klaus asked Aaron to be an advisor. A couple months later, he asked Aaron to be 10X's head of entrepreneurship, and finally, a little while later, to be a co-founder.

Over the years, we (along with our awesome team that hails from four continents) have taught thousands of corporate executives how top Silicon Valley companies innovate at scale and have guided thousands of entrepreneurs from across the globe to connect with the Silicon Valley ecosystem, often traveling to other countries throughout the year. We both liked not only doing business with interesting companies but also experiencing local cultures.

Then the pandemic struck and the opportunities to travel came to a halt.

Upon using the time to reflect and take stock, like many business leaders did during the pandemic, we began to identify the common mistakes companies we worked with made when looking to enter the American market. From not doing proper local market discovery to having unrealistic expectations that entrepreneurs visiting Silicon Valley would basically be handed a check from a venture capitalist at the baggage claim after arriving at the San Francisco International Airport, these mistakes set them on the path to international expansion failure.

Aaron threw out the idea of writing a book to further explore how successful companies do things right and Klaus realized that this would be a great way to continue to explore the world, virtually this time. So we set a goal. Klaus suggested talking to thirty people and seeing if there was a topic worth writing a book on. Aaron skeptically responded that he thought no more than ten people would be willing to discuss the topic.

What came next literally blew both of us away.

In less than one month, we had set up over fifty meetings with some really impressive international business leaders. We learned that there was no book on the topic of global business growth that had really reached the business zeitgeist and that a number of problems existed that battle-scarred business leaders had to figure out on their own. After these interviews, we listened, developed, synthesized, and then went back to all these people and shared our findings. The response was overwhelmingly positive, with everyone saying a book on the topic was sorely needed (or, as Abe Smith, Head of International at Zoom, put it, "This is the book I wish I had fifteen years ago!").

After this initial round of interviews, we realized that we needed to get more of a global scope to ensure the frameworks and concepts we were developing had global applicability. Thus, we went on to universalize our frameworks so they could help a wide variety of companies.

This led us to speak with hundreds more business leaders from more than fifty countries, ranging from top executives with over $100 billion in profit and loss responsibility, to the first person in international markets expanding a business. Many hailed from US-based companies, while others came from companies headquartered in Europe, Asia, Latin America, the Middle East, Africa, and Australia. We purposely spoke with business-to-consumer and business-to-business companies, software and physical product companies, and companies from a diverse set of industries. We spoke to fast-growing start-ups and companies that had a mature global footprint. We found that while the context was different, many of the themes were the same.

After researching, we iterated (as firm believers in agile the process). Looking back, Reid Hoffman would be happy to hear us say that our initial version was cringeworthy, but we kept adapting as we learned, deciding what *not* to focus on (highly company-specific things like market selection that every company seems to have a custom criteria for) as much as what to focus on (building a comprehensive playbook and frameworks that are easy to socialize within organizations) until we arrived at the book in your hands right now.

An Interesting Finding We Didn't Expect . . .

In our research, interviewees mentioned many common themes and insights, but one thing that was never mentioned in hundreds of hours of conversation, not even once, was the word *foreign*.

This might seem obvious when you think about it for even a moment (especially for anyone who has actually launched a company in an international market), but the nuance of this mindset is profound.

The word *foreign* is riddled with negative baggage. *Foreign* precipitates misunderstanding; it screams of differences, smells of fear and doubt. It exudes complexity. It demonstrates a mental barrier between you at "home" and what exists beyond your borders. It creates a nameless/faceless attitude toward the customers you are attempting to reach and a closed-mindedness to cultural differences. All the people we spoke with as part of our research saw global markets in a very different light. Not only as a puzzle to be figured out, but also as an opportunity to connect, engage, and provide value to people.

When pressed during an interview about the absence of *foreign*, Jennifer Yuen, former Head of Airbnb's Americas and Asia-Pacific Marketing, stated that saying and thinking *foreign* creates a barrier on its own. "It's more effective to look for connection and commonality. For example, expanding [internationally] can help you improve your product overall."

In recognition of the importance of this mindset, here and in a single reference at the very end of the book are the only places in the whole book where "the F word" will be used.

HOW TO READ *GLOBAL CLASS*

We realize that there are a lot of concepts and frameworks in the book and that at times it may be a lot to take in (global business is a sizable topic), but we would rather err on the side of giving you more than let this be the kind of business book that fills one hundred pages in describing what could be explained in only five. While we applaud those that can read an entire book in a single setting, we understand that for some it is best to read chapters one at a time, leaving room to digest in between.

To help with this, we have included a summary at the end of each chapter to encapsulate the main takeaways, as well as "Reflection & Action Questions" to help you discover how to apply key concepts and frameworks to your current situation. We have also included a glossary of commonly used terms at the back of the book with definitions of core concepts that you can flip to for quick reference as you are reading. There are also online resources available (like digital versions of the frameworks) at www.GlobalClassBook.com.

Things to Keep in Mind While Reading

Here are some important things to consider as you continue reading:

1. While you might think of many of the companies profiled in this book as established, mature international businesses, we spoke to executives who were part of teams there at the early stages of their international growth. Apple, for instance, was founded last century, but its retail expansion into Brazil, profiled in chapter six, happened around a decade ago. **The frameworks and concepts outlined in this book can be used by companies of all types, sizes, and stages.**

2. Companies selling to businesses (B2B) and consumer-focused businesses (B2C) think, act, and operate very differently, and therefore will adapt frameworks from the book in different ways. The same is true for companies selling physical products compared to software or service-based businesses. A company that sells physical products looking to expand to new global markets has a very different set of considerations than a software business that doesn't need to worry about changes to supply chain, inventory, and physical packaging. Our goal is to offer a broad enough set of principles and flexible tools that apply to businesses of all kinds. You will notice that in certain situations we don't prescribe specific actions and generally don't provide step-by-step processes for global growth. A business's unique considerations, when matched with the unique cultures and regulations of hundreds of countries across the world, can make having an effective uniform process nearly impossible. Instead, we offer a mindset, principles, and flexible frameworks that can be adapted to meet a wide variety of businesses. We provide context for thinking about common challenges to help you come to the best conclusions to apply to your business's specific situation.

a. On a similar note, there are some areas of the global growth initiative planning and implementation process that we don't address directly, namely market selection. We avoid this topic because we have found in our research that the criteria companies use to choose markets to enter can range from highly customized to a specific industry, to directly related to where there is already organic growth, to haphazard (with rationale ranging from selecting locations where investors are located, to picking countries company executives studied abroad in during college or visited once). All companies should evaluate key economic indicators, local market dynamics, and so on to narrow down to a short list of target markets. Outside of foundational elements of mindset and strategy, our tools and frameworks pick up once the decision has been made to expand to international markets and there is a list of target markets to explore.

3. We recognize that writing a book that strives for universal appeal and applicability doesn't come without risk. Please consider the following when reading: We aim not to take a US-centric approach and understand that companies from smaller home markets think about global markets much differently than those from larger markets. We recognize that some markets and regions are overrepresented while others are underrepresented in the book. Being aware of this, we have made an effort to talk with business leaders from every continent and corner of the world to validate that the insights herein are relevant and adaptable for any global market. We admit that at various points we make broad statements about a certain country and culture of its people. We don't mean to assert that these observations represent *all* people in a community, nor do we desire to perpetuate any stereotypes or inaccurate generalizations. We seek to celebrate culture and diversity.

LET'S CONNECT

While the entrepreneurial community is very well connected, we found that the community of people focused on international growth has not been. This is in part because, historically, the exercise of bringing a business to a new country was a solitary exercise, often involving one company representative moving from headquarters to build the business in a faraway land. We strive to make the experience of building a global organization a shared one.

Our goal is to help people, teams, and organizations better connect to international communities worldwide. It is our mission to socialize the Global Class and Interpreneur mindsets among current and aspiring business leaders across every country in the world, helping them become catalysts for positive change, growing economies, and improving lives, both at an individual and societal level.

We hope to connect with you as well and welcome any messages you want to send our way—email us at hello@globalclasscompany.com.

PART 1

EVOLVE

The Global Class

There has been a SHIFT in global business. A new type of company with a new mindset is taking the LEAD. A new brand of leader is also emerging, a TRAILBLAZER who is a catalyst for global growth and scale, cultivated by these leading companies. Together these companies and their leaders ALIGN on a key set of commitments that often mean the difference between success and failure of global growth initiatives.

• 1 •

SHIFT

The World Has Changed

The key to success in Germany is the sausage.

After much success in conquering the American retail market, the retail giant Walmart set its sights on international markets. A new avenue for business growth was the discussion among leadership and employees in the halls of HQ in Bentonville, Arkansas. With a proven track record and dominance in the home market, Walmart's confidence and belief in its own ability to translate local success into global success was a no-brainer—who doesn't want products at low prices, impeccable customer service with friendly greetings, and (said with all the arrogance that once accompanied this mindset) who doesn't *love* America and American products?

While incredibly effective in the US market, the value proposition of low prices didn't resonate with Germans, who already had some of the lowest grocery prices in Europe. Walmart had established operational scale in the United States, but even with the purchase of local retailers Wertkauf and Interspar (two of the largest retail chains in Germany), it couldn't outmaneuver the strong supplier relationships its competitors had, making it impossible to build any kind of advantage.

Walmart also neglected to localize its products and company culture to fit the market. While its prepackaged meats were perennial best sellers for American consumers, Germans didn't like them, viewing them as inherently lower quality. They preferred fresh meat from the local butcher. Neither did German consumers warm to the unfamiliar Walmart-branded products the company promoted in store.

In Germany, people are more accustomed to engaging with store staff only when they need something instead of being proactively (enthusiastically) approached by them. That meant the smiling greeters standing at the door and friendly cashiers at checkout counters was a level of friendliness that was culturally uncomfortable for Germans, instead of creating a sense of community as they do for Americans.

Home turf success and the presumptions it often brings don't necessarily translate into success away from home, and the strategies that work in one market don't always translate to another. Walmart's entry into Germany provides a textbook example of how not to approach building a global organization.

Instead of success in bringing "the American way" to new places, the story was about how Walmart overlooked the nuances of German culture, local buying behavior, and existing market competition. If Walmart had paid attention to these factors, the company would have found ways to adapt their business model to the market (or possibly decided not to enter the market at all). But they didn't, instead serving as a perfect example of how prioritizing the company way of doing things can ultimately lead to failure. In the case of Walmart, it led to a fire sale of its eighty-five retail stores to the local competitor, Metro, at a loss of around $1 billion.

In the end, Walmart learned that there are no substitutes for adapting the business to be an authentic fit in market; as Robyn Larsen, International Growth and Marketing Leader at Shopify, explained, quoting a German partner, "To be good enough it needs to look, taste, and smell like a *German* sausage."

Bottom line, many of the problems Walmart faced stemmed from their mindset when scaling internationally, not being sensitive to local culture but instead prioritizing the Walmart way of doing things and imposing their company values on local employees and consumers—a fatal misstep. Instead of raising an American flag as a signal of success, the company had to raise a white flag of defeat with the admission that it failed to successfully enter the German market, leaving a massive loss, reduced confidence, and questions about whether Walmart's model could work and be scaled beyond the United States.

Challenges like the ones Walmart faced in Germany are relevant whether you have over two million employees or just a handful. Making just *one* of the mistakes Walmart did would have spelled failure for many other companies.

What's clear is that expecting your model to work exactly the same in your home market and abroad is a losing mindset.

You can't lump entering markets across continents and cultural divides into a single bucket. Effective global growth does not stem from a cookie-cutter process that leads to market dominance everywhere. It requires understanding of individual local markets and consideration for local nuances.

As Andy Bird, former Chairman of Disney, aptly said, "There are no flights to international." "International markets" is not a singular place to be lumped together, but a patchwork of diverse economies that operate within unique cultures that can't be addressed with a one-size-fits-all strategy.

Going global isn't a destination, it's a journey. A journey that many companies and executives have discovered on their own on the road to success. Interestingly, our research has found that these companies and their leaders either stumbled upon, instinctively understood, or painstakingly developed effective international growth models through iteration and learning from both successes and failures, often overspending time and money in the process.

As LinkedIn co-founder Reid Hoffman said, "Starting a company is jumping off a cliff and assembling the airplane on the way down." The same applies to building a business beyond its home borders; because to this point there has been no definitive playbook for the next generation of global growth strategies, this book and its frameworks have been created to serve as a map, navigation system, and coordinates to help you scale your business across the globe.

For many company leaders, a global footprint represents a future goal far off in the distance after they've achieved market leadership at home. For some business leaders, going global is the focus from day one. In both cases the recognition is clear—in business today, success isn't merely restricted to the borders where the company was founded. This realization has likely become even more salient as the adoption of technology and the improvement of infrastructure to support and distribute it have proliferated across almost every country.

THERE IS A SHIFT IN BUSINESS

The pandemic has accelerated global trends, offering new opportunities to connect with international markets as companies learn how to interact virtually with both customers and employees alike. The way that companies have successfully built and managed international businesses in the past will be less effective in today's global economy, with the acceleration of distributed work and competition emerging from global markets.

The business world faces another inflection point that will challenge existing models and lead to new best practices. Companies born during and after the pandemic will look and operate differently than companies founded before.

Similarly, companies born before the dot-com boom operated in very different ways than companies founded after. Using the internet as a virtual channel of distribution helped new companies transcend brick and mortar and changed both corporate structure and desirable traits and expertise within the workforce. The rapid adoption of mobile technology (and in particular smartphones) changed how companies operate as well, as did the widespread adoption of the cloud and social media. Each of these trends changed the game but often only affected a subset of company functions: marketing/sales/customer service with social media; software product development and company IT services with the cloud; distribution with the dot-com boom (web and physical products); and product development with mobile. Global expansion touches every business function.

In the same way that business leaders today who look back on the pre-dot-com boom think how absurd it would be to operate a business without the internet, business leaders will soon look at companies that don't maintain a distributed and global workforce and customer base with the same kind of dismissal.

Companies born more recently can have inherent advantages over companies that don't adapt. Not only can they take advantage of access to a larger pool of diverse talent, but they also have local knowledge of how to scale the business in each unique market where their employees reside.

The acceleration of the virtual workforce touches every function of an organization. The ability for companies to expand internationally early in their development changes how they're structured, while the rise of a new set of sought-after skills to support an international footprint affects the company as a whole.

Speed becomes important as adoption curves accelerate and new entrants (both local and international) are more easily able to gain traction in local markets. If companies with strong traction at home don't initiate efforts to grow internationally, then copycats will come along in these markets, making it harder to find traction globally.

Emerging markets are skipping ahead in some ways, bypassing steps more mature markets have taken in building out infrastructure (many countries in Africa, for example, launched mobile networks without establishing robust wireline networks and leapfrogged right to mobile commerce). In many places a smartphone is the access point to the internet—no need to start with desktops or laptops.

Amazon, two to three times the age of most other companies profiled in the book, is structured very differently than post-dot-com companies. Amazon grew its core online retail business country by country because of the physical nature of this line of business (with the necessity for inventory and supply chain considerations), leading to many unique local operating models and an accumulation of complexity (due to local differences in logistics and compliance). This left the company with operational infrastructure that made it difficult to operate single global (software-based) services that didn't require as much country-by-country localization.

The pandemic accelerated a number of already emerging trends: lower barriers to market entry because of lower costs to start and scale businesses; ease of distributing software products (app stores); efforts to solve issues with the archaic global supply chain for physical products (freight forwarding and logistics platform Flexport); access to communities of freelance workers; effective collaboration and productivity software (Zoom and Slack); platforms for running aspects of business (from general, like Amazon Web Services, to industry or functionally specific, like Shopify for ecommerce and Stripe for payments).

This situation doesn't only affect start-up tech companies. It applies to EVERY company, from large organizations with an established global footprint to small upstarts that have only launched in an initial market. Operating models have been challenged, causing Amazon and Google and small businesses alike to revisit workforce strategy, real estate planning, and employee policies. It's also forced them into figuring out how to reach a rapidly changing customer base.

Companies see global opportunities earlier and accelerate faster to meet this new dynamic head-on, and these companies no longer come from one part of the world; they are everywhere. But this is not without risk. Entering new markets is just as challenging as finding traction in an initial market (if not more so). At the same time, rising nationalism has put up some obstacles for building momentum in some countries, further requiring a playbook to navigate these risks.

Despite the challenges, many of these trends make it easier to scale a company globally and will give way to new types of company structures and operating models.

What's also notable is the risk of not acting on this shift in business. For legacy companies, the pandemic has presented a window of opportunity, because employees and customers are less resistant to exploring new ways of doing things given the upheaval of daily life, allowing companies to change their operating models and mindsets to account for the new dynamics of today's global business market. Those who don't adapt risk peril.

Technology, new agile mindsets, and ample capital for new ideas have decimated entrenched industries over the last couple of decades. Uber, for example, started to hit its stride in its initial market of San Francisco in 2013. Over the course of that year, incumbent taxi companies in the city lost 65 percent of their revenue in a single year (not profit, REVENUE). To succeed, companies must now account for not only technology and business model disruption; they must also account for the local cultural nuances of a market. Uber saw the flip side of this when the company was unable to gain a dominant market share over Didi in the China market (even with its vast financial resources). Didi was able to compete by adopting a strategy and culture that better fit with the local nuances of the Chinese market.

GOING GLOBAL ISN'T NEW, BUT IT'S DIFFERENT NOW

For the longest time, "going global" was shorthand for "outsourcing." The exercise involved finding a locale with cheap skilled labor (for IT support or manufacturing) or where accents weren't as pronounced (for customer service). It was an exercise in cost reduction, mainly capitalizing on vast differences in market wages. Today, as economies across the world have grown steadily and swiftly in recent decades, there is a much bigger opportunity to turn the focus on these markets from potential labor (especially as the wage gap has decreased) to target customers. In the last four decades, China, for example, has implemented a large-scale industrial and manufacturing revolution, transforming from a country that had about one-half the per capita GDP as sub-Saharan Africa in 1970 to a technology leader and the second-largest economy in the world (with seven times the GDP as that of sub-Saharan Africa in 2020).

The scale of the opportunity is enormous. For example, a majority of the more than 1.2 billion people in Africa are under the age of nineteen, and the overall population is expected to surpass two billion before 2040. Business leaders who understand that the continent isn't a homogenous place but a diverse region of fifty-four countries, where nearly two thousand languages are spoken, will be well positioned to sell their products to and tap into the talent pools of the more than six hundred million people entering the workforce and becoming the future of the region's rapidly growing economies.

Business leaders involved in these global scaling efforts have changed as well. The classic depiction of an international businessperson was an expat navigating mistranslations and cultural disparities between home and current country of residence, forging partnerships to gain access to new pools of customers. While the expat lifestyle has been lauded, often as a solitary exercise with someone acting as the sole representative on a metaphoric island (or literal one if they were stationed in Hong Kong or Singapore), in recent years new disruptive models have emerged, bringing scale to global growth initiatives. Today, culturally conscious companies build local teams and efficiently balance the needs of HQ with those of the local market.

Moreover, the mindset has also changed. There's a recognition that competition has increased with the rise of these economies and the importance of understanding the local context (just as Uber learned going head-to-head with Didi). Silicon Valley companies have seen the rise of copycats and new business models, recognizing that new entrants are able to compete toe-to-toe with more established players. The internet leveled the playing field and allowed companies to scale much faster than twenty or thirty years ago, just as distributed work and the development of economies across the globe will level access to these markets.

What has also become more clear is that the United States is no longer the dominant market as many other economies emerge and continue to grow at a more rapid pace.

We live in a global world where more people are being educated internationally and going on to build businesses in their home countries, subsequently scaling them abroad. There is a small but growing group of people focused on bringing their companies to global scale; only recently are they becoming more connected with peers with a similar calling. Their unique mindset (discussed in chapter three) is increasingly sought after by companies with aspirations of global scale.

Companies like Canva, Zendesk, LinkedIn, and Flexport proved you can go global and scale quickly. These companies, and many of their contemporaries, have paved the way for your global expansion efforts. While the international teams at companies have been successful, they have also faced painful challenges in international markets and found success only after many missteps. This book will showcase successes but also highlight pitfalls and failures, explaining what *not* to do in order to help you avoid the same mistakes.

So many aspects of doing business have been virtualized as physical interactions have given way to digital ones. Employees working remotely across town once represented a giant step; today, your colleagues may be working remotely across the globe.

Jennifer Yuen, who established Airbnb's brand marketing function in the Asia-Pacific region (APAC) and led marketing across the Americas, highlights how the role (and even concept) of HQ has changed. "HQ is not just a singular physical place anymore, especially related to hiring and mobility. You can find the best talent anywhere now. There is an opportunity to build teams with more diverse backgrounds. When you establish that HQ can be virtual, not only is there less us-versus-them talk but there is also an opportunity to better leverage both functional expertise and local knowledge for a global footprint."

Talent has become more widely available. Smart companies are able to leverage this to establish a global presence. They see remote teams not as cost centers but as local creative organizations that can innovate.

Companies are also beginning to see the potential customer bases in more global markets beyond those traditionally at the top of expansion lists. Less than ten years ago, a country like Indonesia wouldn't be considered a priority target market, but this is changing as the purchasing power of its population of more than 270 million people continues to grow at a rapid pace.

Opportunities in global markets have increased because of four key factors:

1. Improved infrastructure in emerging markets (internet speed and mobility of people). Countries like Indonesia are able to leapfrog more mature markets by being mobile-first.
2. Greater access to talent due to higher investment in workforce development, allowing companies to find the right talent when expanding to new markets.
3. Governments investing heavily in promoting entrepreneurship and company building.
4. Growing middle classes and better-developed consumer markets as economies stabilize.

This has made way for a new era in global business.

THE RISE OF A NEW ERA OF (CULTURALLY CONSCIOUS) GLOBAL BUSINESS

We are at an important inflection point for business. Global citizenship and connectedness are increasingly important, and as Salesforce co-founder and co-CEO Marc Benioff evangelizes, business is becoming more of a catalyst for change. Companies have the opportunity to recalibrate to better consider not only environmental but also human impacts. This notion is having a huge impact in business interactions, within the workplace, and in the community.

To thrive, companies must adapt to be successful and follow the models of the companies that effectively operate at scale globally. A new mindset is not just merited; it's imperative.

A paradigm shift has occurred. Businesses realize that if they are going to be working remotely in different buildings and cities, working across international borders is less of a leap than it once was. Virtual collaboration tools have been adopted out of necessity, and their benefits (and challenges) have led to fundamental changes in how teams function, leading to increased organizational flexibility and a more agile way of working.

Some businesses have changed permanently. A small number have gone completely virtual, like Twitter, but many others have bounced back to something closer to pre-pandemic working models. No matter the degree of change, businesses that survived realized they could leverage technology to operate virtually, often in more efficient ways than before.

HQ is increasingly not a single physical place where all the power and influence are centralized geographically. The pandemic has changed the lifestyle of business professionals, who are no longer tied to a single office complex. Companies are figuring out how to create structures to support this new dynamic.

Legacy companies believe that the most viable customer bases exist in developed countries, while the new breed of company (the Global Class described in the next chapter) sees the market opportunity in developing nations and mature markets alike, and takes a role in helping to develop the former.

Companies must think globally to attract top talent. Confining the search to the geographic area around headquarters or a major office presence is too limiting and will ultimately put companies at a disadvantage as competitors learn how to tap into talent anywhere.

New ways to conduct business virtually were tested until effective methods were proven. While physically covering a global footprint has traditionally meant an executive would live on an airplane, now they can conduct virtual visits on a daily basis, as there is a more even playing field between employees near headquarters and those an ocean away.

Platforms also facilitate rapid international growth and enable companies to run their businesses across borders. Companies in an increasing number of industries don't have to localize every aspect of their business to access millions of customers across the world. Instead, they just need to plug into platforms with global reach. Technology not only lowers barriers but also accelerates disruption. It crosses borders and brings people closer. Platforms like Shopify and Amazon become the cross-border "home" market for emerging companies that can use these platforms to more easily access global markets.

Zoom Video Communications (Zoom), the latest company to become synonymous with what it does (think *Kleenex* over *facial tissue* or *Q-tips* over *cotton swabs*; we don't have a "video conference," we have a "Zoom meeting"), saw incredible growth as the pandemic reached its full force. In January 2020, Zoom had 10 million daily participants and 100 million meeting minutes a month. Just three short months later, in April, the company had 300 million daily participants and was on pace to have 3 trillion meeting meetings per year, a 30x and 2,500x growth, respectively.

The interesting thing for Zoom is that much of this growth came from outside the borders of its home country. More salient is that while the pandemic accelerated adoption and increased globalization, it didn't *start* them. The groundwork had already been laid for success.

CASE STUDY

VIRTUAL CROSS-BORDER COLLABORATION—HEWLETT-PACKARD

Tools that enabled virtual workforces and lowered barriers to building a global presence helped solve problems caused by the pandemic. A doctor in Barcelona was lamenting to a friend who worked at Hewlett-Packard (HP) about how hard it was for the hospital to get personal protective equipment (PPE); the hospital had to wait for factories a continent away to produce mask holders and face shields, which then had to cover dozens of touchpoints in a global supply chain. The friend at HP worked with a team to create a design that could be produced on a 3D printer, going back and forth with iterations for the doctor to test at the hospital. After nearly ten iterations over a single week, an effective face shield design was created. The HP team then shared the 3D print file with its worldwide community so that anyone with a 3D printer could produce this kind of PPE to meet the need in their local area, making a distributed and localized network of production.

This is an exciting example of the potential of this new phase of global business, where cross-border collaboration and working for the greater good of humanity can play a more prominent role in driving innovation than it ever has.

Instead of clinging to the command-and-control mantra of the past, companies are realizing the benefits of making decisions at the edges, especially companies with a presence in multiple diverse local markets. This goes hand in hand with decentralized innovation, where best practices from anywhere can be implemented globally instead of only being top-down from headquarters.

According to a recent Accenture Business Futures report, "71 percent of executives have already decentralized or are planning to decentralize decision-making in parts of their business," and 82 percent said they see their business as operating more like a "broad federation of enterprises," given the "increasingly fragmented" business environment. In simple terms, this means the focus of business operations is shifting from a top-down, centralized HQ model to one based on distributed success and teams with localized missions and focus.

Markets are different, customers are different, companies and the products and services they deliver are inherently different, and there is no one-size-fits-all solution or exact step-by-step guide that all companies can take. People in a number of Asian countries tend to work longer hours compared to Europe, where they tend to leave work earlier and prioritize having more of a balance between work and personal life. This cultural difference drives the local business culture, customs, behaviors, purchasing criteria, and more. The role of work and existence of a social safety net puts job security in a different context, depending on the local culture.

The mindset related to international growth has shifted. The process of evaluating a new market and building a go-to-market plan used to be outsourced to management consultants. Now there is a rising class of business professionals who are bringing their skills and global mindset to companies looking to scale. International markets are seen not only as potential customers but also as test beds for new ideas and products to be validated before being introduced in the initial market. Slack did this when testing out adding a Send button to its platform in Asian markets before launching it worldwide. The rise of competition from local players means that cultural considerations and localization are needed to engage local customers. With endless amounts of information vying for customers' attention, you have to stand out and differentiate.

Culture permeates through all aspects of an international business. You will encounter cultural divergence in how customers make decisions, how business is conducted locally, and how you translate and maintain your corporate culture and core values in a new market. There are endless differences to understand and adapt to when entering a new market, and there are worthwhile ways to celebrate and leverage the diversity that a distributed employee base brings to your whole company.

All of these changes merit the introduction of a new playbook for how to succeed in this new global business world.

WHY DO GLOBAL GROWTH INITIATIVES FAIL?

The reasons why international business growth initiatives fail are almost as numerous as the failure stories. However, ten mistakes that cause these initiatives to fail (or at the very least cost companies more time and money) stand out:

1. **Attempting to be "Born Global."** Seeking growth in international markets is NOT a viable solution or pivot for not being able to find product-market fit at home. Companies cannot succeed when attempting to launch in many markets at once before even finding product-market fit in an initial market. In order to find success in global markets, you must have a foundation in an initial market, where all assumptions about who the right customers are, what they want, why they buy, and the viability of your solution have been validated and scalability is proven.

2. **Failing to establish leadership buy-in.** Everyone in the organization must be on board with global growth. If there isn't support from the very top and cross-functional buy-in, initiatives to scale globally are destined to fail.

3. **Building the wrong team.** During our research, the executives we spoke with highlighted how finding the right people was both the most important but also the most difficult part of building a global business. What mindset and skills should you look for? Hint: Find *Interpreneurs* (more on this in chapter three) and an overlap of company and local knowledges (more on this in chapter eight).

4. **Maintaining an us-versus-them mentality between HQ and local teams.** Companies that aren't intentional about integrating a distributed team don't take full advantage of the organization's talent and rarely find strong traction in new markets. Favoring one over the other creates a divide between HQ and local teams.

5. **Not revisiting customer development and the agile methodology when localizing.** Companies that aren't willing to adopt a globally conscious agile methodology by making their current business and operating models hypotheses to be iterated on in a new market will not capture significant market share globally. Localization is necessary and the process doesn't just involve language translation; business leaders must reevaluate all aspects of the company and its operating model. As illustrated

by Walmart's experience in Germany, when you assume the "company way" will succeed in other markets across the globe, you will fail.

6. **Not managing complexity.** Effective companies work fast and decisively, but they must understand and plan for the complexities that invariably come in diverse international markets; they ignore them at their peril (more on this in chapter six).

7. **Not adapting communication to fit a distributed workforce.** Feedback loops that facilitate constant communication are crucial to the exchange of local market insights and company core values. Companies that don't set up effective lines of communication and don't take advantage of the two-way innovation that can come from local markets will run into issues as they attempt to engage an increasingly distributed (and virtual) workforce.

8. **Not investing appropriate time and resources into global growth.** Like other profitable company investments, building an international footprint takes time and money. Many companies that fail do so because they give up too easily, not dedicating enough resources to the initiative, not allowing enough time for the local team to find traction, or launching and then turning to focus on new markets or other initiatives. Six to twelve months is rarely enough time to find traction in a new market—it often can take two to three years.

9. **Not building the structures to create momentum.** Setting direction isn't enough. Companies that don't develop the right structures and processes to support scaling cannot maintain a thriving global footprint (more on this in chapter seven).

10. **Not universalizing core values and company culture.** The business culture in each country is unique and requires a customized approach. Attempting to push core values that only resonate with the business culture of the headquarters market or conflict with local culture will not engage or empower employees (or customers) in other local markets. Common core values need to be discovered (more on this in chapter ten).

These ten mistakes may characterize why companies often fail, but how can you succeed at running a business at global scale? The secret ingredient is the Global Class mindset (described in the next chapter).

THE GLOBAL CLASS JOURNEY AHEAD

No book before this one has brought together best practices for international market entry and growth from over fifty countries.

While industries, products, target customers, and key business drivers all differ among companies that succeed in building global businesses, they share certain commonalities. To characterize these common traits, we have created the concept of the *Global Class Company.*

This book will help you answer the core questions your company has when growing globally:

- WHO are the best people to build a global organization around?
- WHAT do we need to change about our business to fit in new markets?
- HOW do we implement Global Class strategies and scale our business?

The insights and tools presented here are not meant to be a prescriptive, step-by-step guide that must be followed. Instead, they're a mindset and set of frameworks that can be adapted and applied to a wide variety of businesses. The insights herein reduce the risks associated with expanding in international markets and provide a common lexicon around the next generation of international business.

Most notably, the companies profiled represent some of the fastest-growing companies in the world, which have been able to scale their businesses globally using their own flavors and fragments of the advice within this book.

While your application of key concepts will vary, you will gain the following from reading this book:

- A deeper understanding of what it takes to develop and manage a global organization.
- A common vocabulary related to global growth that can help communicate important aspects of your strategy and highlight key focus areas.
- A set of practical frameworks that can be used not only to provide a pathway to scale but also serve as a troubleshooting tool when things go wrong in existing markets.
- A comprehensive library of concepts and factors to consider throughout the global growth process.
- Case studies, scenarios, and stories that come from the experiences top companies had in scaling globally, which you can use to inform your planning and decision-making.

Planning is key to avoiding common mistakes. Throughout this book you will encounter insights into how to avoid mistakes through expansion stories (failures and successes), practical frameworks, and tactical steps to guide you on your path to success.

No matter which scenario best fits your current situation, this book is designed to provide valuable and practical insights that you can apply to your business.

With the goal of equipping you with the knowledge you need to successfully scale your business globally, let's start by investigating the mindset of the world's most successful companies, decoding what makes them Global Class.

CHAPTER 1 SUMMARY

- The world has changed. We have entered a new era of global business that merits a new (culturally conscious) approach to building an organization at global scale.
- There are key mistakes to avoid when scaling globally that waste time and money.
- Companies who have expanded globally have had to reinvent the wheel. No playbook exists to take companies through *market entry* and *market growth*, until now.

CHAPTER 1 REFLECTION & ACTION QUESTIONS

- How has your view on international recently changed?
- How have you adapted your management practices to navigate the acceleration of distributed work?
- Which of the ten reasons why international expansion initiatives fail is your organization most guilty of?

• 2 •

LEAD

The Global Class Company

Somewhere between multiple extended journeys to Silicon Valley to pitch investors while building a team of engineers and relocating from Perth in Western Australia to Sydney, Melanie Perkins solidified her goal to build a truly global product and company. As CEO and co-founder of Australian graphic design platform Canva, she guided the company to align with the mission "to empower everyone in the world to design." This manifested into a platform that people from all corners of the world could intuitively use to communicate ideas universally.

Having this global mindset came naturally to Melanie, who came from a diverse background; she's the child of an Australian-born teacher and Malaysian engineer of Sri Lankan and Filipino descent. This mindset can clearly be seen in the company's culture, team, product, and operations.

For some companies, going global requires a difficult shift from its current way of doing business. Other companies, often born more recently, build this mentality from the beginning.

Such is the case for Canva. The company was deliberately created with international growth in mind, and the goal to reach global scale has permeated every aspect of how business is conducted. From communications to recruitment to product, the whole company has thought global from day one.

Canva has built a distributed organization—not clustered so that specific teams are in the same physical place (like the whole engineering team being in one office together) but dispersed so that members of the same team are in different geographies. A special effort is made to foster global interactions and collaborations to cross-pollinate ideas and best practices.

The team was globally minded and culturally conscious from the beginning. More than seventy languages are spoken in the company's Sydney headquarters, giving the company a global purview and focus. The company's leadership believes that when you hire international day one, there are less likely to be core value conflicts when entering new markets.

The company's product was designed in such a way that it was easy to localize, in part by providing a customized set of templates and imagery that would resonate with each local market. Naturally, the platform was also built for global scale.

Canva leveraged local market expertise, ensuring translation and content creation was done in-market. The company also made an effort to develop and promote leaders from within local markets, after attempts to bring in leadership from outside the local market failed. This effort to promote from within was a key to Canva's success in building its team in the Philippines.

Canva has expanded at breakneck speed. The company set the bold goal of translating its product and platform (along with customized templates) into one hundred languages within a single year. While it ended up taking a little less than two years to reach this goal, the global scope of the initiative and the work the company did to support a multilingual platform paid dividends with building a global customer base and in keeping the team's focus on running a company with a global mindset.

To keep momentum going, the company has effectively managed complexity, striking a balance between speed (decentralized forces) and efficiency (centralized forces), ultimately finding a way to reduce complexity without slowing the path of progress.

Finally, Canva has developed a new definition of "headquarters" and a unique interaction model between HQ and local market presence, with a concerted effort to break down barriers. For example, the company used to have "HQ" in the name of a number of its Slack channels, but this proved not to support the company's inclusive culture and was ultimately removed, especially when the growth of virtual work increased teams' distribution. Also, because pivotal functions are spread across multiple national boundaries (for example, marketing is spread across Sydney and San Francisco, among other members distributed all over the globe), the company introduced a new concept they refer to as a hub. While the model is still developing rapidly and the company continues opening offices all over the world, team members are tied to (often virtual) clusters to foster inclusivity and establish Feedback Loops (multi-directional lines of communication throughout an organization that facilitate best practice sharing and innovation).

Canva's mission to empower everyone in the world to design reverberated through the design of the company itself, empowering employees, customers, and other stakeholders alike.

Companies like Canva are emerging around the world as access to capital becomes more widespread. Talent is accessible anywhere, and with an increasingly diverse workforce, the move toward internationalization will happen even faster. Melanie and her co-founders Cliff Obrecht and Cameron Adams have built Canva into a perfect example of this.

Canva has been able to execute on a strong global *vision* by leveraging a diverse pool of *talent*, shifting the *role of HQ* to enable distributed teams and enacting a *strategy* that seeks the local way of finding traction and scale.

WHAT IS THE GLOBAL CLASS COMPANY?

Canva isn't the only company taking this approach to building a global organization. A new class of leading global businesses is emerging. They see the opportunities that await in international markets and understand the need to localize all aspects of their business to scale within these new markets. Some of these companies are fast-growing start-ups entering new geographies for the first time, while others are established companies already in many markets that have figured out this formula through trial and error.

No matter where these companies are born, the industries they are in, or the customers they serve, they are all Global Class. We define a Global Class Company as *an organization that strives for, and achieves, global scale by: balancing localization and complexity, building a culturally conscious agile team, establishing the structures and management model to support a distributed organization, and balancing company and local cultures.*

What Makes a Company Global Class?

There are many ways to describe it. It's an action. As Shopify executive Daniel Sullivan puts it, "International is baked into everything and everyone" at Global Class Companies. It's a recognition of the new era of global business we live in. "Products don't have borders; people will look anywhere" for the right solution, as Tomas Kandl, Head of Silicon Valley at Business Sweden, puts it. It's most definitely a mindset and way of doing business.

While nuances for industry and product type (physical versus software) lead to many flavors of Global Class, the core tenets—the WHO, WHAT, and HOW—are very similar.

WHO Do Global Class Companies Employ?

Global Class Companies employ people (at all levels) who cultivate a global mindset and cultural consciousness. Through life experience and empathy, they uphold a sensitivity to the differences of culture and an openness to the new and not yet understood.

The Global Class Company builds a pipeline of this type of talent, placing a premium on local market knowledge and instilling within all members of the local team its company culture and core values. There is a distinct set of skills (built on the foundation of an agile mindset) that the Global Class looks for and nurtures.

While fast-growing businesses in recent years have increasingly sought job candidates with traits related to being agile, Global Class Companies go one step further, looking for candidates with cultural curiosity. As companies start thinking about international markets earlier in their growth journeys, cultural sensitivity and a global mindset will be essential traits at all levels of the organization.

As this new era of global business continues, these skills will become part of the filtering process during recruiting, as more roles will be stretched to cover an international footprint. Over time, this mindset will become so ubiquitous that, in the future, these "global natives" (which we call "Interpreneurs" and describe in more detail in the next chapter) will be the equivalent of the digital natives of today who have not seen a world without the internet and mobile technology.

We also see that culturally minded professionals who have already built (or aspire to build) global careers will form a tighter network than exists today.

They'll find ways to connect with each other and illustrate to others the importance of global curiosity and cultural considerations in building a business—all of which further integrates this mindset into the DNA of top global companies (more on this in chapter four).

WHAT Do Global Class Companies Do?

What do Global Class Companies do to get traction in new markets and reach global scale? To put it as simply as possible, they localize. In their minds, localization is not limited to language translation or culturally tailored marketing campaigns; it seeps through to all aspects of the business. Localization is a way of life.

Growing trends and technology are catalysts for these localization efforts.

Besides platforms that make the localization process easier, new approaches to localization are emerging. Technology helps connect businesses to customers all over the world, in real time. Customization has long been a tool of the Global Class, so customized experiences that help engage customers across the globe continue to emerge.

Most importantly, Global Class Companies manage complexity in the localization process, especially in strategic planning and supporting scaling across a diverse global footprint. Instead of fixing these complexities after the fact, the Global Class plans for and prioritizes mitigating complexities from the beginning. They understand that adaptations to their operating models needed to achieve product-market fit (and beyond) in a single market could be scaled across multiple countries.

Global Class Companies put balancing localization and complexity at the center of the conversation. They don't shy away from this balancing act or the tough conversations and decisions that come along with it (more on this in chapter five).

IMPORTANT NOTE: COMPANY-MARKET FIT

Product-market fit is often the main milestone and measurement of a company's success in entering a new market. While the concept of product-market fit is widely understood (albeit at times with varying definitions), we believe the concept doesn't fully capture the fit that companies need to be successful when entering new global markets. As we'll discuss throughout the book, many aspects of the company beyond the product must adapt to find traction and scale in a new market; the product is only a small part of that.

We define **company-market fit** as *the right go-to-market, operational, organizational, and culture models needed to satisfy the requirements of a local market.* Therefore, companies achieve company-market fit by localizing these aspects of their business while successfully managing the complexities that come along with these changes. As we will discuss, this is a difficult, but necessary, process that is further complicated when factoring in the unique elements of each individual market and the exponential challenge of managing this process across many different countries.

Product-Market Fit and Company-Market Fit

The often-used product-market fit label is focused on identifying a customer need and confirming your product or service meets that need in a scalable and profitable way. While product-market fit is an important milestone in the process, companies must go a step further in international markets by building the right organizational capabilities and cultural fit to reach scale. Throughout the book we will refer to both product-market fit and company-market fit. When we use the term *product-market fit* we are referring to validating the business in a company's initial market and the beginning stage right after launching in a new market as the company searches for early traction. *Company-market fit,* on the other hand, is a longer-term goal, and we use this term to describe the milestone of having validated the go-to-market and operating models in a new country. Further, *company-market fit* includes building the organizational structures to support scale in new markets while finding the right balance of company and local cultures.

This whole book is centered on detailing what it takes to achieve company-market fit and provides frameworks and tools to help companies achieve this goal.

HOW Do Global Class Companies Do It?

Empowering the right team and having the right localization strategy aren't enough. The Global Class leverages a set of tactics and best practices to build a business at global scale. They use an internationalized agile methodology to structure the localization process and find the right model for a new market.

They follow a multistage process both at initial launch and as a troubleshooting mechanism to overcome obstacles in the process of scaling. Their mindset is a muscle that is built over time and constantly exercised.

The bulk of this book outlines agile tools, structures, and processes that Global Class Companies use to transform strategy into international business success, supporting a globally scaled business along the way. From proper planning to removing obstacles, from market entry to market growth, from cultural considerations to a distinct style of organizational management, the Global Class approach is holistic and comprehensive, but flexible to fit the unique realities of your business.

Where does it start? Like developing any new skill or launching any initiative, it all starts with the right mindset.

THE GLOBAL CLASS MINDSET

As Tiffany Stevenson, Chief People Officer at Patreon, says, "there is a difference between being international and being global; global is a mindset."

Having global ambitions is an important aspect of building an international business, but ambition isn't nearly enough. Few companies have attained true global adoption without facing peril from local competition. Despite the sophistication of its product and scale, Zendesk was unable to grab local customer mindshare in India from Freshdesk because of the latter's home field advantage and local brand recognition. Despite seemingly endless resources, Uber was unable to beat Didi in China (although Uber orchestrated a deal to own 20 percent of Didi, which was a big financial win for Uber shareholders). Ample resources, a talented team, and the ability to execute on a strong strategy are important, but the Global Class mindset is the differentiator. The team from Uber learned to recognize the importance of the local perspective from its experience in China. They took a different approach for the company's Middle East expansion, acquiring Careem and keeping the brand intact, allowing it to run as a separate entity and dominate the region. To navigate these challenges and succeed, companies must call upon a new leadership model and mindset.

This distinct mindset serves as a guide for planning and execution alike. It is based on the notion that everyone must be a leader when expanding globally, not just those at HQ. HQ shows leadership by trusting and empowering local teams, manifesting this mindset through a comprehensive management model designed to work with a globally distributed team (detailed in chapter nine). It doesn't matter whether the company is scaling in one country or one hundred; it's about having the right approach to global growth. The mindset's components are numerous, but they fit into four categories:

- Vision
- Talent and Culture
- HQ Role
- Strategy

	Global Class Mindset	Legacy Mindset
Vision	*Think* Global Day One	Home Market Bias
Talent	Distributed Strategy	Centralized/Clustered Strategy
HQ Role	Enabler & Support	Command & Control
Strategy	Local Way	Company Way

Vision

Global Class Companies develop a focused vision. As former Microsoft leader Giancarlo Cozzi puts it, Global Class Companies "choose as much what NOT to do as what to do." Global Class Companies recognize that resources are often limited, so they focus and don't get distracted by shiny objects. With limited resources, these companies know they can't reach a worldwide audience simultaneously. They build their company in a specific way to generate momentum when entering new markets. The Global Class understands the extent of the impact they make when entering a market and the right strategy to successfully get traction and scale.

Global Class Companies Think Global Day One

The most important (and nuanced) part of this mindset is evident in the word *think*. At times in our research, we heard the phrase "born global," and while many companies from smaller countries approach markets outside their borders early in the life of their business, it became evident to us that no company that was successful on a global scale was global from inception. A "born global" company is a myth. Resources are too limited, and local market culture, regulations, and preferences are just too different and fragmented for a company to immediately be ready for global scale day one. Successful scaling is more than just making a product available in a new market. Moreover, finding validation in an initial market is an important first step to have the right foundation to achieve scale in international markets later.

Instead, Global Class Companies *think* global day one by building all aspects of their business—product, team, culture, operations—to localize for multiple markets. They make plans to expand to international markets from the very beginning. Global Class Companies build customizations into a product or service to appeal to the local culture. They build a diverse multinational team of distributed talent and set up distributed support structures to empower local teams.

Global scale is a deliberate process that needs to be worked up to. Mikkel Brun, Tradeshift co-founder and Senior Vice President of APAC, points out, "When you are born global, irrational expansion can happen. The Global Class mindset brings rationality back, even if you already have the right cultural-mindedness within the team."

Global Class Companies realize the importance of having leadership buy-in from the beginning and work hard to procure alignment, adequate resources, and executive champions for international growth efforts. Their leaders realize that going global is as make-or-break for the future of the business as finding product-market fit in an initial market is. Getting validation in an initial market is an important prerequisite.

Today, the notion of building a new business that doesn't have an online presence seems silly. Likewise would be the decision of whether a Global Class Company should "go global"; of course almost every company will do business in more than one country. What was once the mindset of entrepreneurs hailing from smaller markets, thinking global from day one will be more common-place for companies born in even the world's largest markets.

Uber thought global from the beginning. Slack (a company born in Canada) had a presence in Vancouver, Dublin, San Francisco, and New York very early on. Zendesk moved beyond its Denmark borders in its infancy. And while other companies like Roku took years to prepare the right product before executing on their expansion strategies, the company had a global vision early on, taking the long view when implementing.

The "Initial" Market

As this new era of global business proliferates, there continues to be a conver-
gence of how companies from larger markets and those from smaller markets
think about global business.

Companies born in smaller markets begin considering other global markets much earlier in the creation process out of necessity. Business leaders from
Israel, for example, know that their initial market isn't large enough to generate
a huge, scaled-out business, as the market size is too small.

Companies from large markets like the United States, China, or Brazil
begin thinking about international growth much later in the process, given the
vast opportunities within their own borders. These markets have hundreds of
millions of people (or, in the case of China, more than a billion) who have some
of the strongest buying power in the world—places where you can maintain a
multibillion-dollar business without looking to new markets.

To combat this dynamic, companies from smaller markets look toward a
larger market to validate the business and scale. Zendesk, for example, selected
the US as its initial market over its native Denmark so the company could validate its business model and prove scale in a way not possible in its home country.

We have seen this time and time again from companies hailing from smaller
markets, so much so that we have come to believe that it is a pattern for success. Hence, we think a new moniker is merited for the first market a business
is validated in. Instead of referring to it as the "home market," going forward
we will refer to it as the "*initial* market," since the first market the Global Class
scales in may be far from home.

At the same time, this aspect of the Global Class mindset can be a powerful
force for companies born in larger markets. When you divide up the world into
"home" and "international," it leads to an us-versus-them dynamic (mentioned
as one of the main reasons expansion efforts failed in the last chapter) and a bias
toward the first model that finds traction. Businesses built for the "home" market don't factor in flexibilities for localization. The Global Class doesn't think
in terms of a "home" market but instead of an "initial" market whose model
will be localized when scaling internationally.

Over time, Global Class Companies from larger markets will start entering
new markets sooner in their global growth journeys, afforded the opportunity
provided by the more agile idea of an "initial" market (this is how things start

and they will change over time) than a "home" market (this is how things are done at HQ).

Global Class Companies also understand that the *best* initial market isn't necessarily the *biggest*. Niklas Lundsberg, Head of New Markets at Spotify, explained that while all their competitors at the infancy of the music streaming industry selected the US as their initial market, Spotify intentionally chose not to enter the US market first, and that led, in part, to their long-term success. Spotify's native Sweden ended up being a perfect initial market for a number of reasons, namely the local culture around pirating music. iTunes did not expand in Sweden until many years after it launched in the US, so everyone pirated music, leading to a cultural norm that music should be free. This was so ingrained in the culture that Sweden even had a political party, the Pirate Party, whose main focus was on reforming intellectual property laws. This laid the groundwork for a free music streaming service to thrive. Instead of fighting for market share in the US, where it was difficult to get streaming music rights at the time, Spotify let competitors exhaust each other and validated its model in Sweden before expanding across the globe.

The same concept applies to a number of emerging start-ups. Companies like Zipline, which delivers medical supplies via drones, and Yoco, a fintech company that offers online payment and other services, both chose initial markets in Africa, where there was more freedom to implement new systems with less headwind from the existing infrastructure (air traffic control and the financial system, respectively), to validate their models. In the case of Zipline, the company is actually headquartered in Silicon Valley but sees the benefit of first validating the business in African countries.

CASE STUDY

BUILD FOR TWO MARKETS—BLABLACAR

While the "initial market" aspect of the Global Class mindset may seem abstract, there is a very concrete and straightforward way to make the leap: Build your business for two markets.

When you create a business with a single market in mind, you build bias into the foundation of the business. When you deliberately build with more than one market in mind, you consider the nuances of localization and you architect your product, procedures, and culture to resonate more universally. While this mindset is nuanced, it is powerful. When you build with two markets in mind, you make decisions that don't get stuck in the biases and unique circumstances of a single market. Moreover, you are able to scale faster as you enter new markets, since the localization process is less painful, as your business is less entrenched in a single way of doing things.

Note that this doesn't mean *launching* in both markets at once, but *building* the company with more than one market in mind.

This "build for two" framing was spearheaded by BlaBlaCar (the world's largest carpooling platform) founder and President Frédéric Mazzella, whose initial market was France. From the beginning, all aspects of the business were created with two markets in mind: France and Spain.

The team was made up of culturally minded people, hailing from many countries, and all with a proficiency for the English language, helping overcome potential communications issues. Moreover, there was a deliberate focus on hiring people from markets the company planned to enter in the future to integrate a deeper understanding of the market into the team long before market launch.

The company's original brand name was *Covoiturage*, which means "carpooling" in French, to create a frame of reference for what the company did. This would have been an ideal name if Frédéric's goal had been to build a company just for the French market. However, in shifting to this two-market focus early on, Frédéric realized that the name wouldn't connect with many outside of the borders of France, so the more universal BlaBlaCar, which transcends languages better, was adopted.

Talent and Culture

It's not just a solid product and effective strategy that leads to global scale. The Global Class understands the importance of people and culture as well as the humanity that bridges borders. The role of these more human elements is even more paramount and must be deliberately addressed given the rise of distributed work.

A New View on Talent—Distributed and Diverse

The Global Class believes that talent is skills driven, not location driven. For legacy companies, selecting talent used to factor in location as much as skill set.

Global Class Companies focus squarely on the latter. This allows culture-fit to be an even more prominent selection criterion.

The ability to run a distributed organization is an essential muscle all Global Class Companies have developed. They hire where the talent is, understanding that sourcing talent only from their local area is limiting. In fact, at times they intentionally hire team members from abroad.

Legacy companies build clusters of talent focusing on hiring whole offices of people in specific geographic areas. If the company needs cybersecurity expertise, for example, the strategy is to build a cybersecurity center in Israel, where that skill set is prevalent. Global Class Companies, on the other hand, hire talented individuals wherever they are (and get local market knowledge from them in addition to the expertise they are being hired for).

Legacy companies believe that if teams aren't in the same physical space, they can't have chemistry. Global Class teams know that team chemistry and camaraderie can be developed virtually.

They realize that hiring people everywhere gives the advantage of global-mindedness and averts the risk of not being able to adapt when new markets and obstacles challenge the existing model. They know that having local expertise in many markets will help accelerate market entry and avoid pitfalls when the time is right to expand. The Global Class realizes that having people with diverse perspectives can better address local market needs and nuances.

Legacy companies hire people more similar to themselves; the Global Class builds a diverse workforce. Legacy companies value Ivy League candidates or other indications of pedigree. Global Class Companies know that talent isn't related to a diploma. They look at underserved communities for talent, seeking diversity of experience and background. They start hiring employees in global markets early, understanding the positive impact their perspectives can have on the mindset and strategy of the organization.

As illustrated in the BlaBlaCar case earlier in the chapter, Global Class Companies start thinking about building a diverse talent pipeline from the outset and consider what markets they could envision entering in the future. Even employee onboarding emphasizes the organization's role in the world as a global citizen and contributor to society. They also see training as essential to bridge company core values and local context, which is needed for local employees to activate their unique localized context. Global Class Companies establish formalized processes for new hires in international markets to develop a deeper company knowledge, often having them spend time at HQ.

This diversity is essential even when large clusters of employees are geographically close. Forty-two countries are represented among the two hundred Prezi employees located at its headquarters in Budapest. The Global Class intentionally builds multicultural teams and is data-driven in its approach to increase diversity.

Having a "distributed" team has taken on a whole new meaning now. In recent years, a legacy company executive might have said something like, "We have a development team in Estonia," highlighting how a distributed team meant having clusters of employees in geographic proximity based on departments/functions (often based on the reputations certain regions had for specific expertise). Not the case for the Global Class.

Global Class Companies have a truly distributed workforce in which team members of all functions can be in any region, and not always geographically colocated by function. They give their employees more freedom to choose their own schedule, offering the opportunity to adapt work to fit local lifestyle. These companies are able to attract top talent no matter where they are and navigate the challenges of purely virtual interactions. A truly cross-border workforce completely kills the languishing idea of a nine-to-five workday as collaboration melds time zones together and work-life *integration* will become more prevalent than work-life *balance*.

They implement tools that allow for asynchronous collaboration and create opportunities for team members in different time zones to connect. When operating at global scale, it can be easy for employees to feel like they are working 24/7, collaborating with colleagues across the world. Global Class Companies engage their distributed workforce and preempt burnout to keep team members from feeling like they are constantly working.

Finding talent that has a global mindset is key for the Global Class as they prioritize talent that has the potential to acquire new functional skills that are important to execute their role. They see that learning equals engagement and therefore create more learning opportunities, and in particular cross-cultural ones. They provide employees with opportunities for geographic mobility, teaching them about new cultures and connecting them with colleagues from across the globe. They recognize that this builds personal and cultural understanding, all of which improves team productivity and localization.

A Company's Physical Space Still Matters

As Gabriel Engel, co-founder and CEO of Rocket.Chat points out, even when you have a virtual and distributed team, the notion of having a physical space is still important. Instead of occupying space in a high-rise office building, the company's "headquarters" in Porto Alegre, Brazil, is located in a house with a swimming pool, outdoor kitchen for weekly barbecues, and a large indoor kitchen that is a meeting area for company employees. They even kept some of the bedrooms intact to serve as a private Airbnb-like spot for people traveling from out of town to stay in. As Gabriel says, "Even with a company working remotely, there is still the notion of the company having a home, an expression of company values. Everyone doesn't have to go there all the time, but it's an important representation of what the company cares about. Our headquarters is more about finding interaction and building relationships than being designed for people to just do their work."

Company Culture and Core Values

Global Class Companies universalize core values, as Canva did by adopting its core value "make complex simple," given the universal desire for simplicity based in cognitive science and psychology. They find ways to adapt company culture to local nuances while staying true to these core values. In a way, they elevate the development of core values, which may resonate in only a specific region, to "universal virtues" that have more global appeal. Legacy companies that hold an initial market bias find it harder to do this universalization, while Global Class Companies understand the importance of having values that can align with employees and customers alike, worldwide.

Core values even factor into market selection for the Global Class. When considering the Saudi Arabia market, Uber felt that the restrictions on women being allowed to work conflicted with its core values, so it worked to influence the Saudi government to change its policies, leading to women being granted the ability to drive. LinkedIn experienced a similar situation when an international government entity asked that the company add a gender filter to search results as part of an initiative to get more women in the workforce. Realizing this could also be used to discriminate against women, the company declined to make the change.

You may experience a conflict between company and local business culture, which must be navigated when entering a new market and building out a team. When companies don't pay specific attention to the transferability of their core values, they face misalignment with teams in new markets. Global Class Companies are mindful that their company culture and core values must resonate globally. When companies are building international teams from early on, core value conflicts are less likely, since the organization's earliest members will shape the company culture to have universal appeal.

Global Class Companies that have effectively scaled globally have strong company cultures and core values that serve as a guide for hiring, everyday decision-making, and conflict resolution. They have validated the universality of their core values by developing ones with universal appeal and testing their resonance in new markets and ensuring that they build teams of people who internalize these values and support them in how they do business. They allow for local market customs and celebrate the diversity across their global footprint, finding small ways to enhance their company culture with the uniqueness of different locales. A way to do this is to find the time to celebrate global milestones—whether it be opening a new international office, launching product localizations, or recognizing cultural holidays—as a way to promote diversity and inclusion.

OFFEN OVERLOOKED

Celebrating Global Milestones

Treat entering your first global market as a goalpost milestone to celebrate. Kathryn Hymes, former Head of International Product Expansion for Slack, has worked at multiple companies from early days to Initial Public Offering (IPO). She said that in retrospect the first launch into a global market was a turning and inflection point that should be highlighted, often one of less than a handful of moments remembered looking back post-IPO. Celebrating this moment gives purpose to people working on international initiatives and purpose to the company more broadly. Don't short-change it, and don't miss out on a historic moment in the life of the company.

Value the Human Side of Everything

Global Class Companies focus on the human side of company culture, product development, and the operating model alike. They make an effort to build bridges across cultural boundaries and connect to the human condition and how their solution contributes to improving the community and individuals they touch.

Global Class Companies thinking of international markets day one will reduce cultural barriers and foster interconnectedness through localization efforts and deliberately building a diverse team. As Mark Twain said, "Travel is fatal to prejudice, bigotry, and narrow-mindedness . . . things cannot be acquired by vegetating in one little corner of the earth all one's lifetime." With the team getting exposed to other cultures, silos and lack of understanding break down in the face of recognized commonalities and shared humanity.

Similar customer needs exist across borders (with some caveats). As Airbnb learned during its rapid expansion to dozens of countries, consumers are hungry for new ideas, products, and services. These customers recognize they don't have the same access internationally as they do in the United States, but when they are effectively given something new and innovative, they are eager to both engage with it and to make the experience their own.

While this presents an opportunity to access international customers, particularly for B2C and software companies, it's also important to understand that these customers are savvy and detect whether a company truly cares about them. Global Class Companies adapt to meet local customer needs. They show target customers in new markets that they not only "get" them but have also localized their business to support them and will continue to innovate and deliver value in the future. This also extends to the communities Global Class Companies enter as they prioritize having a positive impact on society over no-holds-barred disruption.

The Global Class sees the human side of market selection. In our research, we found that companies typically evaluate new markets based on three core factors:

1. Economic and population indicators and favorability of market dynamics.
2. Already existing customer base established through organic growth.
3. Location of the talent with relevant skills (people driven).

Global Class Companies see a fourth factor—the more human and cultural considerations that are often below the surface, which don't come to light until they build knowledge of the local market. Neglecting these elements can be detrimental to finding scale, but addressing them can uncover new criteria to consider for subsequent market growth initiatives.

- BlaBlaCar built momentum quickly after launching in Russia because hitchhiking is a normal part of Russian culture. This was not a core criterion prior to entry, but became an important consideration going forward after they saw how it led to rapid scale in the Russian market.
- Airbnb fueled its growth by identifying people with common interests or shared beliefs that transcended borders.
- Evernote and Prezi achieved deep penetration in South Korea through efforts that considered the human side to connect with customers. Evernote tapped into the desire of local young professionals to show their status in an upwardly mobile–focused society, giving premium users a physical pin to show off in public. Prezi's efforts to connect with South Korean consumers led to two of the three candidates using the presentation platform in a recent presidential election.

HQ Role

Having the right vision, team, and cohesive culture isn't enough to successfully scale a company globally. The Global Class understands that with a diverse global footprint and workforce, HQ must take on a different role to empower a distributed team to act instead of being the bottleneck for decision-making. They also see that HQ doesn't have to be the genesis of innovative ideas, and, in fact, are often too far removed from customers in local markets to be the driver of innovation.

Two-Way Innovation

In support of many of the ingredients of the Global Class mindset previously discussed (like the notion of an "initial" vs. "home" market), companies that are successful at reaching global scale foster an environment with bidirectional cadence.

For the Global Class, innovation is not something cascaded from HQ on high to the lowly local markets. On the contrary, these companies practice two-way innovation, looking to gather insights from best practices implemented in every local market as much as sharing a best practice discovered at HQ. Global Class Companies use their global footprint to uncover best practices from one market that can apply to other markets (even markets where the local presence is more mature).

Amazon's Seller Flex Space initiative, for example, was born in India, not Seattle. As Jose Chapa, former Director of Product for Amazon's Home Innovation Program in Europe, explained, the supply chain in India was not nearly as developed as it is in many other countries. Establishing the same type of massive fulfillment center footprint wouldn't work, given the different dynamics of last-mile delivery in India. What the Amazon team in India did was launch an initiative to get full coverage of the country through leveraging small stores, which often have space for additional inventory. The initiative turned these small shops into micro Amazon fulfillment centers. This strategy has since been implemented in many other regions with similar supply chain environments.

Because Global Class Companies understand that the best ideas don't always come from HQ, they set up a culture of best practice sharing and mechanisms to uncover the local nuances that can have a large global impact.

HQ's New Primary Role

Compared to legacy companies, headquarters (HQ) in Global Class Companies play a very different role in managing a global organization. Within Global Class Companies, HQ's primary roles are to support and enable local teams, not command and control them, as is the case with many legacy companies.

Given that the Global Class doesn't hold on to the notion of a "home" market, they minimize the us-versus-them dynamic present at many companies, which pits HQ against local teams. They don't maintain an HQ bias or favor their initial market, which can create issues when expanding internationally. This initial market is just the first of many on the path of global scale.

Probably the most interesting area of change for the Global Class is with organizational structures, in particular, the relationship between HQ and local teams. While there are pronounced differences depending on industry, product form (physical or digital), and target customer (B2B vs. B2C vs. B2B2C), among other factors, Global Class organizations that operate (at least in part) with a distributed structure will carve out a competitive advantage from legacy competition.

Which functions are centralized and which are localized will depend on the company and stage of expansion, but the concept of HQ will be similar; HQ will no longer be just a physical place. Global Class companies make an effort to decouple HQ from the operations of the company's initial market to put this market on a level playing field with the rest of the company's international footprint (referenced later in chapter seven). Global Class Companies still have dedicated office locations (or at least coworking spaces) unless they are fully committed to remote-only work, but HQ will change from a physical geography or building location to a virtual power center where vision is set and processes and structure to support localization are created and maintained. All over the world, HQ's influence, as well as decision-making, support, and enablement, is beginning to be distributed as leadership teams now sit in multiple locations. Face-to-face meetings have migrated to interactions via digital tools that capture the company's brain trust. Platforms that create a digital hub in the place of a physical HQ are beginning to proliferate. All of these changes merit a new approach.

The new role of HQ for Global Class Companies is to:

- Support global scaling through implementing mechanisms and dedicating resources that foster growth, creating strong communication channels, and developing trust through granting autonomy.
- Enable the localization process while managing complexity.
- Build a strong team with both company and local market knowledge.
- Facilitate two-way innovation to deploy local best practices globally.
- Balance company culture and local cultures to empower a global team.
- Contribute to the communities the company engages with, while making decisions aligned with core values.

In addition to establishing support and direction-setting structures, HQ must create processes that facilitate progression through the stages of international growth, as well as clear (but customizable) metrics to focus the efforts of the team.

Some companies are even looking to do away with the term *headquarters* completely. As Tiffany Stevenson, Chief People Officer at Patreon, explains, the company now uses the term *hub* in their organizational design instead of *HQ*, explaining how this change creates a new dynamic between local teams and across functions. She indicates, "Hubs are everywhere. They have a specific mission, and different hubs can work together to solve a problem. In this model teams become the center of decision-making, taking the pressure off of an HQ mindset and empowering the greater team."

Disclaimer: Defining HQ

As HQ is becoming the distributed resource whose purpose is to enable the company's presence in local markets, the traditional command and control role of HQ is taking a back seat. This means that how companies are organized could be beginning to change as well, with some companies developing systems of hubs or networks of teams whose shape may look more like a social network map than a traditional hierarchical organizational chart. Regardless, centralized enablement and support mechanisms are needed to be the stewards of the company goals and culture and facilitators of decision-making.

That said, when we refer to "HQ" throughout the book, we are referring more to this new incarnation of HQ (focused on enablement) than the traditional monolithic concept of an HQ (command and control); we are, however, making the deliberate choice to use the "HQ" moniker instead of inventing a new term since the concept is globally understood and this new iteration of HQ is still in flux.

Strategy

While the company way of doing things leads to success in an initial market, this mindset faces challenges in global markets. A new type of strategy is required that considers the local market, is mindful of the downside of disruption, and enables local teams to turn ideas into operations. It is these elements that enable the Global Class to successfully launch and reach global scale.

The Local Way

As previously mentioned, the "American way" of doing things is long gone, and the days are numbered for businesses that let the "company way" drive their efforts. Instead, Global Class Companies strive to find a balance, doing things the "local way," meaning localizing the business to fit the local market while staying true to company principles.

This aspect of the mindset can be particularly difficult for many fast-growing companies, because as we heard many times in our research, culture tops everything. It is a strong company culture that leads to scale, but when layering in the nuances of navigating local culture across multiple international markets, the company way can run into trouble. Since business cultures differ in each international market, how can you expect that your company's core values will resonate universally if built only with your first market in mind?

Global Agile

Adoption of agile principles is key to international success. Global Class Companies use these methodologies to determine what pivots they need to make from their core business and operating model to find traction in a new market.

Instead of using the waterfall approach with a formal market launch, Global Class Companies take a more iterative approach, utilizing the same methodology that start-ups use when validating a new business. They revisit every aspect of the business and label their current way of doing business as hypotheses to be tested (making educated changes based on what is learned when researching a potential new market). Applying agile principles to global markets, they localize while not creating too many disparate modes in each market, which would become hard to manage. The Global Class knows that this requires the right type of talent—employees who fully understand agile and the local market and have a high level of cultural curiosity.

A Different View of Disruption

Disruption and change are table stakes for Global Class Companies. They are willing to discard current models to fit a new international market and navigate shifts in their industry, willing to disrupt their own ways of doing business to maintain their place in the market and better serve their customers. At the same time, they maintain core values and a sense of company culture.

Many legacy companies that have bought into the company way mentality believe that their product (or the jobs they bring to a new market) is enough. They feel like they should be lauded and recognized for entering the market, overlooking all the negative disruption their market entry brings with it.

Companies that think this way are quickly learning that the "ask for forgiveness instead of permission" style of market entry and disruption is a thing of the past. In a way, the by-product of Uber's global success that stirred up strife within the existing transportation systems in cities and countries across the world marked the end of the effectiveness of a "company way" mentality. Local governments that were burned by this brash form of hyper-growth are now more prepared and resistant to this style of growth.

For example, a few years ago San Francisco residents saw an overnight explosion of electric scooters. Teams from Lime to Bird were using the Uber playbook of hyper-growth. In a matter of days, these scooters were strewn across sidewalks, shop entrances, and street corners. After a few weeks, they disappeared overnight, only slowly trickling back in over the coming months.

What happened was that the City and County of San Francisco made it clear that they would not work with any electric scooter company that attempted to skirt current local ordinances or operate without up-front conversations and agreements. If a company didn't follow the rules and engage with the local government before launching, they would be expelled and unable to operate legally. This represented a stark shift from the environment Uber previously operated in when launching.

Unlike proponents of the company way, the Global Class looks at disruption differently. They don't just assume that their product will cure all ills. They see that their market entry disrupts many aspects of a local society, from how people interact with each other to the effect on the local tax base. The Global Class brings in affected stakeholders and builds a coalition of support to navigate any necessary changes to regulations together.

While investigating market conditions and government policy/priorities, Global Class Companies understand that it is important to acknowledge both the positive and negative effects of their market entry. As Thomas Kristensen, former Managing Director of EU Affairs for Facebook, points out, you often think about the value your product brings to the customers, but you don't recognize the disruption you create in countries where you are not a native (he notes this is especially true for internet-based products).

He urges companies to recognize the impact they're making on local communities and find ways to partner with key stakeholders to find solutions. For example, creating advertisement learning programs to help the advertisement industry use technology platforms and adapt their business model was effective for Facebook. Thomas points out that it's better to be proactive about this, as it tends to be more expensive to pick up the pieces afterwards if there is a problem. The publishing industry has political influence in various countries, so Facebook had to think about helping the market players they displaced when entering a new market.

Thomas also suggested that companies outline what their public policy goals are. Is the main driver purely market entry, or is the goal to change regulation or even bolster the company's reputation so as to be considered on the correct side of local policy initiatives? Your goals will dictate the best strategy. Moreover, he suggests that you don't attempt to exist under the radar. Be proactive; otherwise chatter will start, and if the narrative is already set, it is hard to reverse. Develop defenses for areas of weakness and stay in front of them.

For decades the American way of doing business was not only a management mantra but also a point of pride for (legacy) American-born businesses. The days of this mentality are long gone, but the success of companies with strong cultures (even toxic ones) has given rise to the company way of doing things. In this new era of culturally conscious global business, the rising mantra supports the local way, and the companies that will be successful will adopt this mindset and let it permeate all levels of their organization.

A good example of disruption gone wrong was seen in the attempt by professional soccer club owners across Europe to create their own "Super League." Led by a small group of non-European (mostly American) owners, plans were made to create a league exclusively of the highest-performing marquee teams from multiple leagues across the continent. Disregarding the reactions of their fan bases, these owners announced their plans to impose an American sports model in Europe. A revolt immediately erupted, and in order to avoid an international upheaval, the plans were scrapped (in less than forty-eight hours). If these owners had had the Global Class mindset, they would have had more consideration for their customers (fan bases) and wouldn't have forced the American way through their ill-advised scheme.

Legacy companies believe that new locales will love their ideas and effect on the market (disruption is good), while Global Class Companies know that localization is essential and that entering a new market can lead to disruptions and ripples in all corners of the local society.

To put all of these notions another way, Global Class Companies are built *for* the local environment, not just to profit off *of* it.

David Rodriguez, executive at robot delivery service Kiwibot, explains how they "build with the local environment in mind," asking for permission first (and not forgiveness, as market disruptors like Uber had done during their hyper-global growth).

Kiwibot maintains a sensitivity to and respect for local culture, engaging deliberately to build long-term relationships with stakeholders. The company works with local governments to ensure they adhere to local laws with their autonomous delivery solutions. They intentionally build technology that anyone can use, with accessibility not just for rich people, which has been the myopic view of many US-based emerging start-ups.

To package this mindset into one statement, the Global Class practices *local market–conscious disruption*.

A Different View of Corporate (and Global) Citizenship

Global Class Companies aim to contribute to the societies they are part of. Their primary goal is not tax avoidance. In fact, they make an effort to have a positive impact on the markets they sell in, beyond just delivering on their value proposition.

As co-founder and Executive Chairman Peter Arvai puts it, Prezi feels that it's important that this contributor mindset "runs all the way through the company." He points out that making a significant impact goes well beyond localizing a product, and that it's incumbent on Global Class Companies to invest locally.

In addition to addressing problems unique to the local markets they are in, Global Class Companies advocate for more universal issues, like equal pay for women. A great example of this is seen in the Salesforce equal pay policy in its attempts to eliminate any gender- or race-based discrimination in how its workforce is paid.

As you begin to understand the Global Class mindset, the question then surfaces: If my company has a legacy mindset, how do I transition to join the Global Class? The key steps include: revisiting your company core values and culture, evaluating your criteria for talent acquisition and development, measuring your diversity, building channels for effective communication, and creating processes to support global scale, all of which must start with securing leadership buy-in for being dedicated to reaching global scale. The chapters to come create structure and a common vocabulary around how to become Global Class so that you can become a catalyst for change within your organization.

It's clear that the Global Class thinks, plans, builds, and acts differently than legacy companies. **To the Global Class, culture is a path (and linchpin), processes are tools (table stakes for creating momentum), and people are catalysts (driven through purposeful and universally resonating company culture). At its core, the Global Class mindset is about balance: balance between HQ and the local teams, balance between speed and managing complexity.** That is why balance is a running theme throughout the book, and the remaining chapters are dedicated to mitigating problems in the process of achieving this balance.

Throughout this book we will take an even deeper look at the WHO, WHAT, and HOW of Global Class Companies, their unique mindset, and the methods they use to translate it into global business success—with the goal to help companies of all industries and stages achieve Global Class status. Since a strong team is the catalyst for any successful global growth initiative, let's start by looking at the *who*, the people Global Class Companies are made up of: Interpreneurs.

CHAPTER 2 SUMMARY

- In this new era of global business, a new type of company has emerged that is achieving global scale as never before: the Global Class Company.
- The "company way" is dead, giving way to a new mindset: the "local way" that involves adopting a new *Vision*, view on *Talent*, the *Role of HQ*, and overall *Strategy*.
- A new approach to disruption is needed to beat local competition while finding scale and acceptance in international markets.

CHAPTER 2 REFLECTION & ACTION QUESTIONS

1. Does your leadership team *think* global from day one?
2. Where does your HQ sit on the spectrum between command & control and enablement & support?
3. Which aspect (vision, talent, role of HQ, and strategy) of the Global Class mindset is your organization best at? Which does it have the most room for growth with?

· 3 ·

TRAILBLAZER
The Interpreneur

Nearly thirty years ago, American Abe Smith ventured off to teach English in a tiny fishing village located near the southern tip of Kyushu, Japan, in the Nagasaki Prefecture. Connecting with the locals in a rural town with a population of fewer than three thousand gave Abe a new lens on life, and an appreciation for the intricacies of a world beyond his American borders. Back at home everything moved relentlessly fast, but here in Japan, centuries-old traditions like sencha green tea ceremonies and slow, deliberate meals of local fish, heirloom vegetables, and seaweed, prepared by local families, opened Abe's mind to another, more purposeful way of life. The experience created a cultural curiosity in Abe and planted a seed that cemented the importance of cultural-mindedness and set him off on a global career.

The next lesson for Abe came in the form of a mentor who was a pioneer selling bagels and other food products in Japan. Seeing opportunity in the Japanese market, Abe worked with his mentor to build the business, constantly iterating as new challenges arose as the company (which was ultimately sold to Quaker Oats) navigated cultural barriers and local market nuances. The endless pivots gave Abe a sense of grit and a firm belief in the importance of the agile mindset in growing businesses in global markets.

Transitioning to a more corporate career track, Abe worked at Webex, where he took on leadership roles in the company's Latin America (LATAM) and Asia-Pacific (APAC) regions and built a relationship with a young engineer named Eric Yuan. As an employee working at multiple companies, Abe built a company mindset and the ability to drive change and innovate in the bureaucracy and complexity of established organizations through coalition building and collaboration, leading the team to focus on key drivers of global growth.

Other career opportunities led Abe to relocate his family to London, where he headed international growth for a fast-growing company. Coming back to the US, he was handpicked by Eric, now the CEO and founder of Zoom, to be the Head of International. Abe's identity as a global citizen, as well as his leadership philosophy, gave him patience, empathy, and a sense of purpose he would not have developed if he'd stayed in the continental United States. This was the driving force behind Eric asking Abe to lead one of Zoom's most important teams.

Through his career journey, Abe gained the combination of entrepreneurial mindset, company mindset, and cultural mindset that is the hallmark of successful global business leaders driving Global Class Companies.

Almost every executive we spoke with highlighted people as one of the most important differentiators in the success of their expansion initiatives. As Jorn Lyseggen, founder and Executive Chairman of Meltwater, put it, "It's less about *what* to do in each market and more about *who* you hire to do it."

Leaders like Abe Smith and others in similar global growth roles don't seek the spotlight. They often work under the radar, but it's their ability to translate successful business models to global markets that is a company's key to achieving international scale.

Now that you're equipped with an understanding of how Global Class Companies think and act, it's time to better understand the specific type of person these top companies call on to lead and support their international growth efforts. We would go as far as saying that the archetype profiled in this chapter is the template for the successful global businessperson of the future.

For the purpose of simplicity, we found it best to offer a moniker for these international-minded business leaders. In doing so, we call on all the characteristics that make them effective at scaling businesses internationally, as outlined in the rest of this book. The label we landed on was "Interpreneur"—"inter," as in *international*, and "preneur" to evoke the mindset of today's business innovators.

We recognize the trite nature of this label but knowingly proceed, given the mindset overlap between Interpreneurs and other "preneurs" that are commonly canonized and criticized in business today. In a way, Interpreneurs are an evolution of the agile innovators of today, who must now operate within a distributed workplace that is becoming increasingly global.

WHAT IS AN INTERPRENEUR?

Functionally, an Interpreneur is a business professional who recognizes global business opportunity, rallies the team around scaling internationally, and contributes to the organization's adopting and maintaining a Global Class mindset.

Interpreneurs are in fact a fusion of entrepreneurs and intrapreneurs, with a little something extra mixed in.

Interpreneurs are *entrepreneurial* because they are agile, quick to adapt, and willing to not only face but actively take on the unknown. They maintain a growth mindset, knowing that applying agile methodology in new markets is vital and believing in the importance of constantly learning, even amidst failure.

Interpreneurs are also *intrapreneurial* because their roles require them to navigate the complexities of an established organization with set policies, along with varying levels of bureaucracy and internal politics, while building a coalition to support their internationally minded goals, goals that are often merely a small subset of the organization's greater focus. As Christina Lee, Vice President of International Growth at Chegg, puts it, you need to be able to "innovate something from within the box."

Early on in the life of a company that is growing in new international markets, it is a huge challenge to get the resources and attention of the leadership team needed to find product-market fit (and ultimately company-market fit) in other countries. Intrapreneurial skills are needed to work within the existing organizational rules to get the assigned resources to get things done.

It's also important to note that Interpreneurs aren't just the people who pack up their lives and move to a new country to open a new office. Interpreneurs can be located at HQ. They can be part of any business function and at any level from CEO down to entry level. Interpreneurs don't limit their connections within their own borders. As Mads Faurholt, former Global Managing Director and Partner at incubator and company builder Rocket Internet, points out of successful global business professionals, "they often connect more with others across countries than those in their same location; what defines them is cross-border," a mindset that is well suited for distributed work.

Interpreneurs are able to take what is often a complex and challenging process of scaling internationally and frame it in the positive, communicating the ROI and getting buy-in while advocating for competing budget items. Interpreneurs are facilitators who are extremely effective at listening and learning. To echo a mantra from Marc Benioff, co-founder and co-CEO of Salesforce, Interpreneurs constantly have a "beginner's mindset" and are able to listen *deeply* to things beyond what confirms their biases.

Finally, and most importantly, Interpreneurs have a *cultural* mindset, which is a combination of cultural consciousness, cultural curiosity, cultural sensitivity, and Cultural EQ, the latter being when cultural intelligence meets emotional intelligence, granting the ability to understand and empathize with other cultures. This aspect of the mindset includes the ability to develop understanding and empathy necessary to localize a business for a new market. This cultural mindset is the key ingredient Global Class Companies use to scale globally. It's also a mindset that governments want to nurture, thereby developing and attracting Interpreneurs. They recognize that building ecosystems

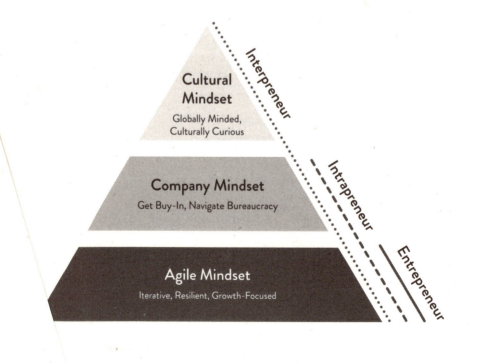

of Interpreneurs can have positive societal impact, becoming a catalyst for economic and social development.

Put another way, Interpreneurs put a global layer on top of entrepreneurs and intrapreneurs.

You can visualize the combination of these mindsets as a pyramid, where an agile (entrepreneurial) mindset serves as the base, a company (intrapreneurial) mindset is layered on top, with the cultural mindset resting at the apex, encapsulating and building on a foundation of the other two. These three mindsets combined are the interpreneurial mindset.

To put it more simply, an Interpreneur is someone who has the *global* mindset to interpret culture, the *agile* mindset to resiliently overcome obstacles with creative solutions, and the *company* mindset to sustain support and buy-in to get things done. Interpreneurs take a vision (theirs or someone else's) and bring it to the world.

WHY IS INTERPRENEURSHIP IMPORTANT?

As outlined in chapter one, the pandemic has changed how businesses operate, accelerating many nascent trends, forcing companies to activate distributed workforces and rethink operating models, decision-making, and strategy.

All the right strategies and processes will not lead to success without the right people implementing them. Put another way, attempts at adopting a Global Class mindset at a company level will fail if the individuals involved aren't Interpreneurs (or at least if they aren't tapping into the interpreneurial mindset). The Global Class mindset is manifested at the *individual* level via the interpreneurial mindset just as the proliferation of an interpreneurial mindset among individuals in an organization is what drives the Global Class mindset at a *company* level.

Because there are developed economies in so many places and an increased importance of localizing to connect with customers in these markets, a mindset built on cultural consciousness is as important as product quality or speed to market.

It also takes the right mindset to identify opportunities. Lazada co-founders Maximilian Bittner, Mads Faurholt, Stefan Bruun, and Raphael Strauch decided not to launch the business in their native Europe but instead in Southeast Asia so it could access rapidly growing ecommerce markets there. Interpreneurs aren't automatically convinced that their home market must launch first. In fact, they don't think in terms of home versus international at all.

We believe this interpreneurial mindset and corresponding traits and skills will be the most sought-after assets companies seek in employees over the next decade, just as a desire for an agile mindset and entrepreneurial skills has rapidly increased over the last decade.

Right now, interpreneurial skills can be hard to find, and the community of these global-minded professionals has been disconnected and scattered across the globe. With the rapid adoption of virtual and distributed work, Interpreneurs will be in demand, and this community of business leaders will become more connected. In distributed organizations, Interpreneurs are needed to influence others in the organization from afar and collaborate across diverse cultures to get things done.

This is all happening just in time, as Global Class Companies see the importance of this mindset and start to use it for talent pipeline development. In our research, we heard of the growing importance of this mindset multiple times (although without a moniker like Interpreneur). Executives at companies like Amazon and Shopify now include international experience in their conversations about promotion of senior leaders and in building a pipeline of talent. A number of Global Class Companies are starting to require international experience as a prerequisite for executive roles; they see themselves as global organizations and acutely see the importance of an international mindset as part of the collective psyche.

We even heard from high-level Asian government officials that this mindset will be particularly crucial for their ecosystems because of their aging populations and relative decrease in local talent. Developing the interpreneurial mindset within their emerging workforces can be an effective means for technology development, supporting social safety net programs and keeping their country relevant in the global ecosystem.

In a more distributed world, organizations need Interpreneurs who are agile thinkers and who can do real-time learning, while also being able to influence the organization from within and from afar, all with a cultural mindset able to understand how to localize the business.

Global Class Companies recognize these trends and believe that the Interpreneur's mindset is a North Star, guiding them in team building as well as culture and mindset building.

CHARACTERISTICS OF EFFECTIVE INTERPRENEURS

When interacting with successful Interpreneurs, we found that they weren't attracted to global business merely for the cultural experience or frequent flyer miles. Abe Smith called his focus on building international companies a "calling"—not a part-time or temporary thing but a passion and labor of love that involves resilience to navigate what he referred to as a "tough journey."

Many of the Interpreneurs we interviewed have made a career of expanding companies internationally, showcasing the skills they have built in this nascent (but increasingly important) functional niche, much as an executive with merger experience would go from company to company guiding them through a core aspect of the M&A process.

The Interpreneur's global mindset allows them to navigate new cultural environments. They possess the cultural awareness ("Cultural EQ") that allows them to connect with and understand local conventions, dissecting differences while at the same time finding common ground. Further, they understand the importance of community and work to find the ways their company can improve the society in new markets it enters.

Imre Hild, seasoned executive and Hungarian start-up ecosystem ambassador, also highlights the broader role Interpreneurs play. "Interpreneurs are often also early adopters who drive ecosystems in addition to fueling internationalization." They are the drivers of new ideas and innovations.

Interpreneurs are open-minded, culturally conscious, and agile, able to adapt to new settings and build strong relationships with people outside the home environment. Klaus, for example, developed a passion for international markets by venturing out in the jungles of Bolivia, studying language and culture in Chile, doing strategy development and market launch support in northern Vietnam, and moving from Denmark to San Francisco. To illustrate this even further, Klaus intentionally selected a role in Silicon Valley that was focused on helping entrepreneurs from across the globe (albeit not his native country, Denmark). Aaron's international trek across three continents between college and starting his career, teaching students from across the globe through the Berkeley Haas Global Access Program experience and traveling to nearly forty countries, contributed to his global-mindedness.

In addition to having the characteristics that come with the agile and growth mindsets, Interpreneurs:

- possess a global mindset and see opportunities.
- value diversity and inclusion.
- take educated risks.
- are open, sharing, and always learning.
- display cultural curiosity and creativity.
- seek to understand and are sensitive to culture.
- have a builder's mentality.
- think in terms of focus.
- commit long term.
- are global citizens.

Global Mindset, See Opportunities

Scott Coleman, former Head of Global Growth and International Product for Pinterest, highlights how Interpreneurs recognize unique perspectives across cultures and have an appreciation for diversity. They see each market as distinct and different. They don't lump a whole region together, instead appreciating the nuances of each country and city within. Interpreneurs embrace the adventure and optimistically think in terms of opportunity. That doesn't mean neglecting risk considerations but instead planning and executing to identify and take advantage of opportunities.

Value Diversity and Inclusion

In the minds of Interpreneurs, diversity and inclusion are table stakes, not just a business trend. Interpreneurs value diversity in thought, experience, and background. They seek differing opinions and look to bring those with diverse perspectives into conversation, strategy development, and decision-making.

Take Educated Risks

Interpreneurs are willing to step outside their comfort zones. When part of a local team, this means not only uprooting their lives (and families) to move to a new place but also stepping away from the corporate and political epicenter of the company at headquarters, where influence is wielded. When part of the HQ team, this means being an evangelist for international growth initiatives, building a coalition of support, and securing necessary resources.

Interpreneurs understand how big the opportunity is. Jennifer Yuen from Airbnb highlighted that we often develop bias for the things close to us. We make assumptions quickly, especially if we come from a large market. This bias makes it difficult to understand other international markets. It becomes hard to understand the potential velocity; hard to understand the scale of countries like China, for example, which is multiples larger in population than the United States. Interpreneurs look past this, eager to go where opportunity is.

Open, Sharing, and Always Learning

All of the Interpreneurs we interviewed were quick to accept our offer to contribute to this book. There was little pushback and a general excitement to learn from their fellow Interpreneurs. Interpreneurs are avid learners who always embrace additional insights and improvement in real time. The classic "it's always day one" mentality coined by Jeff Bezos from Amazon permeates through the Interpreneurs interviewed for this book. Elise Rubin, Global Head of Program Management, Internationalization, and Product Launch at Google Nest, puts herself in situations to learn and experience new things, staying in home-sharing accommodations instead of hotels during international business trips, and staying in multiple smaller cities and not just major metro areas to truly see what life is like for target customers.

Cultural Curiosity and Creativity

Jennifer Yuen explained, "Interpreneurs maintain a mindset that suspends bias and taps into curiosity. They seek to understand people (colleagues and customers alike). An Interpreneur is able to get things done because of their passion and determination, often with limited guidance and resources."

As Dan Himelstein, lecturer in global business and former Executive Director of the undergraduate program at UC Berkeley's Haas School of Business, puts it, "In today's business world, the separation of dollars and quality between businesses is so small, cultural curiosity makes you stand out. It's a differentiator." He continues, "Genuine curiosity is a heck of a lot more important than the ability to build a financial projection. There's not a million people in the world who are Interpreneurs, but plenty of people can manage your finances. What's hard is finding someone who can navigate a 2 AM karaoke session."

Seek to Understand and Are Sensitive to Culture

Interpreneurs search for commonalities. They *embrace* differences and view any challenges as opportunities. They can find "belonging" in otherwise unknown places and are unfazed by unfamiliar situations. They can translate customs and beliefs from a different market into keen insights about the local culture, bridging them with shared values and creating common ground.

International-mindedness and cultural sensitivity make Interpreneurs aware of the cultural similarities and differences that exist between people without assigning these differences a value—positive or negative, better or worse, right or wrong. Troy Malone, international expansion executive for companies like Evernote, Weebly, and mmhmm, labeled it as not being "presumptuous," but mindful. He points out that this approach is more effective at driving long-term results than throwing endless amounts of money at attempting to get a market to bend to the ways HQ does things.

This can work at all levels. When Troy was at Evernote, local press often asked him about the meaning behind the company's elephant logo. In anticipation of this, he would do research on the symbolic nature of elephants in the local culture. Instead of offering an American-centric answer—that the logo relates to the American saying "an elephant never forgets" (symbolic of how Evernote remembers all the notes and thoughts you add to it)—he would localize his answer to fit the country he was in, calling on the local mythology surrounding elephants. Being perceptive and making an effort to adapt to local culture is vital to building high-quality relationships.

At the same time, Interpreneurs are conscious of the other important type of culture fundamental to global growth: company culture. They are able to translate the company's core values to the staff and customers in a local market.

Have a Builder's Mentality

Interpreneurs are builders. They help build the company's presence in local markets (when part of local market teams). They help build a home for international within the organization (when part of HQ). They are adept at building relationships.

Interpreneurs are keen to build long-term bonds with local market stakeholders. They have the soft skills to communicate their cultural awareness and the ability to build trust with people. They are effective communicators, capable networkers, and stewards of other soft skills that aid in solidifying relationships at lightning speed. They aren't transactional but play the long game, effectively using positive framing to build an internal coalition that buys into their plans.

Think in Terms of Focus

Interpreneurs focus. They are able to identify the things that truly matter and aren't distracted by the many small things. As Paul Williamson, Head of Revenue at Plaid, points out, "They are truthful about alignment with values," using these principles as a guiding light for where to put time, attention, and resources.

Committed, Long-Term View

Interpreneurs play the long game. This is seen in their proficiency in building relationships, but also in how they make strategic business decisions. They look for the *right* partner, hire, or customer, not the first one that comes along.

Christina Lee from Chegg accurately points out that "the stuff you built yesterday is not good enough for tomorrow." When taking the long view, Interpreneurs focus on iterating and constantly improving all aspects of how their business is run to increase the likelihood of success long term.

Global Citizenship

Interpreneurs are truly global citizens. They see humanity before nationality. They don't think of things through a lens of "my home country" versus "abroad." They connect with people in any geography and bridge gaps in culture through their empathy.

One final observation, which is interesting but not necessarily universal among Interpreneurs, is that many we talked with had unique backgrounds or experiences that affected their perspectives on the world. This often set a nonlinear path to international business—in other words, these Interpreneurs didn't follow some cookie-cutter path working as a banker or consultant, going to business school, and then entering the corporate world.

For one executive it was starting out as a passionate photographer; for another it was a life-changing church mission in South Korea. Many had curiosity for the arts or an educational background in social sciences, while all had some form of immersive experience outside their home country.

CASE STUDY

HOW INTERPRENEURS NAVIGATE LOCAL CULTURES

Elise Rubin has seen firsthand the differences in business cultures outside of the United States. Despite her extensive experience, her youthful look and being female means that she's had to navigate many occasions when her role didn't fit local cultural norms. Serving as the Global Head of Program Management, Internationalization, and Product Launch at Google Nest, Elise travels on business and carries Google Nest devices to showcase them to potential partners. In a number of countries, a youthful-looking woman carrying smart home devices is incongruent with local gender norms and raises alarms at airport security checkpoints, leading to lengthy searches and background checks. A man with the same cargo would often be allowed to pass free of concern or major hassle.

When meeting with business leaders in certain countries, like Japan, specifically, Elise has had to adopt the practice of attending meetings in these markets with a male colleague. During meetings, local business leaders would look to her male colleague, instead of her, for answers to questions. Being conscious of these cultural nuances, Elise would often have to coach her male colleague how to answer these questions, even though he was more junior than Elise. Over time, through sheer determination, willpower, and deft communication skills, Elise has been able to win over skeptical male leaders abroad who are used to placing the opinions of men above women.

While this is a reality for female Interpreneurs and fits within the typical gender roles accepted in some societies, it is our hope that in this new era of global business and with the upsurge of Interpreneurs, these barriers will be removed and lead locals to respect the culture and freedoms of individuals from other societies who are guests in their country, and in particular upholding principles of diversity and inclusion for women, ethnic minorities, and those from underserved communities.

HOW TO BE AN INTERPRENEUR

Besides working hard to sharpen the mindset and attributes highlighted in the previous section, there are some additional ways to build your interpreneurial muscles. Just as companies aren't "born" global, people aren't "born" Interpreneurs; they evolve and gain experience and perspective over time. It's a learned and practiced mindset.

Leaders we spoke with discovered their inner Interpreneur along the way, at times unintentionally. The experiences that lead to your global-mindedness and cultural curiosity matter less than the fact that you are developing Cultural EQ.

Interpreneurs adopt agile methodology and seek out more entrepreneurial-minded communities, picking environments that allow professional development. They travel and experience other cultures and value diversity and collaboration, in the process gaining credibility and influencing their organizations on the path to global scale.

To become more interpreneurial, you should first and foremost intentionally seek international experiences and opportunities to interact with people outside your borders. This is the most direct and straightforward way. Step outside your comfort zone. Work in another country, connect with other globally minded people from different countries, follow international media sources, and track global trends. While leisure travel can assist in some ways, it's not a substitute. It's hard to understand differences in mindset and cultures if you haven't lived or worked abroad.

Next, default to openness and suspend judgment. Interpreneurs don't use their home country as a baseline to measure right/wrong or normal/different. There is no us-versus-them to Interpreneurs; there is only a shared humanity and a desire to bridge commonalities.

Finally, truly evaluate your aptitude according to the ten attributes listed above. Where you have gaps, work mindfully to eliminate them.

THE GENESIS OF INTERPRENEURSHIP

The formative experiences that lead Interpreneurs to careers in international are as diverse as the Interpreneurs themselves.

Whitney Bouck, former COO of Dropbox's HelloSign business, found her inner Interpreneur at an early age. Whitney's grandparents developed modern sewer systems for international governments, leading her family to live in Indonesia and Sudan when her mother was growing up. When they returned to the United States, Whitney's grandparents brought back a chef to live with them, introducing Whitney to new cuisines. Her family's global-mindedness led them to support Whitney living in Europe for a period of time as a teenager.

Similarly, Troy Malone, former General Manager of International Expansion at Evernote, is a highly curious business leader with exceptional cultural awareness and sensitivity. He led international growth efforts in both APAC and LATAM, clearly personifying interpreneurial principles. Troy lived abroad as a student at Brigham Young University when he completed a two-year church mission to Seoul, South Korea. These early international experiences craft business leaders of the future, creating Interpreneurs who are in growing demand for companies of tomorrow looking to break into global markets.

HyunBin Kang, Executive SVP of Global Business Development at Line, had a similarly diverse experience. Early in his career he worked for an American company and had the opportunity to interact with many colleagues and stakeholders across continents while working on projects in China, Japan, South Korea, Southeast Asia, and Europe. While working for Naver, South Korea's number-one search portal company, he had the opportunity to gain further international experience, which gave him the right global mindset to succeed in his role at Line.

The mindset and capabilities of Interpreneurs are very well aligned across the world, despite their unique career and life journeys.

HOW GLOBAL CLASS COMPANIES NURTURE INTERPRENEURS

It is common for executives at legacy companies to fear Interpreneurs because they bring in a new way of thinking and challenge the company way. Global

Class Companies, on the other hand, not only embrace this mindset but actively seek it out and work hard to develop it. Global Class Companies look for cultural curiosity, global-mindedness, and cultural sensitivity over educational and professional pedigree.

Having regard for this interpreneurial mindset affects how these companies hire (they seek diversity of background and experience), how they create their products, and even how they build their core values and company culture.

As part of their recruiting process, Global Class Companies intentionally screen for the interpreneurial attributes outlined in this chapter. Zendesk intentionally recruits employees from underserved communities, not only to give opportunity to these talented people (many of whom have an inherent resilience built through overcoming obstacles that those from privileged backgrounds don't face), but also to ensure their solutions aren't just tailored toward the elite. Building teams of Interpreneurs and those with diverse backgrounds helps integrate empathy into the product and operating model.

OFTEN OVERLOOKED

Company Policies and Structures Can Nurture Interpreneurs

In addition to building company cultures that value interpreneurship, Global Class Companies also develop structures and processes to develop interpreneurial talent.

Chris Murphy, CEO of Thoughtworks, North America, a software consultancy with forty-eight offices in seventeen countries, highlights that companies increase their likelihood of international success when teams are intentionally global and multicultural. Successful companies remember to monitor the global leadership team mix, know what the company's global growth drivers and model are, and design the growth strategy with these factors in mind.

Thoughtworks intentionally makes an effort to rotate its team members through multiple international markets so that everyone has an interpreneurial mindset. Moreover, in the early days of expanding into a new country or territory, the company usually ensures that a portion of the local team is from outside that country's borders to ensure a global mindset is applied to all work done in the country.

Even temporary trips where employees co-locate in international offices for a couple of months are fruitful.

Interpreneurs are an emerging type of business leader who have a global mindset and cultural curiosity, maintain a vision for growth in international markets, and possess agile and intrapreneurial skills to make expansion strategies a reality.

Now that we've highlighted *who* Global Class Companies employ, let's look at *what* they do to successfully scale across global markets.

CHAPTER 3 SUMMARY

- Interpreneurs have the *global* mindset to interpret culture and the empathy to understand new markets to effectively localize a business, a key advantage Global Class Companies utilize to succeed in international markets.
- Interpreneurs also have the *agile* mindset to resiliently overcome obstacles with creative solutions and the *company* mindset to sustain support and buy-in in complex and bureaucratic organizations to get things done.
- Interpreneurs are catalysts to help companies reach global scale. Recognizing this, Global Class Companies take specific steps to nurture Interpreneurs within their organizations.

CHAPTER 3 REFLECTION & ACTION QUESTIONS

1. What actions have you taken to develop your own interpreneurial mindset? What are three actionable steps you can take right now?
2. How prevalent is the interpreneurial mindset within your organization? In what ways is your organization fostering this mindset?
3. How are you hiring and nurturing a (distributed) team of Interpreneurs?

• PART 2 •

SCALE

Effective International Growth

G iven the diverse nature of global business, there is a greater need to customize in order to connect with customers in international markets. Frameworks are needed to navigate these changes. Global Class Companies go through a process of LOCALIZATION, putting a global layer on widely used innovation methodology. To keep balance, they manage COMPLEXITY and concurrently build structures that navigate market entry and market growth, generating MOMENTUM and scale.

• 4 •

ALIGN

The Four Commitments for
Successful Global Growth

As Vice President of International for Apple, John Brandon crisscrossed the globe, facing many challenges as he rallied teams across continents and time zones to uphold Apple's core values and work toward the company's lofty goals of extending its global reach and scale. While Apple has been extremely successful at maintaining a unified branding, customer experience, and suite of products worldwide, the company has had to navigate the numerous differences of each region it operates in.

John regularly came face-to-face with some of these differences in the course of managing his teams. Some differences were easier to accept, like a local custom or conflicting political belief, while others directly conflicted with company values and had to be addressed head-on.

In the course of reviewing financial results for the People's Republic of China operations, John and the team at HQ discovered a few discrepancies. An investigation was conducted, and it showed that numbers were fabricated to hide mistakes stemming from the local general manager's poor judgment. The GM gave no admission of guilt, and his staff supported him, alleging that the figures were accurate. This was a perfect example of how, in China's business culture, priority is given to respecting hierarchy, saving face, and making the boss look good over being forthcoming.

This breach clearly conflicted with Apple's culture, which valued integrity and protecting the company and brand over the boss, crossing the line in both scale and significance. In the end, the company's core values prevailed. Apple's efforts to scale in China were almost derailed, and John had to fire 75 percent of the existing local team, rebuilding with a staff (and in particular a GM) with values that aligned more with the company than with local norms.

John learned from this experience, deciding to pair local market GMs with finance team members from other markets going forward. This created a Feedback Loop, granting someone from a different business culture (with less bias toward local business norms) visibility into local operations.

If you don't align on fundamental principles (like integrity), you risk failure at a global scale.

• • •

Developing the right Global Class mindset and building teams of Interpreneurs are crucial for effective global growth, but having the right team and mindset isn't enough.

Global Class teams dedicated to global growth initiatives must rally around a set of commitments to increase their likelihood of success: a set of pledges related to culture, team building, and focus aligning both the company and its Interpreneurs.

Aligning with company culture and collaborating with HQ on goal-setting allows local teams to grow the business in their markets. To support global growth efforts, company leadership must commit to supporting local teams. A set of agreed-upon promises can serve as a North Star for local team/ HQ decision-making as international growth initiatives hit roadblocks.

Entry into global markets is the inflection point where the organization proves whether it works better in a single market or if there is truly global applicability and opportunity.

Global market entry is in fact harder than most domestic expansion because of an extra variable that companies don't have to consider during entry and growth in an initial market—namely, culture. When companies first launch, they have the latitude to operate flexibly, searching for the right model that will scale profitability in a single market; there is no basis you have to adapt from, no baggage or initial market bias. When launching and growing in new markets, established companies have their successful initial model (go-to-market, operating model, culture, and norms) as a basis that everything is compared to and that the whole company to this point has supported. Entering new markets causes companies to diverge from the current model, requiring that they juggle multiple ways of doing things; there is no longer only one *right* way of doing things.

Having a set of commitments grounds Global Class Companies and directs the team toward a specific set of priorities that truly matter to successful scaling, helping them avoid wasting energy on other distractions with lower ROIs. These commitments become important reminders and the foundation for a set of operating principles delineating what both HQ and the local market team need to effectively scale internationally.

HQ and local teams may have very different mindsets, set ways of doing things that map to company culture for HQ teams and local culture for those in-market, as well as occasional competing priorities. Therefore, a common set of commitments and pledges sets expectations so that all those involved in global growth initiatives can focus on effective market entry, localization, and scale.

One of the reasons these internal pacts must be made is that local teams will undoubtedly require support as they face new and complex challenges. They need to operate like a start-up in a new market (entrepreneurial); navigate competing interests at HQ (intrapreneurial); and of course adapt to fit the new market and its culture (interpreneurial).

The commitments must be flexible enough to nurture market entry while later being the fuel for market growth, in alignment with agile principles.

THE FOUR COMMITMENTS FOR SUCCESSFUL GLOBAL GROWTH

From our research, we recognized patterns in the commitments that successful companies make to ensure effective global growth. These Four Commitments for Successful Global Growth guide their success:

1. **Resource Alignment**—Funding and team members from HQ focused on supporting global growth initiatives

2. **Trust and Autonomy**—Freedom granted to local teams to find company-market fit and recognize added complexity

3. **Communication and Clarity**—Effective channels of communication established and maintained between HQ and local teams

4. **Global Agile Methodology**—Ongoing utilization of agile principles by local teams and HQ (in partnership) that adapts the business to address differences in local markets

These Four Commitments must be upheld for both effective market entry and market growth. They are oxygen to global growth efforts; without them, initiatives are much more likely to fail.

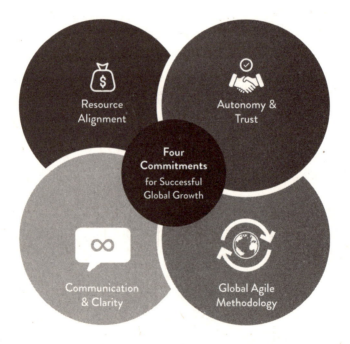

Resource Alignment

To succeed, companies must dedicate resources to global growth initiatives. This includes funding to build up a staff and ample capital for marketing strategies. It also could include focus from the executive team, HQ functional resources, or support for a specific partnership. As discussed, leadership buy-in for international growth is crucial for success, and the manifestation of this support is the resources committed to these initiatives.

Many stories of international growth failures share a common theme of inadequate resources and focus. Companies may send an executive from HQ or bring on a few new hires, expecting to see results in six to nine months, only to find that by then there are more questions than answers. The executive team then looks at the current business in existing markets, sees how more investment there will have more predictable profitable outcomes, and decides it wasn't meant to be.

HQ must fully commit to global growth (before and after a new market has been validated) to be successful. They must be willing to feel uncomfortable (and lose money) for two to three years before seeing even a slight ROI or sign of traction. It is crucial to stay the course and dedicate enough resources and focus to see the initiative through.

OFTEN OVERLOOKED

Effective Resource Allocation

The key to international expansion resource alignment is often misunderstood. Instead of focusing on the total amount allocated to global growth initiatives, the more important consideration is how resources are allocated over time. It's important that these initiatives have resources over a multi-year period and not just for a few months before and after launch. Ramsey Pryor, former Head of International Expansion and Sales at Branch Metrics and founder of Port of Entry Partners, suggests that unlocking resources when local teams reach milestones can be an effective strategy to empower these teams. He points out that in addition to revenue milestones, building a strong sales pipeline, securing local government approval, or establishing key local partnerships could serve as milestones that unlock additional resources.

To assist with estimating the level of financial commitment it takes to launch a new initiative, we have developed a Total Cost of Entry (TCE) Formula, akin to the "total cost of ownership" equation many companies use in selling their products. The TCE Formula will be discussed in more detail in chapter six.

At the same time, be warned; these estimates can be more art than science. You may need to double or even triple (in both time and dollars) the cost to enter a market, break even, and pay back original investments; there are that many unknowns.

As Kathryn Hymes, former Head of International Product Expansion for Slack, explains, "It's really tempting with international growth to think you can fully calculate out answers, putting a number to the potential impact of an investment. Besides being inaccurate, it sets a false sense of security. Numbers can be deceiving. Don't tailspin conversations around data. It's more important to determine whether it is strategically the right thing. Data can inform, but it cannot solve."

An important complement to resource commitment is setting clear performance metrics that measure the right things. Clear performance metrics represent a strong determination of what the goals and focus are for the local team and how results will be measured. Moreover, the answer is not for HQ to provide local teams with whatever they ask for. On the contrary, additional resources can be directly tied to milestones.

Chang Wen Lai, CEO and co-founder of Ninja Van, Southeast Asia's largest tech-enabled express logistics provider, uses an analogy of mountain climbing to articulate his view on HQ resource commitment. He explains that it's HQ's responsibility to point the local team to the right mountain to climb but to allow them to take whatever path they want. At the same time, he gives them the right amount of food (funding) for the journey—not too much so they start climbing other mountains (lose focus) but enough to scale the mountain HQ sets them at the base of.

OFTEN OVERLOOKED

Don't Launch and Leave; Build Sustainable Models

Global expansion is not just about launching in a country and hoping for the best. It takes long-term commitment. As Kathryn Hymes explains, companies have a natural temptation to leave once they launch, letting their focus wane. Before finding a sustainable growth model, they begin looking to new markets for additional growth opportunities. While this appetite is healthy for any company with global aspirations, it is important that HQ continues to keep close watch on the budding local presence to ensure they reach local company-market fit. Building for sustainability and scalability has to be part of the strategy and resource allocation must provide a sustained investment in a new region; otherwise you are setting yourself up for failure.

Why this commitment is important: The resources you expend are a manifestation of your commitment to, and focus on, global growth initiatives. Instead of focusing on an amount, focus on alignment and how resources can be unlocked over time as local teams reach goals and hit key metrics. Without ample resources and strong buy-in for international scaling, your potential for failure is higher. It is difficult to launch a new market as it is (in some ways it's similar to starting a brand-new company). It's exponentially *more* difficult without executive team engagement, a commitment of people on the ground, ample funding, or a dedication by HQ to remove obstacles.

Oracle, for example, was not successful in gaining widespread traction in China with one of its marketing products because leadership didn't commit ample resources or give the right level of focus to the market. Although crucial, the team didn't invest in language translation, nor did Oracle integrate with WeChat, an essential platform widely used by customers in the Chinese market.

Related to metrics, all parties need to agree to the rules of the game and how performance will be measured. This doesn't mean that HQ dictates everything from a pedestal on high; rather, it's a collective effort where the local market team also determines what is being measured.

Performance metrics will vary by company, but early on, during market entry, the right metrics aren't purely revenue and profitability related. Finding product-market fit, establishing key partnerships, and building government relationships, for example, are more relevant and applicable to setting the foundation for scale. During market growth this transitions into more traditional profitability metrics and achieving company-market fit.

Throughout this chapter we present "Pathways for Success," crucial considerations for adopting each commitment.

To successfully align HQ and the local market leadership team around required resources, here is a set of steps to set you on your path to success:

Pathways for Success

- Determine the time needed to explore the market and gain traction. Commit long term, two to three years or more. It always takes longer than you think.
- Estimate resources required to be successful. This applies to both HQ and in-market.
- Calculate the total cost of entry and tie it to future ROI. Build in a buffer and always remember to frame the cost as an investment, defining estimated ROI.
- Ensure executive visibility and check-ins/status/updates to show process and ensure continued dedication of resources.
- Set realistic and simple metrics. Identify no more than three core metrics, defined jointly by HQ and the local team. When both sides are involved, they are more engaged and committed.
- Stay iterative and agile as you learn more about the market and business in the local office matures. Metrics are more qualitative to start, aligned with company-market fit, then shift to profitability in later stages. As facts on the ground change, company metrics should follow suit.
- Customize targets and metrics for each market to meet unique market opportunity and complexities.

Trust and Autonomy

One of the other biggest challenges your teams will face in the expansion process is balancing the desire to replicate the magic that led to growth in the initial market with the need to allow local teams to chart their own path and customize the business for the new market.

This commitment involves offering foundational support and creating a sense of trust between HQ and the local team while maintaining the proper amount of autonomy. Local teams must have autonomy to adapt the business to find company-market fit in the new country, and HQ must trust them to figure it out. At the same time, the local team must trust that HQ will be there to support them, help them solve problems, and provide direction through challenges.

Why this commitment is important: As Tiffany Stevenson, Chief People Officer of Patreon and former Chief Talent and Inclusion Officer at Box, puts it,

"Autonomy allows for scale to happen." There is ample research expounding on the virtues of trust within organizations, so we won't spend much time on the topic, but autonomy is equally crucial.

It is not possible for HQ to make every decision from so far away, nor is it possible for those decisions to always be right without firsthand knowledge of what is happening in the local market. This is where trust comes in. HQ shows its trust by granting autonomy to the local team, and the local team leverages this autonomy to make the right decisions that will increase the likelihood of successfully scaling in the new market. This trust and autonomy should extend to all aspects of local operations, from localizing the business for the new market to hiring and so on. Note that trust comes first, as the local team must earn and maintain the trust of HQ to continue to be granted autonomy.

Core values are an important vehicle for focusing the team and channeling efforts, not discounting local culture and forcing something as the only way (the "company way"). The Rakuten team found this in their expansion overseas. Leveraging an acquisition strategy, Rakuten, an ecommerce company headquartered in Japan, purchased a company in the European region and kicked off the relationship by insisting that the Rakuten way was the best and only path to success. The Rakuten team didn't take a step back to build trust or seek ways to capitalize on the acquired team's local market knowledge to build more traction in the country. HQ did not offer ways for the local team to influence the local go-to-market strategy through sharing key insights, instead focusing the team on speed and execution of the plan HQ established. This hindered the growth until the company adapted, beginning to take key learnings from local customers and employees alike to localize for the market.

Looking to bridge the gap, Seichu Masatada Kobayashi, Rakuten's co-founder and head of the region at the time (now Chief Well-Being Officer), met with the local team face-to-face and asked them to write down all of their former company's core values. He then put up a poster with Rakuten's core values and they discussed the similarities between them, showing how they were linked. Communicating the crossover between local business culture and Rakuten's company culture led to improved results and better office morale. The local team started to gain momentum and achieve greater market penetration once HQ built trust with them after ensuring core value alignment.

Finding the right balance of autonomy with local teams helps HQ manage a growing global footprint, and it also helps expansion efforts progress from market entry to market growth. If a local team is given the latitude to adapt the business and find the right model for the market, they will be more successful, faster. Scott Coleman, formerly of Pinterest and Google, points out that there is one big caveat: local teams don't have to reinvent the wheel. Tools that come along with *resource alignment*, such as a Global Growth Playbook and various processes (more on this in chapter seven), can help guide the team away from creating unnecessary complexity or spending precious time on activities that have less impact on finding traction and scaling.

At the same time, Scott is first to point out that local teams should be able to pursue small-scale initiatives with speed. HQ should strike a balance between providing the tools to local teams to implement previously learned best practices while granting local teams autonomy and instilling a sense of empowerment so that local teams take swift action to adapt the business to be successful in the new market.

The flip side of autonomy is bureaucracy, which can become frustrating to local teams. It's difficult to stay as flexible as a start-up while finding the right model, and adding time-consuming processes won't help them get there. We see this bureaucratic organizational challenge when working with the local offices of Japanese clients burdened by too many time-consuming administrative procedures, leaving them little time to interact with and engage the market they have been asked to lead. Organizational bureaucracy hampers any team focused on global growth from being successful, and micromanagement can often lead teams to focus on the wrong things.

Enabling people is paramount. Trust and autonomy fuel the empowerment that leads to traction in new markets. Local market teams need the ability (and resources) to make decisions without gathering approval for every little thing (nor does HQ want to make some of these more minute decisions). HQ needs to trust that these decisions are the right ones. Fostering trust starts with hiring the right people in the local market and within HQ (Interpreneurs).

The Autonomy Curve

A helpful framework to manage the balance between autonomy and control at each stage of the process is the Autonomy Curve. While there will be nuances that will affect the degree of autonomy, depending on your industry and company culture (among other factors), the curve can directionally guide how much autonomy to grant local teams at each stage of scaling globally. The

Autonomy Curve breaks global scaling into three categories: market entry, market growth, and market maturity, each meriting its own degree of autonomy. Each local market travels along this Autonomy Curve independently since each is likely at a different point of entry or growth, so multiple regions aren't necessarily judged together, although HQ will likely consider the scalability of its efforts across regions during market growth for reasons described below.

Expansion Stages Defined

There are three distinct stages when entering international markets, each marked by its own core objective.

- **Market Entry**—This stage includes pre-launch planning and launching in the new market up until product-market fit is achieved where the team validates the localized version of how to operate the business in-country and the go-to-market, proving the business model is profitable and scalable.
- **Market Growth**—This stage is focused on building momentum and scale to build a global footprint and operate the business without creating too much complexity in how the business operates across borders. During this stage, companies strive for and achieve company-market fit.
- **Market Maturity**—In this stage, companies focus on further penetrating an existing local market. Often during the market entry and market growth phases, the company isn't getting deep penetration or capturing the full market potential. The goal is to get a more dominant market share through further localization and scaling best practices to other markets.

During market entry, autonomy is the oxygen that allows the local team to focus on and discover the right model to find product-market fit locally. This is where autonomy should be at its highest (although never at 100 percent full autonomy, given the need for alignment). If HQ doesn't feel comfortable granting this autonomy, it is likely an indicator that trust is lacking with the local team, that the organization is not ready for expansion, or that the Global Class mindset hasn't been internalized.

During market growth, autonomy goes down (although notice that it never goes down to a complete command and control level because HQ still wants to tap into the knowledge of the local market that the team on the ground has).

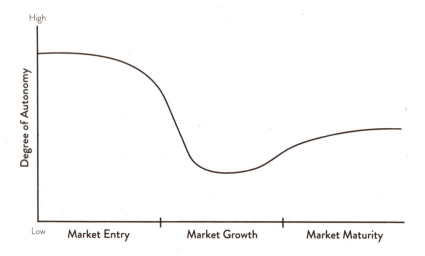

This reduction in autonomy is less about an individual market and more about a global footprint across multiple countries. The organization's focus during this stage is managing complexity and controlling the amount of localization being done. Here, the organization has to consider multinational momentum and scale and not individual market fit, which is why this is where additional processes and structures can be implemented to foster this momentum. By nature, these processes will put up guardrails and reduce autonomy.

During market maturity, autonomy goes back up. It likely doesn't reach the same level as during market entry because teams are utilizing the structures and standardizations adopted during market growth, but additional autonomy should be granted so the local team can further penetrate the market. During market entry, companies typically only penetrate the surface of the market potential; during market maturity, the organization can capture a more dominant position in the market through deeper localization work (like product customization).

In parallel, strategy and key performance indicators (KPIs) follow a similar path. During market entry, the KPIs and strategy need to be fairly customized for the area and not benchmarked against mature markets since the local market nuances, localizations required, and path to company-market fit can vary. During market growth, KPIs and strategy become more aligned with HQ and other regions at a similar stage (as does strategy, although to a slightly lesser extent). Finally, in market maturity, some KPIs and strategies become more localized to align with the goal of deeper market penetration, all of which are supported by the organizational processes built during market growth that cultivate momentum.

Pathways for Success

- Build strong relationships between HQ and the local team.
- Give the local team autonomy to discover the uniquely successful model for that market.
- Build a culture of trust through open communication. Share successes and failures, with corresponding lessons learned.
- Establish processes that give HQ some level of visibility and influence on local operations without hindering the quest for company-market fit and required localization.
- Ensure that local teams internalize company culture and core values, and that HQ understands the unique culture and market dynamics of the local market.
- Balance priorities by allowing the level of autonomy to change over time. Let the local team find company-market fit in their individual market, but create processes and cultural norms that enable HQ to manage the company at scale across many markets. Utilize the Autonomy Curve to find the right balance at the right stage of expansion.

Communication and Clarity

If trust and autonomy fuel empowerment and traction in new markets, communication channels are the highways the team uses to get there. Clarity is the signage that guides the journey.

Similar to any team environment, effective communication is essential for the success of global teams. Communication is even more crucial in a global company than it is in a company with only a domestic footprint because of cultural and linguistic barriers. Global Class Companies develop a communication network that is structured more like a brain, with endless interconnections instead of a hub-and-spoke model with HQ sitting at the nexus. Local teams and people across functions can connect, share best practices, and support one another.

When operating a distributed cross-border team, Global Class Companies are mindful of differences in communication style that arise from local business culture. In many Asian business cultures, for example, hierarchy is highly valued; disagreeing with your superior is seen as insubordination, while Scandinavian business culture highly values directness. Effective communication channels and practices help navigate these cultural nuances to ensure everyone can communicate appropriately.

Global Class Companies establish strong communication links between HQ and local teams. HQ uses these links to set expectations, confirm alignment to core values and goals, and measure progress with local teams. The Global Class also ensures these communication channels are two-way, allowing HQ to gather market intelligence to help with business planning, resource allocation, uncovering required localization, and removing obstacles for local teams. We refer to these two-way communication channels as Feedback Loops (discussed in more detail here and in later chapters).

Global Class Companies understand that communication channels must be both synchronous and asynchronous, allowing for those on different time zones to be part of the conversation. These companies understand that effective communication channels are a great equalizer so that all team members have a voice and no team or individual has an outsized influence due to geographic proximity.

Global Class Companies realize that implementing effective communication tools is only part of the process, and that set structures and processes must be set up to ensure effective communication. At Slack, the GM of South Korea connected with the GM of Japan, knowing that the company's presence in South Korea would benefit from all the knowledge accumulated from the launch in Japan. These cross-team connections allowed the team in South Korea to have relevant data from another country in the region. Understanding the level of investment needed in Japan and the growth that ensued was extremely valuable in planning for market entry in South Korea.

Clarity can best be achieved through transparency. Global Class Companies work to create transparency—in decision-making, in building playbooks and best-practice sharing, and in tracking and measuring progress.

Feedback Loops are a great way to foster communication and clarity.

Feedback Loops

Transparency and knowledge sharing that come from effective two-way communication temper the tug of work between HQ and local teams, saving time and empowering all parties.

The best way to create effective communication channels between HQ and local teams is by establishing Feedback Loops. Feedback Loops are established lines of communication that allow for a transparent, multi-directional exchange of ideas and information, functioning as a lubricant that helps the gears of the company—its internal processes—move faster and gain momentum.

Feedback Loops allow both local teams and HQ to share market intelligence and solve problems. When they work effectively, local teams share lessons and observations from the local market to help the HQ team and executive leadership determine necessary localization and understand progress toward gaining traction and reaching company-market fit in the new market. Equally important, the team at HQ can translate core values to the local team and ensure company culture is being internalized. The HQ team is able to share best practices with the local team and search for efficiencies, scaling the most effective innovations when they see patterns across multiple markets.

This alignment is important at Global Class Companies like Slack. As Dawn Sharifan, Senior Vice President of People, explained, the company has created set processes to manage alignment between local teams and HQ. First, the company ensures there are multiple sources for keeping a pulse on the engagement of local market employees and adherence to core values. If only one person interacts with HQ (which can naturally happen with the local market lead acting as go-between) this can distort what is truly happening on the ground in the local market.

Slack facilitates this by having team members from a couple of key functions based out of each local office, namely HR and Legal. Moreover, Slack has a "cultural ambassador program," where approximately three to five non-HR people in each local office have a direct connection with HQ, whereby they can share the vibe and latest happenings through regularly scheduled cadence.

Feedback Loops are important mechanisms for managing communication. But merely setting these structures up isn't enough. Jennifer Cornelius, Chief People Officer of Ritual and former Head of Organization Design for Apple's Retail Division, shared the best practice of identifying gaps and creating solutions by explicitly answering the question: What happens within and outside of the Feedback Loop?

At its best, effective implementation of Feedback Loops isn't about HQ keeping a tighter grip on what local teams do. Instead, it manifests in local teams being empowered to share insights and best practices, and HQ having the foresight to implement best practices found in one market across an entire global footprint. Feedback Loops help Global Class Companies gather insights and feedback across the organization, both domestically and internationally.

Offering some level of autonomy to the local team is important, but Feedback Loops create a strong communication link and system for local teams to ensure they aren't re-creating the wheel or being left alone to solve a problem, taking focus away from finding company-market fit, growing the customer base, and scaling operations.

Effective use of Feedback Loops is also an antidote against complexity. Effective implementation of two-way communication channels reduces localization premium, go-to-market, and operational complexities (Organizational Premium in particular, all of which will be defined and discussed in chapter six) when entering new markets and scaling.

At their core, Feedback Loops are more about an exchange among equals leading to new insights, a catalyst to move forward, as opposed to a mechanism for HQ command and control. This means being open to change and not getting attached to the way things are done at HQ. As Mark Parry from Zoom's international strategy and operations team puts it, the way to be a Global Class Company is to remove obstacles found within legacy systems/processes, as well as any (seen and unseen) cultural biases to enable the right narrative for change. Ideally, when legacy systems/processes are updated or replaced, the company maintains a global mindset in both design and planning.

Effective two-way communication also illuminates imbalances such as unconscious legacy bias toward HQ or localization bias toward local markets, which are among the major reasons why international expansion efforts fail.

Feedback Loops shouldn't just exist between HQ and local teams but also between local teams and even within a single local team. We refer to the latter as "small loops," Feedback Loops from within an individual local market team. These communication channels are important because they often represent where the dialogue about what elements of the business need to be adapted for the new market and what doesn't need to be customized occurs. It is also where insights about the local market and new innovations are first discovered and validated before being shared with HQ through larger Feedback Loops. It's important that these small loops maintain a balance between the company perspective and the local perspective.

Why this commitment is important: If the local team isn't able to communicate which changes are required according to what they learned from first-hand experience in the local market, then HQ won't support these pivots and thereby won't dedicate resources to adapting. Without open lines of communication, HQ (and other regions that have launched) won't be able to help the local teams overcome obstacles previously conquered in other local markets or ensure alignment, nor will the team achieve company-market fit.

As former Flexport executive Jan van Casteren put it, "This is another situation where the eighty/twenty rule applies. Eighty percent of the company's model works in a new area; 20 percent needs to be figured out through iteration"—a construct codified in Uber's launch playbook, which we will reference in chapter seven. Leveraging a collective industrial mind (the accumulation of the entire team's experiences and lessons learned) within the company is key to figuring out this 20 percent. The driver for creating this collective mind is effective communication.

Besides upholding Apple's core values, as outlined in the story at the beginning of this chapter, John Brandon also created a collective mind among Apple's international team through communicating a set of ten rules ("JB's Rules for Success"). To ensure these rules were understood and stayed top of mind, the managers in his organization, unprompted, printed a laminated card for employees with the list of the rules that could be attached to their company badges. These principles were so well known and followed internally that a former Apple employee shared them with pride online, stating of John, "He really seemed to live by these rules and made the whole organization feel like something really special, even when Apple was still climbing out of 'beleaguered' status." This kind of clarity and communication around core principles is important for ensuring global alignment.

Pathways for Success

- Assign ambassadors from local teams to keep a pulse on what is happening in the market. They should be employees rather than members of the local executive team to get a more diverse set of opinions with no intermediaries.
- Establish appropriate communication channels and platforms (structures and processes).

- Ensure that Feedback Loops are set up for fast response and iteration.
- Safeguard two-way communication. Overcome any local business culture aversion to transparency and share failures while making sure the local team is in the loop about relevant issues.
- Establish a reporting structure and cadence for all sides to be able to track progress.

Global Agile Methodology

The fourth and arguably most important commitment Global Class Companies make when scaling globally is to continue leveraging the agile methodology to achieve company-market fit and scale in new international markets.

Global Class Companies understand it is rare for a product or operating model to work the same across all geographies; the world is just too diverse. They recognize that instead of pushing the company way and insisting that local markets must bend to their orbit, Global Class Companies view their current model, which was validated in their initial market, as a set of hypotheses to be tested and iterated on, understanding that pivots will need to be made to find traction and scale.

Moreover, like any company that has validated its model in its initial market, Global Class Companies know they may not get it right the first time and that failure is part of the pathway toward success.

An internationally focused version of the agile process is the key driver for localization (as detailed in the next chapter). It is important during market entry, for initial iterations on the road to product-market fit, and market growth, to optimize operations to build momentum and scale on the path to company-market fit.

This lean mindset factors into multiple aspects of the organization, from product development to the local team. Troy Malone spoke of a "minimum viable team," a small group of scrappy Interpreneurs effective at finding traction in a new market. Kathryn Hymes talks about leaning into small scale and setting up processes that won't necessarily work across a larger footprint or with a higher volume of customers, but are crucial for validating a new local market early on. Once you find product-market fit in the new market, then the focus of agile shifts to finding company-market fit, scaling, and optimizing the go-to-market and operating models.

Why this commitment is important: Often, companies in growth mode have finite resources and a limited number of things they can focus on. Agile methodology can help by limiting the amount of resources expended during validation, saving them for scaling once company-market fit is achieved.

In addition, many companies have a tendency to start shedding agile principles once their business has been validated in an initial market. This happens because many of the core questions about the business have been answered: Who are our customers? What is our go-to-market strategy? and the like. Moreover, as organizations grow, people with more functional expertise outnumber those who were part of the initial customer development process.

OFTEN OVERLOOKED

The Role of Agile in Global Growth

As will become clear in the next chapter, it is crucial to continue to communicate the importance of agile across the business in local markets. It applies well beyond product-market fit in an initial market. Business is ever changing, and Global Class Companies know they need teams with this mindset to be able to innovate, overcome obstacles, and find growth opportunities in these new markets.

Keeping a commitment to agile throughout the process of building a global organization will provide the flexibility needed to find both company-market fit in a single market and scale across many markets.

If you think that agile only applies to smaller companies entering new markets for the first time, think again. It is a secret weapon of Global Class Companies of all sizes at different stages of scaling globally.

Case in point: Google was focused on the competitive American home voice assistant market, where all players were taking aggressive action to lock in market share and build a more robust ecosystem. After seeing data that highlighted the opportunity in Latin American markets, an untapped market with limited competition, the Google Nest team pivoted, seeking a first-mover advantage. The Google team jumped into action, recalibrating the prioritization of international markets and launching its Nest products into eleven countries in the region, all the while taking an agile approach. Effectively navigating different technical specifications per country (like voltage requirements) and bringing on key partners who had expertise in the local markets, some with different models, Google was able to capitalize on a first-mover advantage of its own in the region.

Pathways for Success

- When building a team focused on international growth efforts, choose members who are fluent in agile. This applies to team members in the local market and those at HQ who are supporting growth efforts.
- Reward the utilization of agile methodology until the local operating model is validated over adhering to set plans and timelines.
- Recognize that agile methodology is the clearest pathway toward identifying the localizations necessary to find traction (and scale) in new international markets.

CASE STUDY

EFFECTIVE ADOPTION OF THE FOUR COMMITMENTS FOR SUCCESSFUL GLOBAL GROWTH—FLEXPORT

Flexport effectively embodied the Four Commitments for Successful Global Growth in its expansion to, and growth in, Europe. As founder of Flexport's European business Jan van Casteren explained, the support from HQ in these core areas allowed for finding company-market fit and achieving scale.

Resource Alignment

Flexport had executive and stakeholder alignment around expansion. They understood the global nature of their industry (freight forwarding) and that a presence in Europe was needed to attract and serve larger customers. Recognizing the importance of long-term investment in the region in order to get traction, the executive team waited on expanding until after the Series A funding round was closed and funding was available (limiting the risk of needing to "launch and leave"). The local team in Europe was very committed to the expansion. The local office expanded from sales, client success, operations, and legal/regulatory compliance to include procurement, recruiting, finance, human resources, product, and design over time, giving Flexport a strong local presence.

Interestingly, Jan explained that during market entry the Flexport Europe team was given specific goals but wasn't assigned a specific budget. The stated goals were to identify company-market fit, get commercial traction, and serve the existing clients whose operations were underserved in Europe. This strategy led resource allocation to be customer driven. And, as such, headcount was granted by the executive team to build a solution to meet these customer needs.

Trust and Autonomy

One of the keys to Flexport's success in Europe that might go unnoticed was the relationship between Jan and Flexport's COO, Sanne Manders. Jan and Sanne knew each other from their days working together in Boston Consulting Group's Amsterdam office. This relationship not only helped lead to Jan joining Flexport, but also gave him an executive champion at HQ. On the flip side, Sanne had already built trust with Jan, an important aspect of good relationships between local teams and HQ, which is discussed further in chapter eight. While Jan was given many freedoms to build out the European operations, HQ did put up some guardrails for what was localized and centralized (product being the latter).

Communication and Clarity

In the beginning, most of Jan's communications back to HQ related to commercial traction and was between him and Sanne. Over time this expanded to communications with other members of HQ and other global team members. Each month, Jan would send an update to the executive team and collaborated with HQ and the rest of the global team in important decisions—from hiring to large expenses to investments made in new clients, explaining how the decisions were made and not just the expected outcomes. This also provided an opportunity to share local nuances, making requests for localization more accepted. Jan also hosted executives who traveled to see the European office every other month and in turn Jan visited HQ bi-monthly.

This provided more formal communication structures, and "GM Weeks" were established when all the general managers across the United States, the head of Asia, and Jan would meet face-to-face, leading to greater team building and communication. For example, a Google Sheet with all the localizations/project functionality requests from each region was created to help with getting priority for regional product change requests. This led to the hiring of a technical program manager whose role was to collect and track product needs for the local teams (this is a lightweight and targeted version of the Localization Resource Team concept, which we will discuss in chapter seven). This team member was located in Europe but reported to the global product team's leadership at HQ, something that Jan mentioned was a key reason why the role was effective.

Relevant Note: Jan's experience with Flexport's global growth journey aligns well with the organic way most successful expansions progress. During market entry, Jan's main channel of communication was through an executive champion (Sanne), which then gave way to more global communication (although mostly through individually driven behaviors like office visits). And as Flexport got further into the market growth stage, more formal structures like "GM Weeks" were established, as well as the technical program manager resource.

Nowadays, Flexport has a clear playbook outlining all steps and requirements (including legal, HR, and the like) and the decision process for entering a new market. Communication and meeting structures have also matured. The Europe, Middle East, Africa (EMEA), and APAC regions are seen as on par with North America, and all three regions run weekly global problem solving meetings together with Flexport's global functions.

Global Agile Methodology

Flexport provided Jan with the freedom to utilize the agile methodology in reaching company-market fit in the European region, iterating on many elements of Flexport's go-to-market and operating models. Since the product was tightly managed by HQ and a centralized product team, most of the iterating was focused on the rest of the playbook. Iterations and pivots occurred, including bringing on a partner for UK operations at first and needing to localize policies (German salespeople were given cars, something which is uncommon in North America, but an important perk in German business culture).

Combined, the resource alignment, trust and autonomy, communication and clarity, and use of global agile methodology were key ingredients for Flexport's success in Europe and worldwide.

WHY THE FOUR COMMITMENTS FOR SUCCESSFUL GLOBAL SCALING ARE IMPORTANT

The Four Commitments, visualized on page 84, establish a bridge between HQ and local teams, set parameters for collaboration, and provide framing for the elements HQ needs to put local teams on a path to success.

The Four Commitments are crucial to the success of global growth initiatives because without the proper implementation of and ongoing adherence to these commitments, companies run the risk of falling prey to the ten most common factors that cause global businesses to fail (as outlined in chapter one).

- Failing to establish leadership buy-in (#2) comes from inadequate **resource alignment** from HQ, as does Not investing appropriate time and resources into global growth (#8), Building the wrong team (#3), and Not building the structures to create momentum (#9).
- Maintaining an us-versus-them mentality between HQ and local teams (#4) manifests when there is a lack of **trust and autonomy** granted to local teams.
- Problems localizing [Not revisiting customer development (#5) and the agile methodology when localizing and Not managing complexity (#6)] and Attempting to be "Born Global" (#1) stem from abandoning the **global agile methodology**.
- Not adapting communication to fit a distributed workforce (#7) and Not universalizing core values and company culture (#10) grow out of a lack of commitment to **communication and clarity.**

The Four Commitments facilitate this balance by setting the local team up for success and ensuring HQ has a mechanism to both support and guide local teams. From Feedback Loops to the global agile mindset, the mechanics of these commitments are meant to foster and keep alignment between HQ and local teams.

From a practical perspective, these commitments help companies find product-market fit during market entry and help build momentum to achieve company-market fit during the market growth phase and scale in market maturity (more on this in chapter seven).

Moreover, the Four Commitments are all interconnected.

- A commitment to establishing strong **communication** channels allows for the **agile** iteration that is needed to localize a business for a new market.
- **Communication and clarity** foster the necessary **trust and autonomy** for effective growth. Trust fosters even better communication links.
- **Effective communication** channels also optimize the use of **resources committed** to global growth initiatives so that local teams utilize resources in ways most appropriate for the local market.
- **Trust and autonomy** optimizes the use of **resources** (people and funding).

Adoption of agile enables iteration of the other three commitments to support an ever-changing organization as it goes from market entry to market growth (finding product-market fit and company-market fit, respectively) and into market maturity, where deeper localizations and ongoing optimizations are fueled by agile. The importance of how the commitment to agile enables the other three commitments cannot be underscored enough. The role of agile is so important that it must not only be utilized; it must be adapted to specifically confront the unique complexities that arise when needing to localize and then scale a business across a diverse global footprint, where each country has unique market conditions, cultural nuances, and rules.

With full alignment among the leadership team on the Four Commitments, it's time to put each into practice.

The *global* flavor of agile is detailed in the next chapter.

CHAPTER 4 SUMMARY

- There are four key commitments that companies must make (and uphold) to have success with global growth initiatives:
  a. **Resource Alignment**—Global Class Companies dedicate financial and people resources to global growth initiatives over an extended period of time, ensuring there is alignment with company leadership who is actively engaged in the initiative.
  b. **Trust and Autonomy**—Global Class Companies foster trust between HQ and local teams, granting the local team the appropriate amount of autonomy for the specific expansion stage (*Market Entry, Growth,* and *Maturity*) using the *Autonomy Curve* as a guide.

c. **Communication and Clarity**—Global Class Companies establish *Feedback Loops* so that there can be two-way communication and innovation that occurs across a global footprint.

d. **Global Agile Methodology**—Global Class Companies use a modified version of the agile methodology that accounts for the challenge of finding company-market fit across multiple countries.

- These four commitments build a bridge between HQ and local teams and facilitate interactions and strategy implementation.

CHAPTER 4 REFLECTION & ACTION QUESTIONS

1. Which of the Four Commitments is your company's leadership most bought into? Least?

2. Describe the dynamic between HQ and local teams in your organization. Is it balanced?

3. Do you have alignment among the leadership team and key stakeholders around your expansion?

LOCALIZATION

Global Agile Part 1: Discovery and Hypothesis Development

*W*e *understand that homelessness is the community impact area headquarters focuses on, but it doesn't really resonate with us,* thought Zendesk's budding team in Singapore.

Zendesk is a very community-minded company headquartered in the Tenderloin neighborhood of San Francisco, where employees come face-to-face with homelessness on a daily basis. From homeless people camping out at street corners near the company's main office to drug addicts roaming the neighborhood at all hours, the Zendesk team saw the effects of homelessness and made a focused effort to address poverty through the Zendesk Foundation.

This neighborly mindset became an integral part of Zendesk's core values and global growth strategy alike, as the company looked to have a positive impact on the communities it has offices in. Initially, this was a mindset deeply rooted in the homelessness and poverty challenges native to the company's San Francisco HQ, and the company addressed this social concern wherever Zendesk offices popped up.

The only problem was that not every city Zendesk expanded to was hampered by the effects of poverty. When establishing an office in Singapore, the local team remarked that homelessness was not as prevalent in the city-state, and so this community focus didn't connect with the local team.

Singapore does, however, have a problem with depression within its senior citizen population. In order to encourage full employment, Singapore's Ministry of Manpower mandated that the retirement age be sixty-two at the time (unless a worker qualified for an exemption). Without the social interactions of the workplace, many senior citizens felt isolated and became depressed. Given the pervasiveness of the problem, it was an impact area that Zendesk's Singaporean team was passionate about solving.

As Zendesk continued on its journey of global growth, the company began to localize its community impact focus to align with each locale and the passions of the employee base there.

Besides showing the positive role Global Class Companies can have on society, this serves as a great example of *what* Global Class Companies do to reach global scale; they localize. It also illustrates the breadth of what localizations should be considered and how multifaceted the path to achieving company-market fit can be.

The thing that sets Global Class Companies apart from companies with failed global growth initiatives is the scope of these localizations. It's easy for companies to think about localizing marketing campaigns or customer service, but only the most successful companies allow localization to permeate through every aspect of the company, like Zendesk's community impact.

THE IMPORTANCE OF LOCALIZING

With recent shifts in business, global opportunities are more apparent, but speed and agility have become even more important. And with a diverse set of market forces and cultural nuances in each market, Global Class Companies realize they must revisit their model, since the way things are currently done likely won't work exactly the same in a new market.

It's the Interpreneurs at these companies who see opportunities to connect with local markets and become the catalysts for localizing aspects of the business to engage communities and empower local employees.

Without the purview of Interpreneurs, the scope and importance of localization are often misunderstood. Admittedly, a number of business leaders don't see localization going much beyond language translation, but Global

Class Companies that put planning and resources behind localization truly reap the benefits.

Localization is a core vehicle for companies to gain traction in a new market through pivots and iterations. It is paired with culture in the Business Model Localization Canvas (BMLC) detailed in this chapter because the two are closely connected, culture being one of the drivers for localizing an aspect of the business and a key influence on what the localization is.

Localization is the output of going through the agile process in a new market. It is a proxy for all the pivots necessary to arrive at company-market fit in a new market.

A contradiction lies in the fact that a deep level of localization unavoidably creates complexity. This will mean that some aspects of localization will be worth doing and other aspects won't. Yet without this customization, customers are less likely to connect and engage with your brand.

Despite the complexities they create, localization efforts can help reduce barriers to growth in other areas, such as enabling sales teams to close deals much faster with marketing material that is localized and resonates with customers. While this time and attention expends marketing resources, it optimizes the sales process, since this collateral can be repeatedly used to overcome obstacles and shorten sales cycles.

Daniel Sullivan, Head of International Content and Localization for Shopify, believes that if you want to see the true potential of localization, you need to shift from considering it a *cost center* to viewing it as a *strategic business unit* and *process* that can drive customer engagement and sales. Equally important is that you make an effort to be local and speak local (which is where having a team with local knowledge is key).

Localization is even more crucial as we enter the new era of global business. As Muhammed ("Mo") Yildirim, former General Manager of International Expansion for Middle Eastern food delivery platform Talabat, shared, "Ten years ago, just being a US or European brand was cool to consumers in the region. Now, unless the product is localized, it doesn't matter. Localization is no longer a decision; now it's a must."

Why is all of this important? Because without the implementation of a comprehensive localization strategy, you miss out on top-of-funnel opportunities and ultimately won't capture the full ROI available from expansion. Or worse.

LOCALIZATION GOES BEYOND
LANGUAGE TRANSLATION

Many legacy companies believe that language translation is the first and (almost) only step to localizing their business for new markets. These are often the same companies that have an altogether too simplistic view of the best international markets to enter, prioritizing countries that speak the same language as their initial market instead of looking at the many factors that could have a more important impact on success in a new market.

In the standard scenario of the legacy company, there is an (often overly simplistic) language translation done that doesn't resonate with target customers in the local market. Tableau saw firsthand what happens if your localization efforts are rushed. Immediately after translated website content was released, German customers began to tear apart the language, sending the company corrections and in correspondence saying things like, "You gotta be kidding me . . . you think I am buying your product when you can't even translate to our language?" As Walmart also learned, to be good enough for the local market, it needs to look, taste, and smell like a German sausage.

People's desire for new products isn't boundless, and if you don't make an effort to meet customers in international markets partway, you can turn their goodwill into criticism. Customers respond when you make an effort to connect with them, and translating content into their native language is the most straightforward way to do this. As Slack's localization team puts it, "Localization builds trust with our customers in a language they understand, with cultural references that are familiar to them." But this is just a start.

In reality, it is better not to define localization solely by a language or cultural reference point but instead by outcomes. As Chang Wen Lai, CEO and co-founder of Ninja Van, puts it, "Localization comes in two forms: how you win local demand, and how you craft an operational strategy that makes sense on a local level."

The two core areas Chang Wen mentions (go-to-market and operational) match the structure of the Localization Premium Analysis framework introduced in the next chapter, which together supports the goal of controlling the negative outcomes that result from localizing.

HOW TO LOCALIZE

While localizing your business for a new market is an important step toward finding traction and scaling, the process shouldn't be followed blindly. As Jan van Casteren, former Head of Europe for Flexport, puts it, "The most important thing to avoid is *arbitrary uniqueness*; being unique just because you can. Only try to be unique when your clients or the local market structure demand it."

Eric Ries, author of *The Lean Startup*, points out, "When you enter new global markets, the 'product' is no longer the actual product you sell, the 'product' becomes the whole playbook that you need to use to get traction in that market, all the localizations and changes to your core business model that must be iterated on to achieve product-market fit in the new market." This is why we use the term *company-market fit* to characterize how localization extends beyond the product and go-to-market strategy to include all company operations. As outlined in the case study from the previous chapter, Jan from Flexport validated this point when he explained that most of the iterating he did to get traction in Europe was not related to the product (which was centrally managed by a product team at HQ), but instead with the rest of the playbook— the other aspects of the go-to-market and operating models.

Localization involves both *product* and *process* changes to effectively operate in the market. Processes can include adhering to local business customs but more generally include changing your operating model to find company-market fit (at first) and then scale (over time) in the new market. Success comes from re-examining the playbook that worked in the initial market and adapting it to fit the nuances of the new local market.

Effective localization does not mean changing just for the sake of it. All changes should come from market insights and validation. Industry, target customer base, and country all matter.

So what are the core tenets to consider when localizing?

First and foremost, Global Class Companies understand that adherence to the Four Commitments outlined in the last chapter is essential. Localizing any aspect of a business costs money (*resource alignment*), requires effective communication to share best practices and progress (*communication and clarity*), needs to be done with the local context in mind by someone with a deep (ideally native) understanding of the market, which requires the local team's discretion (*trust and autonomy*), and necessitates iteration to get right (*global agile methodology*).

Localization isn't a one-and-done process. You use the same agile (interpreneurial) mindset to constantly iterate and improve on translated go-to-market strategies and localized business operations. This takes a concerted effort to revisit and adhere to the customer development process that is often used by companies finding company-market fit in their initial market. As Eric Ries shared, "I've seen companies that plan to launch in twenty-two international markets at once, asking whether doing this can be done successfully. The more relevant question is, can you manage twenty-two customer discovery processes at once?" Utilizing the agile methodology during global market entry, growth and maturity takes focus and resources.

Don't overthink things. Global Class Companies realize they don't need to roll out the whole playbook right away. While putting resources into localization efforts is very important, things don't have to be perfect at launch. You can enter a market with the marketing materials you have (but make sure your product works). You will discover information as you go and can adapt from there. Localization discovery is ongoing. With this mindset, localization becomes an iterative process that pays for itself, versus doing all the work up front. Up-front work increases expectations and lowers the ROI from the beginning.

Don't think of individual localizations in a vacuum; relate them to other core aspects of the business. Because of the importance of company culture, for example, all localization needs to align with core values. Sometimes this will mean that you consciously choose *not* to localize aspects of your business. Core values can be a guide to what can be changed and what can't.

To better direct your localization efforts, recall BlaBlaCar's "build for two markets" strategy mentioned in chapter two.

Legacy companies build with their initial market in mind. The product, operating model, and team are all tailored toward the initial market the business scales in. Decisions are made with this one market in mind and hard-coded into the DNA of the company. When this approach is taken, it becomes very difficult to make changes suited for new markets.

Recall from the case study in chapter two, instead of building the product and company solely with its native French market in mind, founder and President Frédéric Mazzella directed the BlaBlaCar team to build the product and operations for both France and Spain simultaneously. This had a profound effect on many aspects of the product in particular.

The product was built to work in two different languages. When coding the tech stack/infrastructure for the platform, developers already had two languages in mind, French and Spanish, given the company's plans to enter Spanish-speaking markets after finding product-market fit in France. This approach made integrating a third and fourth language much easier. Think of simple elements you don't consider when you are building a software product for a single language, like text placement within the user interface. Words are different lengths in various languages, and some read from right to left instead of left to right.

Note that you don't necessarily have to physically build the product for two markets at once. When you do the research to understand the nuances of the second target market, you make decisions that build flexibility into the product and operations, making localization easier in the future. The company becomes more like a template or platform that can be adapted instead of a closed system.

THE KEY TO EFFECTIVE LOCALIZATION IS A GLOBAL VERSION OF AGILE

The agile methodology has proven effective in helping companies both large and small. This approach helps start-ups validate their business models and find company-market fit, just as it helps established organizations experiment, innovate, optimize, and scale rapidly.

The methodology (sometimes referred to as the lean methodology) refers to an iterative approach to product development, business model generation, or completing any project; in the case of Global Class Companies, this would be finding traction and scaling in international markets. Instead of developing a rigid and comprehensive plan that doesn't account for uncertainty and change (the waterfall methodology), agile methodology allows teams to change as they become more familiar with a new market. Plans are flexible and tests are conducted to validate which research and hypotheses are accurate and which are not, leading to well-informed improvements to the expansion strategy.

Just as companies appreciated the effectiveness of iterative processes, so too do Global Class Companies see their value in the context of global growth. Applying agile methodology to globalization initiatives is an effective way of making the agile mindset and tools compelling in an international context.

In particular, a global flavor of agile is a catalyst for identifying, building, and scaling localizations required to succeed in each market.

Effective Market Entry Starts with Revisiting Customer Development

As mentioned in the last chapter, to succeed at global scale, companies must stay agile. Returning to agile can be tough for organizations that have stepped away from iterative processes in favor of the waterfall method as they have grown to sizes that require more process and structure. However, the pure agile methodology isn't effective at localizing for multiple international markets because the pathway of agile is to iterate and pivot in whatever ways necessary to find the right model for a market. This is fine to do with one market, but doing this for ten different markets would lead to ten different operating models, which would be overwhelming to manage and difficult to generate momentum with. Adding back a globally conscious version of agile can help recalibrate the organization for the mission of building a global footprint.

In support of the notion that *global is the new agile* (mentioned in the introduction), we are seeing that in the same way start-ups have moved away from strict plan adherence and formal launch dates when bringing their products to market, so too are Global Class Companies moving away from formal international market launches. Opening offices with large teams up front is being replaced by a more organic market entry that seeks more validation and initial traction before a more public launch.

Herein lies the greatest challenge of them all. How do the local team (a team focused on a single market) and HQ (a team with a global purview) find ways to adapt and dance at the same pace without stepping on each other's toes?

This is a big challenge that requires the next generation of agile, a global layer that addresses these fundamental issues. We define the global agile methodology as *the process of localizing a business for a new international market in an iterative manner while managing the complexities that go along with implementing these changes. The ultimate goal of the process is to reach company-market fit in new international markets.*

In outlining the global agile methodology, we break the discussion into two parts. The first, *discovery and hypothesis development,* is discussed in this chapter and covers the initial stage where a company takes actions to better understand a new market and then develops a baseline for how they believe they will adapt their business to succeed in the new market. The focus of this step centers on *localizing* the business. The key framework for completing this stage is the Business Model Localization Canvas exercise detailed in this chapter. The goal of this step is achieving product-market fit.

Chapter six covers the second part of the global agile process, *preparation, validation,* and *implementation,* where a company does a deeper analysis, builds a plan to make required localizations, and then implements the plan. The focus of this step centers on *managing the complexities that come along with the localizations* uncovered in step one of the global agile process. It also considers how the changes made for this market fit into the global growth pathway of the whole company. The key framework for completing this stage is the Localization Premium Analysis process detailed in the next chapter. The goal of this second step is achieving company-market fit (as defined on page 40).

Agile in a Global Context

At its core, the main tenets of agile in an international context are the same as the agile methodology used when searching for product-market fit in an initial market, with a couple important differences.

- *Hypothesis testing* is superior to market research alone, since all localizations start with a hypothesis to test and change to validate changes to your business model to fit a new market.
- During discovery and market entry, team members with *customer development* skills are more effective than those with deep functional expertise, since many questions need to be answered about the localizations required for the market.
- *Observations* of *customer behavior* are still preferable to opinions.
- Road map adherence is secondary to *iterating and pivoting* based on key insights uncovered through testing.

- The finished products/services already sold in the initial market become the *Minimum Viable Products* (MVPs) that need to be validated in the new market for the new global market by putting them in front of customers to get feedback. In other words, you should have the mindset that your current product in your initial market is an MVP for the new international market.
- Confirming *problem-solution fit* and *product-market fit* are still the main goals of step one in the global agile process, as local teams look to transition from market entry to market growth. Then, in incorporating the global context and active complexity management, the main goal of step two is achieving company-market fit as companies go from market growth to market maturity.

Testing is an important aspect of agile methodology and is particularly important in the context of expanding into global markets. Although most companies going global are a long way from the days they first validated their business model through measured tests, that doesn't mean they should revert to the waterfall method, where every aspect of a new market launch is planned and built based on assumptions from research. Testing is one of the most effective methods to optimize time and money invested into expansion efforts. Consider when the opposite happens.

For example, a United States–based company selling point of sale (POS) systems didn't effectively test when entering the Australian market and jeopardized their entire expansion initiative.

In Australia, air shipping distribution is not as advanced as in Europe, Asia, and the United States. Before launching, members of the launch team conducted a test of the country's shipping system to ensure product and packaging integrity, along with calculating estimated shipping times. This was part of a broader pre-launch testing initiative that also included changing labels/stickers since every country and even individual retailers can do it very differently.

When it came time to launch, Australia Post refused to ship the POS terminals (which had lithium batteries, something many postal carriers don't allow) via air. The team hadn't uncovered this in all the testing conducted since the test products were shipped via ground service. Even though the product was certified with the International Air Transport Association (IATA), adhering to its centralized universal standards, in attempts to internationalize packaging, the decision came down to one Australia Post employee who wouldn't permit the item to be shipped.

Effective testing would have helped avoid the delays, operational limitations, and additional costs incurred by the company. Then, just like with the standard agile methodology, as results from measured tests garner key insights, hypotheses around planned localizations are changed. Constant iterations then occur until the new localized business has been validated by the market.

OFTEN OVERLOOKED

Rediscovery in Existing Markets Can Increase Market Share

If your company is already in one or more international markets but wants greater market share, it may be worthwhile to take a step back and conduct further localization discovery (explained in detail later in this chapter), where you go back to the search phase to understand the market better to reevaluate and then recalibrate your current strategy. We often find companies rush ahead to get traction and are unsure what to do when growth has stalled or fit hasn't been found. Doing this rediscovery is an important step to take before going through the global agile process. It also can uncover localizations necessary to improve performance in the market.

In order to avoid common mistakes and effectively reach global scale, Global Class Companies must utilize this new version of agile that accounts for the collective nature of finding company-market fit in multiple international markets. As mentioned, the standard agile process is about finding fit at all costs. This is great for an initial market, but if this methodology is used in five, ten, twenty, or more international markets, managing all of the disparate models and permutations of the business would be untenable.

Moreover, during this first stage, this globalized version of agile considers two lenses through which all aspects of a business must be viewed: government regulation and culture.

Government Regulation Filter

Government policy, local laws, and the current political environment play outsized roles in a company's likelihood of success during market entry. This category covers a wide variety of elements related to operating your business legally in a new country: establishing an entity, licensing, intellectual property rights and protections, regulations your products have to adhere to, location and ownership of customer data, taxation, and more. It can include policies as simple as regulation around the location of customer data storage (Germany), or it could be as disruptive as requiring you to partner with a local company or have local board members to legally operate (India), or charging import taxes that make your product far less attractive for locals (electronics in Brazil).

Government regulation can also affect market dynamics. Some industries garner more government attention than others; the liquor industry is one of them. When targeting the Vietnamese market, Carlsberg realized that working with the government was critical to the company's success. Local law mandated that the Vietnamese government own a controlling equity stake in local breweries, so Carlsberg's typical strategy of buying a majority stake of a local brewery to enter the market proved to be difficult. Instead, the company had to pivot its go-to-market strategy, building a long-term relationship with the Vietnamese government to be allowed to buy a minority share in local breweries and then having to wait to buy additional shares of the business over time.

Why it's important: A rising tide lifts all boats (and vice versa). Choosing the right "ocean"—country—to launch in is one of the biggest factors contributing to success or failure of a global growth initiative. Government policy can either be welcoming to your business, directly contributing to your ability to scale, or it can hinder your ability to operate profitably. And while government regulation may not directly outlaw your company from operating, it may use creative means to inhibit your operating model or product features.

To stress the importance of government regulation as a filter, we've seen public policy teams begin to play an even more crucial role in the success of validation and growth in new markets. A disruptive government policy could be a singular reason to not launch in a country. China's requirement to share intellectual property has strong financial implications and has been a big concern for companies looking to enter the market. Local laws requiring a local joint venture (JV) partner instead of direct ownership, political dynamics, or an industry-specific regulation all can have a strong effect on market attractiveness. These policies may affect how a company operates, limiting profitability or preventing the use of a specific business model. It could also be something that clashes with company core values or culture.

For example, Vivino, which sells wine online, couldn't utilize its primary revenue model in Russia or South Korea because the company's research found that it's illegal to sell alcohol online in those countries. Similarly, the company delayed its expansion in Brazil for years because of how difficult it is to get money out of the country.

The Middle Eastern country of Oman has its "Omanization" initiative, which requires companies operating within its borders to hire only Omani nationals for some roles (like HR), while other roles, such as sales, can be filled partially by expats. At the same time, a certain percentage of company employees need to be Omani nationals for the country to grant visas for the expat employees. Mo Yildirim, former Managing Director of International Expansion for Talabat, explained that this created issues for Talabat, since locals lacked certain skills the company needed. It slowed hiring and required the company to invest heavily in training.

Because of Uber's disruption of the regulated taxi and delivery markets, the company faced a great deal of pushback from various governments (both national and municipal). That is why they developed their green/yellow/red market segmentation based on local regulations, prioritizing the (green) markets with the most friendly regulatory environments. While the company successfully operates in many markets, they were blocked from doing business in others. The Hungarian government, for example, suspended Uber's operations in Budapest with a 2016 law that allowed the Hungarian national communications authority to block all internet access to "illegal dispatcher services." Uber was forced to pull out of the Danish market after the country required fare meters and seat occupancy sensors in all vehicles providing taxi service, something Uber was unable to operationalize profitably. Regulation, governments, and politics all matter.

Outside of head-on disruption, government regulation can affect business models, the competitive landscape, customer data privacy, distribution channels, and the ability to move cash in and out of a country.

When planning to enter a new market, run all aspects of your business through a government regulation filter. This will help you account for how politics and regulations will affect your market entry strategy. Global Class teams avoid wasted time and money by establishing an accurate estimation of how the company will have to pivot so that localizations can be built in advance and by building a productive relationship with the local government.

OFTEN OVERLOOKED

Local Legal Counsel

In order to be most effective at complying with local law, it is best to have a local legal counsel to help you navigate. It's not something that can be strictly handled at HQ. A legal department representative can assist in selecting and communicating with this local counsel, but it is best not to use an attorney from your home country as primary counsel in a new market, since they may lack the expertise to effectively practice law in international markets. In other words, it's best to have your counsel at HQ learn how to manage local counsel in many countries, instead of having the legal team build its own local legal knowledge. As Thomas Kristensen, formerly of Facebook, points out, "You need to be able to look at the details and the big picture, seeing things from both a thirty-thousand-foot scope and a hundred-foot scope," which is difficult to do for multiple complex legal systems.

Culture Filter

The other layer to run all aspects of the business through is a cultural filter. Global Class Companies growing in new markets are sensitive to local nuances, including language, local traditions, customs and rituals, history, the trust-building process, unique decision-making criteria and buying processes, particular distribution practices, the local view on money and payments, as well as the local team's interactions with members of the local community, to name a few. In some markets, being perceived as an international (outside) brand can be a positive (Vietnam), while in others it can be a hindrance (Germany), although this can vary by industry within a single country.

Why it's important: Adjusting to local culture is crucial for product adoption and for effectively maintaining a local presence in the market. It enables your target customers to communicate with your business and connect with your product enough to want to use it.

Culture can even change the product you offer, if not at least core functionality. Prior to focusing on Asian markets, Slack's messaging platform didn't have a Send button, opting to have users click the Enter key on their keyboard. In some parts of Asia, businesspeople tend to send very detailed instructions/narratives rather than quick messages. Not having a Send button created a sense of anxiety in Asian business professionals, since being prepared, detailed, and lengthy in communications is part of the local business culture, and they were fearful of accidentally hitting the Enter button and then having to edit a message they sent prematurely, being thought of as unprofessional. This flew in the face of Slack's focus on improving the speed of communication since it added an extra step to the messaging process, making it a difficult decision for the Slack team. Given a spike in accidentally sent messages by users in Asian markets, a Send button was added. The product team subsequently set default preferences for the Enter key/Send button based on where the user was from, but ultimately offering both options to all users worldwide.

Despite the massive penetration Google Search has in many parts of the world, the company hasn't been able to gain much share in South Korea. One of the core reasons local search engine Naver continues to hold a strong market position is culture. South Koreans care deeply about democracy and maintaining freedom. Naver has successfully positioned itself as the people's search engine, which doesn't run the same kind of paid advertising system that Google Search does. Naver prioritizes searches less according to who pays to be at the top of the list (Google's "sponsored listings") and more based on relevance to local customers, which resonates with the local customer base.

Framing a solid understanding of the local culture allowed Airbnb to create a bridge to their target customers by highlighting specific experiences that would appeal to them. Customers in some markets in Asia would embrace unique places to stay (castles and tree houses, for example), while others are more conservative. Seeking new ways of traveling and considering relative risk are concepts that are approached quite differently in various markets. This baseline understanding directly affected the experiences shown in the app and influenced customer communications, providing more detailed information in some markets to reassure potential customers, for example.

In our interviews, Japan was regularly singled out as a country where cultural differences were notable and localization efforts were paramount for reaching company-market fit. In order to get a large enough inventory of rooms to meet demand early on in the company's expansion there, Airbnb had to combat the apprehension that Japanese hosts had for posting a room listing if the space they were offering wasn't "perfect."

Cultural paradigms and local market trends can be catalysts for growth as well. One of the primary concerns in Japanese culture is the aging population. DocuSign played on this trend, explaining how Japanese corporations needed to enable digitalization technology to deal with the upcoming labor shortage and how the company's solution could help. With more of the population retiring, younger generations had to finish more work with fewer resources. DocuSign aptly illustrated how its digital signature solutions improved productivity and aligned with the Japanese government's own no-paper policy that was accelerating digital transformation, resulting in DocuSign changing its value proposition. Klaus saw this firsthand when in Japan in 2014. When visiting a client's offices, he saw stacks of papers piled high on every table at the office. After the government implemented its no-paper policy, the stacks of paper disappeared almost overnight.

When planning to enter a new market, running all aspects of the business through a filter to account for how culture affects go-to-market helps Global Class teams improve speed of adoption, avoid cultural faux pas, and better position the company as an organization that values and supports local culture, improving brand equity.

GLOBAL AGILE IN CONTEXT

Before going into more detail about the effects government and culture have on a business that is localizing for a new market, it is important to understand where the process of localizing fits within the greater context of applying agile to international growth.

During the initial customer discovery that occurs when a company is first founded, the starting point is a set of hypotheses about who the target customer is, what the solution (product/service) will be, and an estimated business and operating model. When expanding to new international markets, the starting point is the validated model in the initial market. When recalibrating in an underperforming market of an existing global footprint, the starting point would be the failing product/model that needs to be iterated on or pivoted away from.

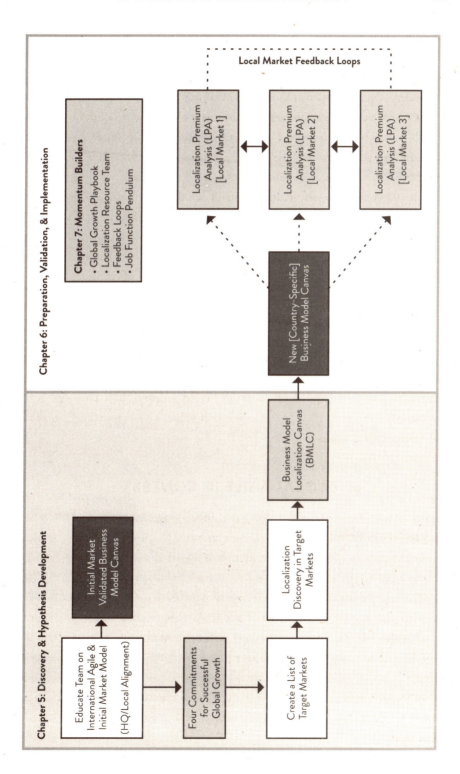

Chapter 5: Discovery & Hypothesis Development

Educate Team on International Agile & Initial Market Model (HQ/Local Alignment)

Initial Market Validated Business Model Canvas

Four Commitments for Successful Global Growth

Create a List of Target Markets

Localization Discovery in Target Markets

Business Model Localization Canvas (BMLC)

Chapter 6: Preparation, Validation, & Implementation

Chapter 7: Momentum Builders
· Global Growth Playbook
· Localization Resource Team
· Feedback Loops
· Job Function Pendulum

New [Country-Specific] Business Model Canvas

Localization Premium Analysis (LPA) [Local Market 1]

Localization Premium Analysis (LPA) [Local Market 2]

Localization Premium Analysis (LPA) [Local Market 3]

Local Market Feedback Loops

During market entry, the goals are to validate the new market, uncover required localizations, and gain traction, with the main milestone being product-market fit. When a team embarks on its global growth journey, it is important that all team members involved (both at HQ and in local markets) are educated on the operating model validated in the initial market and that everyone has bought into the Four Commitments discussed in chapter four, ensuring HQ/local team alignment.

The next step is to outline key questions that will help you evaluate a new market and determine how the model validated in your initial market will need to change to fit the unique aspects of a new market. For example, answering the following types of questions can be helpful in identifying hypotheses for what the model of a new market will look like:

- Can we target the same types of customers in the new market?
- Do we need to adapt our channel strategy in distributing our product to customers in the new market?
- How do we need to adapt our revenue or pricing model to gain traction in the new market?
- Does our value proposition resonate with target customers in the new market?

Localization Discovery

From there, the team starts strategy development, planning, and market entry preparation. This first involves taking the list of target markets and conducting a localization discovery exercise to answer these key questions and uncover the nuances of the market and scope the likely localizations needed. As Kathryn Hymes, former Head of International Product Expansion at Slack, suggests, look to understand what growth means in your initial market and understand the drivers of your business model. Then look for similar signs in other markets.

While research done at HQ can garner a number of key insights, it is insufficient on its own. You must go a step further and *validate* this data on the ground. During the research phase, the *voice of the customer* is often sacrificed at the feet of global vision. Gaining the voice of the customer involves talking with your target customers directly, not just researching them from afar. This helps mitigate the bias that is often part of the consideration and selection of target international markets.

Ideally, market analysis conducted at headquarters (and in-market) should deliver a prioritized list of target countries and ideas on how to localize. In practice, it may lead to a list of countries but also a number of new questions.

As with the customer development process companies go through to discover product-market fit through the standard agile methodology, localization discovery is a process that shouldn't be outsourced. Zoom's Head of International Strategy and Operations, Mark Parry, accurately points out that market readiness must be internally driven, not outsourced. Someone who will be involved in the expansion efforts (who will either be responsible for international growth at HQ or is part of the local market leadership team) should be part of the localization discovery process.

While talking with potential customers is a core part of the process, it's important that conversations go far beyond target customers. We recommend you include the following within the scope of your localization discovery process:

- Target customers (and current customers already in the target market)
- Investors
- Entrepreneurs and connected business leaders
- Prospective partners
- Potential new hires
- Local government agencies
- Local trade associations
- Universities
- Potential suppliers
- Thought leaders and market analysts
- Banks and financial system representatives
- Local media
- Everyday people

Localization discovery is a crucial step whose importance cannot be overstated. Things as mundane as the size of mail slots can affect packaging sizes and distribution choices, just as alphanumeric zip codes or the need to invoice in multiple currencies can challenge legacy systems. The former actually caused the delay of a company's entry into the South Korean market. The team didn't talk to the local post office to understand the postal system and local standards. A week before the launch, the launch team learned that their box didn't fit in the standard mail slot in South Korea, causing the company to push back the launch, scramble to redesign the packaging to fit, and stifle the planned (and paid-for) launch marketing campaign.

If not understood ahead of time, these little factors can incur delays and additional costs. These small nuances can even mean failure if your team utilizes the waterfall approach and overinvests without validating the right operating model for each market first.

At its best, localization discovery includes conducting in-person visits, during which key members of the team go in-market, talking to key stakeholders face-to-face and experiencing the market firsthand.

A great example we heard of the benefits of localization discovery comes from conversations with locals conducted by Troy Malone, former General Manager of International at Evernote. His initial research involved simply engaging with everyday people in taxis and in regular interactions at restaurants and hotels. The data uncovered during his remote research on India as he evaluated market entry in 2014 uncovered that the upwardly mobile young professionals (Evernote's primary target demographic for its premium product) had high credit card penetration, a great sign for Evernote, which used credit cards as their primary payment method. Interestingly, during conversations Troy had with everyday people in India, he heard time and time again what he referred to as "Auntie Stories."

Almost every young professional seemed to have an "auntie" who told stories of a relative who got a credit card, racked up a lot of debt, and *ruined* their life. Because of these stories, it was true that many people had credit cards, but no one ever used them out of fear of getting into debt and ruining their lives. The data uncovered during initial "behind the desk" research showed great promise for credit card payments, but reality from a boots-on-the-ground perspective showed that this data was unfounded. This in-market discovery not only helps validate (or invalidate) market research; it also uncovers new ideas for localization.

In the case of Evernote, it was a combination of Troy's interpreneurial cultural curiosity and local market expertise that led to effective marketing tactics, which helped Evernote cut through the noise by doing the unexpected. While exploring the Indian market with a local colleague, Anirban Mukhopadhyay,

Troy saw workers carrying around large crates full of buckets that were balanced on a wooden plank on top of their heads. When asking Anirban more details, he learned that these workers (dabbawalas) were delivering lunches ("set boxes") to white-collar professionals (Evernote's initial target customer base) in the area. Troy got the idea of a hyperlocal marketing tactic, printing a card with an advertisement on it promoting Evernote's premium service to augment the other digital advertising the company was doing. The strategy was successful and never would have been discovered without Troy's interpreneurial mindset that led him to explore the local market and experience it firsthand and Anirban's local knowledge. This clearly demonstrates the importance of having both local market knowledge and company knowledge when expanding to new markets (discussed further in chapter eight).

It's important to note that the localization discovery process should continue beyond this initial investigatory phase. In fact, Global Class Companies understand that ongoing localization discovery is needed even after initial market entry to gather additional insights about the local market and accelerate finding company-market fit.

CASE STUDY

EXPERIENTIAL EXECUTIVE BUY-IN—AIRBNB

When launching in APAC, Airbnb co-founder and CEO Brian Chesky wanted to observe people using the company's mobile app in one of the first countries the company launched in, South Korea. Jennifer Yuen, the company's former Head of Marketing in APAC, planned a trip around the holiday season that year for the company's entire C-suite to gain insights into the region's consumers firsthand (on-the-ground localization discovery at its finest). As part of the trip, Jennifer assembled some focus groups of South Korean customers for the executive team to observe.

Through a one-way mirror, the executive team was able not only to see the body language of customers but was also able to "look over their shoulders," watching how they interacted with the app.

Having the company's CEO observe this was incredibly valuable. It offered him a live experience showcasing the challenges of the app and the delight that the consumers in the new market had when interacting with it, bolstering buy-in for the expansion initiative. The executive team was able to see firsthand how locals immediately connected with the photo-heavy mobile app, despite the text not being translated into Korean. This reinforced the market opportunity and provided insights into what ways the product would need to be localized to fit the local market.

Moreover, this trip was a great tool to help the executive team better understand the differences in culture and market dynamics in this new region and buy into the updates to the product and strategy that the local team was proposing.

Building on the insights uncovered during localization discovery, the next step is to develop a new set of hypotheses for how the business will operate in the target market.

The Business Model Localization Canvas

Applying a global version of agile methodology starts here. The best way to create accurate hypotheses for the new market is to run the business model already operating at scale in the initial market through the two filters detailed earlier in the chapter (government regulation and culture), informing each with insights from localization discovery.

To assist with this, we have created the Business Model Localization Canvas (BMLC).

As a starting point, choose categories from the Business Model Canvas, created by Alex Osterwalder, used by many start-ups as they navigated initial product-market fit. (The Business Model Canvas is available at Strategyzer.com.) You can also use categories in the Localization Premium Analysis discussed in the next chapter, or you can design your own list of elements (BMLC templates are available at www.GlobalClassBook.com). The goal is to compile a comprehensive list of elements of your business and operating model and run them through the government regulation and culture filters to develop a new set of hypotheses for how your business will operate in the new market. By nature, this will highlight the required localization needed to find traction as well.

Interpreneurs shine in this process. Their cultural-mindedness and sensitivity to local nuances help solidify how government and culture dictate changes that need to be made to the business.

From here, you can transfer the new country's anticipated go-to-market/ operating models (your new local market hypotheses) into a country-specific Localization Premium Analysis template—a comprehensive framework that visualizes changes required to gain traction in new markets, part of the second stage of the global agile process (described in chapter six)—while using a country-specific Business Model Canvas (or other tracking tool of your choosing) to track changes to your hypotheses as you iterate in the new market. Then, follow the rest of the standard agile methodology—conduct measured tests using the Build-Measure-Learn Feedback Loop (described in Eric Ries's *The Lean Startup*), iterate based on key learnings, create initial versions of strategies and processes, pivot when needed—until you reach product-market fit (and ultimately company-market fit). Each country should have its own separate Localization Premium Analysis/Business Model Canvas (in the case of the former, multiple countries can be layered on a single template for comparison purposes).

This exercise is important to do for each individual country you are entering. You should then continue to run all aspects of the business through these filters during market growth to optimize operations and results. As you scale and begin operating in multiple countries, it may make sense to use markets you are already in as benchmarks for new markets, since the localization you did for your current footprint may be scalable in new markets (the concept of a "linked market" is discussed further in chapter six).

Filling out the BMLC

To complete the BMLC, write out the element of the business model validated in your initial market in the far left column. Then conduct the localization discovery if you haven't already done so. Next, list out the relevant aspects of government regulation and culture that may affect each element of the go-to-market or operating model in that country. Then, in the far right column, formulate and write out the locally conscious hypotheses for the new market. These hypotheses then become the basis for testing and iterating as you prepare for and launch in the new market. This then feeds into the Localization Premium Analysis process in step two of the global agile process.

Country: _____   Date: _____   Completed By: _____

Business Model Localization Canvas

Version: Localization Premiums		**Validated Model in Initial Market** List the validated model for each aspect of your business that has been proven in your initial market.	**Government & Regulation** How do government, regulations & local political environment affect each aspect of your business?	**Culture** How do local market culture, norms, beliefs & values affect each aspect of your business?	**Local Market Hypotheses** After running each aspect through a Government & Regulation and Culture filter, what new hypotheses should you test for the new market?
Go-to-Market Strategy	Sales Premium				
	Product Premium				
	Marketing Premium				
Operational Strategy	Admin. Premium				
	Infrastructure Premium				
	Org. Premium				

Country: _____   Date: _____   Completed By: _____

Version: Business Model Canvas	Validated Model in Initial Market List the validated model for each aspect of your business that has been proven in your initial market.	Government & Regulation How do government, regulations & local political environment affect each aspect of your business?	Culture How do local market culture, norms, beliefs & values affect each aspect of your business?	Local Market Hypotheses After running each aspect through a Government & Regulation and Culture filter, what new hypotheses should you test for the new market?
Customer Segment				
Value Proposition				
Channels				
Customer Relationships				
Revenue Streams				
Key Resources				
Key Activities				
Key Partners				
Cost Structure				

Business Model Localization Canvas

GLOBAL AGILE/BUSINESS MODEL
LOCALIZATION CANVAS IN ACTION

Culture and government regulations can have profound effects on localizations required to find fit, as well as on legally and culturally accepted models. Culture and government regulations cover every block of the Business Model Canvas in addition to product (as well as every category on the Localization Premium Analysis detailed in the next chapter). To explain the extent of the impact, here's an outline of different examples that showcase these filters:

Product. Zoom goes through a process of localizing its product when launching in a new market, or what Head of International Abe Smith dubbed a "localization of tech." This has led to product changes that reflect sensitivity to local culture and increased adoption of its video conferencing platform. In Asia, during face-to-face meetings, the exchange of business cards is a ceremonial custom where cards are passed and accepted with two hands and are inspected at length as a sign of respect. Taking note of this, Zoom has a feature that allows for the virtual exchange of business cards to make virtual meetings fit the culture of in-person meetings. Moreover, the company allows the windows of each video stream to be rearranged to account for the formalized seating arrangements customary in Asian in-person meetings, where the most senior attendees are placed in the most prominent seating positions (or, in the case of video meetings, position on the screen) to communicate their level of importance.

Revenue Model. Culture has a notable effect on pricing. In Mexico, companies typically offer zero-cost loans on products purchased. In Japanese business culture, price negotiations are standard practice (with discounts of as much as 90 percent being normal), so list prices are artificially high. In B2B industries in China, the last invoice is often not paid, a practice accepted by a vendor to offer a signal of the commitment to the future of the partnership. The vendor signals that they plan to build a long-term relationship with their client by not sending a final invoice. If you don't price to factor this in, you may quickly start to do business unprofitably—something the Thoughtworks team had to learn the hard way.

Value Proposition. Since it's typical for German employees to spend much longer stints at the same company, building a profile on LinkedIn, a platform whose value proposition in the United States was primarily around job search, was thought of as being disloyal. LinkedIn had to change its value proposition to position itself as a relevant professional development tool. The company worked to downplay the job search aspects of its platform, communicating that updating your profile or status didn't mean you were looking for a new job and showing how the platform can be an everyday knowledge tool to improve the skills necessary to succeed in one's current job.

Channels. Wine app Vivino has an ecommerce model where the customer's wine order is shipped directly to their door. This worked in a number of European countries, like Germany, but was rarely done in France because wine shipping costs ran up to 70 percent higher than in other markets, and consumers were used to a "click and collect" model, where they would pick up a wine order from a central location. The Vivino team adapted by creating a distribution system that allowed for a "click and collect" option to serve the French market. In other markets where selling alcohol online is illegal, as in Russia or South Korea, the company had to reevaluate and adapt its revenue model.

Understanding governmental and cultural landscapes can be a competitive advantage and even direct a company's go-to-market strategy, as proven by DocuSign's entry into the German market.

CASE STUDY

A PARTNER FOR THE GERMAN MARKET—DOCUSIGN

Germans are used to high-quality domestic brands and therefore prefer to buy from local companies (as illustrated by the story of Walmart's failure to gain traction in the market in chapter one). This makes getting Germans to adopt a new product or service from an international company difficult.

DocuSign was undeterred by this challenge. Understanding the local culture, they saw the need to secure a go-to-market partnership with a well-known German enterprise with vast reach across the market. The team targeted inking a deal with SAP, Allianz, Deutsche Telekom (DT), and others. In the end, DT seemed like the best fit, with its ten-thousand-person salesforce, an amazing distribution channel to tap into. DT also sought technology integrations so that DT mobile devices would have DocuSign esignature capabilities as well as customer data storage with DT data center, given that German customer data needed to be stored in-country.

To show commitment to the market, DocuSign crafted a comprehensive partnership proposal that included the partner investing in the next round of

DocuSign's fundraising, a resale partnership, tech integration (such as mobile device signature for DT), and a mutual customer relationship where employees of each company used the partner company's solutions. This four-pronged approach of distribution, mutual customers, investment, and tech integration would be a big win for DocuSign, but also an opportunity for DT to improve customer experience, gain revenue for its cloud business, and benefit from an investment in the rapidly rising value of DocuSign for helping grow the business in Germany.

As partnership conversations with many large organizations tend to do, talks progressed slowly. In June that year, DocuSign's then-CEO, Keith Krach, found out that DT's CEO, Tim Hodges, and about fifty of his top executives were going to be taking some executive education courses at Stanford University, near Docu-Sign's headquarters in San Francisco. With the Fourth of July holiday approaching, Keith invited all the DT executives to his (self-proclaimed) "beach shack" along the California coast near Santa Cruz to celebrate. The DT executives attended, exchanging formal business wear for shorts and short-sleeved shirts. The group enjoyed some BBQ (which *should have* been hot dogs but were bratwursts, comically enough) and fireworks. Because of the relationships built at the gathering, the partnership agreement was finalized shortly thereafter.

The partnership was incredibly successful. Not only did DT benefit from the profitable investment in DocuSign, but they also were able to include DocuSign as a value-added service on top of its network solutions. Within a two-year period, DocuSign started to hire a direct sales team in Germany to support the additional customer base and new market opportunities that the partnership laid a foundation for. The game plan was a winner because the entire strategy was built on an understanding and adoption of German cultural practices.

Localization is the key activity and focus of Global Class Companies as they expand to new markets. It spells the difference between success and failure. As outlined in the previous chapter, localization is both difficult and broad in scope. Besides getting you traction in new markets, localization also adds complexity to how you operate your business.

The burdensome fact is that the way you do business will change when you branch out internationally. Whether it be a change to your product or operational model, you will need to adapt when entering a new market. Some of this is driven by necessity (local laws and regulations), some by market factors (i.e., the need to change to get traction in the new market), and some by culture.

Whatever the change may be, our research indicates that business leaders often only understand this complexity in part, and not usually as part of a comprehensive and straightforward framework to plan around and socialize within their organization.

The Flexport team, for example, experienced an "aha" moment during their global growth initiative preparations when they compared how to price and sell their ocean freight products in the United States versus the various markets in Europe. Pricing and contract models are quite different. For example, the market rate for filing import customs is significantly higher in the United States versus (most of) Europe, and certain European markets have special port surcharges the United States does not have (and vice versa). In the United States, fixed contracts typically start in May and have an annual validity (a contractual rate lock), while in Europe annual fixed contracts are more likely to be closed around year end, and commonly have quarterly and half-yearly fixed validities. In order to fit each market, Flexport had to adapt its pricing model and realign its sales cycle to ensure the company could operate globally. These changes invite complexity into the business. What may start as two different pricing models may turn into five or six when a company establishes a global footprint along with multiple legal entities, different value propositions in each country, diverging sales or support models, and various internal technology integrations, not to mention translation and marketing changes to localize.

The addition of localization requires a new framework for tracking, communicating, and implementing the customizations you have validated through the application of the global agile methodology. With a stronger hold on how to localize in your quest to achieve company-market fit in global markets, let's investigate how to manage the complexity that comes along with these changes to your business, step two of the global agile process. The next chapter will explore a framework that will help you do this and achieve company-market fit.

CHAPTER 5 SUMMARY

- To succeed in reaching global scale, Global Class Companies utilize a modified version of the agile methodology (global agile) that helps them navigate the localizations (changes to the company's go-to-market and operating models) required to achieve product-market fit (the goal of step one) in a new market and ultimately company-market fit (the goal of step two). Step one involves conducting localization discovery and developing a new set of hypotheses for how the business will operate in the new market.

- Localization goes beyond language translation and marketing to include all aspects of a company from product to processes, from business model to local community engagement.
- There are two filters to run all aspects of a company's go-to-market and operating models through (as part of the *Business Model Localization Canvas*) prior to market entry: government regulation and culture. This process helps uncover hypotheses for what the model will look like in the new market that can be tested.

CHAPTER 5 REFLECTION & ACTION QUESTIONS

1. How are you uncovering and tracking the localizations required to enter new global markets?
2. What did you discover the last time you took a step back to evaluate how your company has localized for international markets?
3. How have the filters of government regulation and culture factored into your localization strategy during planning?

• 6 •

COMPLEXITY

Global Agile Part 2: Preparation, Validation, and Implementation

As Gonzalo Begazo, co-founder and CEO of logistics and delivery platform Chazki, guided his company's expansion to an eighth market, he realized he had a problem. Aspects of the business he'd spent so much time shaping in the company's first international market, such as operational model and office culture alignment, had been deprioritized as more urgent matters and a push to find a unique company-market fit in each market had taken priority. Now these issues were creating obstacles, preventing further scale and momentum as his team was taxed with operating many different models at once. He needed to not only solve some of the current issues at hand but also do a better job of creating commonalities among the models for each country and be more purposeful about evaluating the nuances of each market before committing to launch there.

Gonzalo was not alone. Amazon's online retail business was built out in an earlier era of global business. It operates almost like twenty separate companies abroad, each country with its own processes, logistics, go-to-market strategies, and value propositions. Even though Amazon's website looks similar in different markets, each site stands alone, and the products sold on each can be vastly different. This level of complexity keeps Amazon from truly reaching its full potential and higher level of optimization.

A battle is fought every time a company decides to enter a new market—a fight over which aspects of the business change and which stay the same. This is a battle that companies of all sizes, of all industries, and in all regions must fight, from global behemoths like Amazon to rapidly growing start-ups like Chazki. The result can be catastrophic, with Chazki's potential growth stalling and Amazon leaving itself susceptible to new local market competition. The effect of the balance struck between complexity and customization can lead to traction or failure in any single market, but when many markets are in the mix, the stakes are even higher.

As we specified in chapter five, localization is more than just language translation; it involves adapting all aspects of your business to fit the culture, regulations, and other distinct nuances of a local market. But these changes also breed complexity. After detailing step one of the global agile process, discovery and hypothesis development, now we will focus on the next step that helps you manage this complexity: the preparation, validation, and implementation step.

Each company has its own way of describing the complexities that come along with making necessary changes: A saying at Slack is "Every 'Yes' is a sacrifice." At Zendesk, it's "You can't be all things to all people." For others, there was even the tired reference to the inability to successfully "boil the ocean."

Focus, simplicity, and concerted efforts to avoid (what are often unavoidable) complexities are important factors to keep top-of-mind when growing globally.

Step one of the global agile methodology can help uncover the changes needed to find traction in a new market, but the mentality can't be product-market fit at all costs, because that mindset creates complexity and hinders momentum, efficiency, and scale. Instead, it is important to manage the complexity that comes with global growth.

It's imperative that you balance the localizations required to get traction in a new market with the complexities that come along with making these changes. Global Class Companies effectively use the global agile methodology to achieve this balance.

The imperative for this balance is encapsulated in what we call *Localization Premium*—a new agile concept that allows organizations to manage localization strategies while managing complexity as they scale globally.

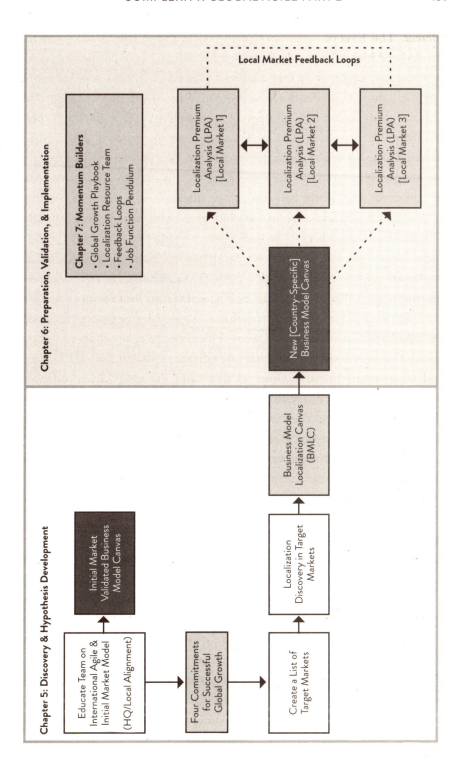

Chapter 6: Preparation, Validation, & Implementation

Chapter 7: Momentum Builders
- Global Growth Playbook
- Localization Resource Team
- Feedback Loops
- Job Function Pendulum

Local Market Feedback Loops

Localization Premium Analysis (LPA) [Local Market 1]

Localization Premium Analysis (LPA) [Local Market 2]

Localization Premium Analysis (LPA) [Local Market 3]

New [Country-Specific] Business Model Canvas

Business Model Localization Canvas (BMLC)

Chapter 5: Discovery & Hypothesis Development

Initial Market Validated Business Model Canvas

Educate Team on International Agile & Initial Market Model (HQ/Local Alignment)

Four Commitments for Successful Global Growth

Create a List of Target Markets

Localization Discovery in Target Markets

Ultimately, this is the goal of step two of the global agile process—to manage the complexities that come along with localizing your business for a new market on the way to achieving company-market fit.

WHAT IS LOCALIZATION PREMIUM?

Built into the core of the localization premium concept is an essential recognition that you have to adapt your business in some, if not many, ways to successfully penetrate a new market.

The word *premium* is used to connote both the benefit the company gets from making the necessary change (traction in the new market) and the added cost (in time, financial burden, or human resource effort) required when doing so. The benefit comes with a burden. **At its core, *localization premium* is the amount of complexity incurred in the process of localizing to achieve company-market fit in a new market.**

There is additional cost or time investment if a company chooses to create a quicker and easier solution, as opposed to a better solution that takes longer to implement at the beginning. There is a trade-off between speed and scalability, and longevity of the end result. In turn, accumulated localization premium creates issues that multiply and must be fixed later, often intensifying the longer they aren't addressed.

These operational and go-to-market changes and the premium they incur can be both big and small. If, for example, you allowed the team in every new country to use its own customer relationship management (CRM) technology, payroll systems, proposal building, and pricing tools, and let them enact different intellectual property strategies and maintain different legal entity structures, the operational management of your global footprint would be unbearable, and an effort to integrate it would be overwhelming.

Conducting a Localization Premium Analysis (detailed later in this chapter) can help you achieve company-market fit and scale faster in a new market. It directs you to the changes you need to make to your current model to be successful in the new markets and helps scale these changes across multiple local markets. This makes the Localization Premium Analysis a catalyst for finding company-market fit on a broader scale worldwide. The concept of localization premium can also serve as a common language and framework for companies to understand the changes involved with scaling to new markets and how the added complexity needs to be intentionally managed.

With this in mind, Interpreneurs should put a positive spin on localization premium and the higher ROI associated with global growth initiatives, keeping the concept at the forefront of the team's efforts. You can think of the cost associated with each localization as an investment that, when done right, can be scaled to other markets, thereby allowing for scale to happen faster. Regardless of how well complexity is managed, a company that goes through the process of scaling globally will change in many ways (many of them positive) as it stretches to reach a global audience.

The goal of this chapter is to help you optimize localization premium from the beginning, first by making you more aware of it, and then by giving you constructs and insights to help you manage it better. The idea is to ingrain a set of beliefs in your team and establish processes to simplify complexities instead of cobbling together customized quick fixes. Having these structures and clear lines of communication can give local market teams insight into how others have structured their regions and solved problems.

Paul Williamson, Head of Revenue at Plaid, sees localization premium as akin to the statistical concept of standard deviations, in that changes to how you run your business take you standard deviations away from your core focus. Traveling farther away from your primary focus by adding complexities and multiple ways of operating takes away from solving problems at the core. Measuring proposed changes in the context of standard deviations helps business leaders put guardrails around the decision-making process and highlights the often-overlooked negative effects that even small changes will have.

As Paul continued on the topic, he referenced how, without standard deviation guardrails or a perspective of localization premium, you can "Frankenstein" your product; instead of continuing to be a valuable solution to your target customers, you become a non-specialist to everyone (and have high Product Premium). Product changes just scratch the surface of localizations required to capture a significant share of a new market. Changes to other aspects of your business are also often essential. Focus matters in the beginning, whether you are at the early stages of a business or launching into new markets.

While you can think of localization premium as a proxy for complexity, it is more than that. We see it as a physical and graphical representation of how your business must adapt your current model to best attain company-market fit in a new market.

Localization premium is a conversation starter and a common language and framework, allowing you to quantify often amoebic elements. The Localization Premium Analysis framework explained in this chapter will help you balance revenue potential and necessary changes (which require resources). It allows for comparison between multiple elements of your business. More than anything, it is a helpful heuristic for navigating international scaling.

WHY LOCALIZATION PREMIUM MATTERS

James Sherrett, former Head of EMEA Sales at Slack, describes the complexities that lead to localization premium this way: "Every decision and change has downstream effects."

It's important to understand and track localization premium. If left unchecked, it will compound, slowing down your company's growth, sucking resources from your core, wasting time and money. It can even jeopardize your core business in your initial market.

Managing complexity is also the key to progressing from market entry to market growth and ultimately market maturity.

Moreover, the concepts of localization premium and complexity align closely with the Four Commitments for Successful Global Growth.

As previously referenced, despite all Amazon has done to make the lives of its customers easier worldwide, they have done so by making it very difficult on themselves to operate the company at global scale.

Amazon began launching in international markets at a time when many of the tools and structures to minimize complexity didn't exist. As the company grew, it amassed considerable localization premium.

Ethan Evans, former Vice President of Amazon's Appstore for the Kindle Tablet, describes Amazon not as a global company but instead as a multinational one, technically running quasi-separate businesses and with different operational strategies for delivering goods in each country. The company began with physical goods in a single country, then expanded country by country. So while Amazon uses one operating model and set of guiding principles, the online retail business in each country is unique. This highly localized approach allows the local entity to be agile and fit the needs of the local market (great for achieving company-market fit), but at the same time it creates many different ways of running various parts of the business (increasing localization premium).

Apple is one Apple, but Amazon has Amazon.com, .jp, co.uk, and so on; while they have a similar look and feel, the product offerings and processes behind each marketplace are different. Because the company deals with physical goods, it needs to have a physical presence in-country, in addition to a localized website. This model requires customizations for the import/export of products, corporate real estate, local labor laws, political concerns, and local regulations.

If you were to study Amazon's services, you would find that they have a localized-per-country offering in about fifteen to twenty major commercial markets, and a global offering of the American online experience for the rest of the world. Hence, Amazon is divided into twenty marketplaces and a "rest of the world" group. As time goes on, Amazon slowly shifts some of the countries in the rest-of-the-world group into individual markets as well.

In running a technology-based part of the business (Prime Gaming and the Kindle Tablet)—one that could theoretically run across borders—Ethan was still tied to each country's separate legal entity and the online experience customized for each country, increasing the complexity of launching in new markets. Layer on differences in infrastructure, cultural nuances, localization, and local market regulations, and operating in multiple countries can be cumbersome.

Ethan explained it this way: "Amazon has built a house, neighborhood, and a city. You can't neglect the structure that is there. You can't avoid what already exists. You have a legacy structure you have to reconcile with"—a detriment—although he did point out that Amazon has a huge advantage in scale and distribution, which has helped it be incredibly successful despite these complexities.

While companies like Amazon may have the resources to persevere despite these complexities, it is best for you to avoid making them from early on so you don't face the "no turning back" scenario Amazon is in, as at this point it would be nearly impossible for the company to reorganize its operations into a less complex model globally.

As you enter the phase of building a global organization, keep your eyes wide open. Understand that you have to sacrifice and ask yourself the tough questions ahead of time. As Scott Coleman, formerly of Pinterest and Google, suggests, ask and answer questions like:

- What would we need to change?
- What are we willing to sacrifice?
- How does it affect go-to-market strategy or operating model?

OFTEN OVERLOOKED

What Happens When You Prioritize Speed Above All Else

When you launch in multiple new markets, you may experience a dead zone in your timeline where short-term speed takes priority over managing complexity. Such was the case for Gonzalo Begazo when expanding Chazki into new markets. After launching in a few international markets, important factors were deprioritized. Gonzalo spoke of how maintaining a consistent company culture in Chazki's first international market was as important as establishing a strong company culture in their initial market; this took a back seat to other priorities in the next few markets. Often companies focus on implementing a strong company culture and ensuring core value alignment in an initial market and even in the first couple of international markets. As a company enters markets three, five, seven, however, this is deprioritized in favor of speed-to-market and finding traction. Core value alignment returns to focus only later, when leadership identifies a handful of markets that aren't well aligned with core values. This forces the team to make painful decisions, taking more time and focus away from customers. Utilizing the localization premium concept can help you avoid this by keeping a 360-degree view of all elements of go-to-market and operational strategies in focus for every single market entry.

Mastery of localization premium mitigates issues with scaling later by ensuring you build things right the first time through effective planning, strategy development, prioritization, and ongoing tracking.

LOCALIZATION PREMIUM ANALYSIS USE CASES

The Localization Premium Analysis (LPA) is a relevant exercise for a number of use cases and can solve problems many companies face when going through both market entry and market growth phases.

New Market Analysis

Prior to market entry, completing the research and preparation in step one of the global agile process not only gives you visibility into potential localization premium (the localization discovery discussed in chapter five), but it also gives you important criteria for selecting the best countries to expand into. The LPA provides a checklist of all the factors you need to research before deciding to commit to a market. It is best paired with the market research typically conducted that evaluates market size and other economic indicators to create a more robust and multifaceted analysis. The typical research metrics are quantitative (population, economic growth), while the LPA provides a qualitative counterbalance. The LPA then becomes a tool the organization can use on an ongoing basis to track the localizations for all international markets. The LPA described in detail below is the main tool companies can use to complete step two of the global agile process and is the main facilitator (along with the momentum builders discussed in chapter seven and Three Pillars for Achieving Global Scale detailed in part three) to reach company-market fit.

Market Prioritization

Paired with data on market size/opportunity, the exercise of determining the overall composition of changes required to enter a new market is an effective tool for determining which markets to prioritize. Countries with a lower localization premium may be the right focus in the short term, but in the long run it may make sense to prioritize a market that requires more localization because these changes could be scalable in other related markets, thereby increasing momentum and leading to faster penetration in multiple countries. This is the Linked Market concept discussed later in the chapter. Troy Malone suggests bucketizing each market based on the amount of localization premium market entry would incur into either:

- **Available Markets**—Markets that would incur little premium to enter
- **Emerging Markets**—Markets that incur more premium and would require overcoming some obstacles
- **Challenging Markets**—Markets that are problematic and would incur extreme premium

Naturally, the criteria for how to classify each market is highly dependent on go-to-market and operational models and can vary wildly from another company's classification.

Communication Tool

Complexities of entering a new market and required changes to the current model can be difficult to visualize and explain. The LPA makes the discussion more straightforward, highlighting required changes in the context of how different a new country's model would be and serving as a high-level overview that can foster deeper discussion and more buy-in. This framework is particularly effective in offering a comprehensive yet easy-to-understand explanation of required localizations for C-level and board-level audiences. This also ties directly into the communication and clarity commitment of the Four Commitments for Successful Global Growth.

Visualization of Risks

Executives and boards of directors often think in terms of risk: regulatory, reputational, political, financial, and security, among others. The LPA visualizes required changes, which can naturally lead to a discussion highlighting the corresponding risks of each.

Overcoming Myopic Viewpoints

Without a comprehensive snapshot of all the aspects of a company that need to be adapted to localize for a new market, executives and team members alike will default to think mainly about the scope of the changes that affect their functional area (sales, marketing, HR, etc.). The exercise of mapping out every premium helps minimize role bias (especially if your company is driven by a specific function, like product). It is important to communicate a holistic set of changes so that each team is given the proper focus and resources to execute on.

Road Map Alignment

Strategy must link to implementation. The LPA highlights the changes that need to be made so that relevant teams can be engaged and these changes can be built into their road maps.

Foundation for a Global Growth Playbook

The localizations mapped on the LPA, along with insights from localization discovery, become the basis for a Global Growth Playbook that can be iterated on by the team focused on global growth.

Implementation Tracking

Post launch, the key to success becomes establishing effective Feedback Loops. The process of estimating localization premium is not just a valuable exercise in quantifying the amount of complexity a company must take on; it's also an effective tracking tool. In addition to forecasting localization premium, you can return to this exercise after launch to track how far off the actual complexities incurred are from what you estimated, helping you set better expectations for future market entries and encouraging efforts to foster consistency (seen in the case study of Evernote's entry into India described later in the chapter).

Moreover, using the LPA to evaluate the localizations and complexities of markets where you already operate can uncover new success factors, helping you identify new criteria to consider when evaluating additional markets. Revisiting the case study from chapter two, identifying the cultural acceptance of hitchhiking through filling out the LPA for their entry into Russia could help BlaBlaCar identify a new cultural criteria they can use to evaluate new markets in addition to other economic, demographic, governmental, and market dynamic criteria.

When the LPA is used to indicate different models being implemented in multiple international markets, it can showcase how many distinct models the company is juggling and highlight ways to reduce complexities and streamline operating models, whether through implementing best practices between markets or optimizing organizational structures to support your current and planned global presence.

The Localization Premium Analysis Isn't Just for Launching New Markets

To be clear, the LPA is a valuable exercise not just when launching in new markets, but even when you have an established footprint. Besides uncovering insights to help with future market selection, having multiple local teams maintain LPAs allows a cross-border team to have visibility into what has and hasn't had to change in each market, a transparency that allows for best practice sharing, scaling of innovation between markets, and the foundation for a Global Growth Playbook to accelerate momentum of expansion initiatives (more on the latter in chapter seven).

Linked Markets and Pattern Identification

Tracking effective localizations in existing markets can uncover trends, best practices, and patterns that can help with future market selection and strategies for entering new markets. The LPA can be used as a tool to help see markets that influence each other, where an operational or go-to-market change can help multiple geographies.

MAPPING OUT YOUR LOCALIZATION PREMIUM

As Whitney Bouck, former COO of Dropbox's HelloSign Division, aptly highlighted, "People generally under-appreciate the breadth of international expansion." This is why we have developed a comprehensive framework to map out the wide scope of potential premiums incurred when entering new markets.

In conceptualizing localization premium, we found that using a spider chart can visualize the various subcategories of localization premium and help you understand how far the changes in each area pull you from your current way of doing business.

Each of the premiums in the analysis represents an area of the business that may need to be localized to achieve company-market fit in the new market.

Localization Premium Analysis

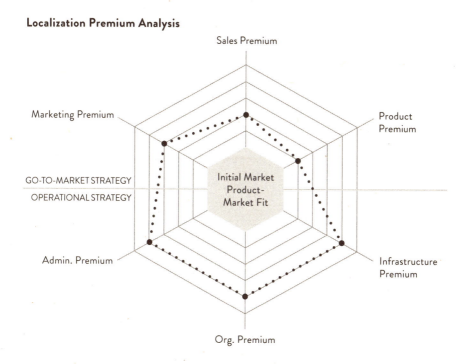

At the center of the chart sits your core model, which could also be referred to as the product-market fit in your initial market. As previously mentioned, having product-market fit and proving scale in an initial market are essential stepping stones to achieving effective international expansion.

Without product-market fit in your initial market as a foundation, your core is constantly shifting. This throws your operations into flux, since there is neither a steady base nor a pivot point that local teams in new markets can operate off of. Before confirming product-market fit in the United States, Microsoft's Workplace Analytics team was also quickly drawn to the Japanese market, seeing that they could ride a tailwind and be one of many solutions to a recently launched government-backed initiative that asked Japanese companies to address concerning work practices (including the problematic and tragic issue of karoshi, or "death from overwork"). Still lacking clarity on the appropriate customer use cases and more comprehensive value propositions in the United States (initial market) made it exponentially harder to find traction in Japan beyond pilot engagements without a core reference point that had been validated in the initial market.

Surrounding the core are various layers, which you can think of as standard deviations (as characterized by Paul Williamson from Plaid), or degrees of difference from the core. The larger the overall surface area among the points on the chart, the more localization premium is being accumulated.

Each point on the chart represents an area of your business and its operations where premiums can accumulate. The subcategories on the top half of the chart represent elements that are part of a company's *go-to-market strategy*, while the elements on the bottom half represent a company's *operational strategy*, scaffolding that supports local operations—both sets of which need to be localized to gain traction in a new market.

Subcategories that together make up localization premium include:

- Sales Premium
- Product Premium
- Marketing Premium
- Administrative Premium
- Infrastructure Premium
- Organizational Premium

Let's look at each in more detail.

GO-TO-MARKET PREMIUMS

The Go-to-Market Premiums (Sales, Product, and Marketing) represent the customer-facing elements of a company's business model that may need to be adapted to find traction and scale in a local market. Think of these premiums as the visible tip of the iceberg. While government regulation can affect these categories, they tend to be more driven by differences in culture.

1. Sales Premium

Sales Premium refers to the changes that companies must make to sell, distribute their product, and support customers. This includes changes to channel distribution (direct sales/local retailer/value-added reseller), pricing/revenue model, sales model, sales/support teams, and customer service.

Workday had the opportunity to close a sale with Samsung corporate in South Korea, but they had to hire a dedicated sales and support team made of native South Koreans. This included changing their support model to include an additional services team dedicated to the Samsung account.

Japanese business leaders believe that products with high up-front costs are better, and they reject paying for add-ons and extras. For instance, they will pay a higher price for a product or service but expect that things like twenty-four-hour support and warranties are included.

Global Class Companies take into account differences in competition, anticipated competitor response, and how they must adapt to differentiate.

2. Product Premium

Product Premium is accumulated when you have to make changes to your product or service, including adding/subtracting features, bundling or integrating with other solutions, and product localization to fit cultural differences. Changes can be as slight as adding or subtracting a feature or as vast as revamping an entire product.

At times, LinkedIn needed to make drastic product changes to fit other markets. For example, in India, mobile networks have slower speeds than those of other countries. This meant that it would take a long time for the graphic and image-heavy content on LinkedIn's mobile app to load. While this wasn't a problem directly created by LinkedIn, it was a reality they needed to contend with; if left unaddressed, customers would begin to complain about the bad user experience or stop using the app altogether. To avoid this, the LinkedIn team created a new, less-bandwidth-heavy version of the app, which it internally dubbed "LinkedIn Lite." It replaced images and graphics with a more text-heavy experience that loaded faster and met the constraints imposed by local mobile networks.

OFTEN OVERLOOKED

Leadership Bias Can Prevent Growth in New Markets

Evernote considered itself an Apple shop, with HQ maintaining a heavy bias toward Mac devices. In conducting research for a launch in Asia, former General Manager of International Troy Malone found that 95 percent of the population used Windows. This meant that the Windows version needed to be at parity with the Mac application, which would require additional resources and time for the engineering team to revamp the Windows application. The company's pro-Apple mindset temporarily obstructed the company from seeing the customer need and perspective. Eventually Troy convinced CEO Phil Libin to dedicate the resources to improve the Windows version by getting him to use only a Windows PC to access the existing Evernote app for a week. Through this experience, Phil understood the need to improve the Windows PC app experience. While this did incur Product Premium, the investment in improving its Windows version led Evernote to grow in the region. Moreover, it was the more direct path to success; it's easier to change the Windows PC version of the app than to have to convince target customers to buy a Mac computer AND use Evernote.

---

3. Marketing Premium

Marketing Premium includes differences in target customer, changes in value proposition, changes to use cases, market segmentation, competitive landscape, differences in demand generators, brand changes, differences in customer purchase decision-making criteria and marketing strategies/advertising channels (user acquisition, retention, and growth), public relations and branding changes, as well as language translation and beyond.

As mentioned in the previous chapter, LinkedIn had to change its core value proposition in order to gain traction in Germany, from career advancement and connecting recruiters and job seekers (i.e., an online resume and job candidate filter) to positioning LinkedIn as a place to explore their intellectual curiosities and, as Sankar Venkatraman, LinkedIn's Chief Evangelist of Global Customer Advocacy and Sales Transformation, puts it, "help you do better at what you are already doing."

Branding changes were a consideration for a number of companies we researched. Yes, changes in branding do accumulate Marketing Premium, but it's hard to be taken seriously if your brand name sounds like slang words for poop, as was the case for South Korean company Kakao when translated into a number of other languages. One of their main products, Kakao Talk, may turn heads if local customers interpret the name as "shit talk." This made it more difficult for people to connect with the brand, which was not a problem competitors like Line and WeChat had to face.

When considering market segmentation, recognize that launching in new markets presents an opportunity to reposition your brand; Budweiser positions itself as a mass-market mid-tier brand in the US while in China and other markets the company positions itself as a premium brand charging higher prices, a standard strategy in the beverage industry.

Fitting "Business Model" and "Delivery" into Premiums

While an effort was made to categorize each element into a go-to-market or operational category, some concepts transcend a single category—namely, business model and delivery. Because of the all-encompassing and multifaceted nature of the label "business model" (and its various accepted definitions), it was not possible to fit it into a single category. By one definition, the business model fits into the category of revenue model in Sales Premium, while by others it would include Product and Marketing Premium (covering all go-to-market strategy). Similarly, the concept of "delivery" also touches multiple premium categories, like product/service delivery that is supported by Infrastructure and Product Premiums as well as distribution channels and customer service housed under Sales Premium.

OPERATIONAL MODEL PREMIUMS

The Operational Model Premiums (Administrative, Infrastructure, and Organizational) represent the back-end elements of a company's business model that may need to be adapted to properly operate the business in a local market. Think of these premiums as the bulk of the iceberg below the surface of the water. These premiums tend to be underestimated and can be harder to uncover during localization discovery. While culture can affect these categories (Organizational Premium in particular), they tend to be more driven by differences in government regulation.

4. Administrative Premium

Administrative (Admin.) Premium is both the most often overlooked and the most complex. The category includes government regulation and compliance, payroll, taxation (including tariffs), customs, licensing, legal entities, protecting intellectual property, political considerations, corporate real estate, utilities/communications services, and everything related to operating a local office and having employees (human resources policies and otherwise). Reputational risk, accounting differences (such as separate profit and loss statements), and other financial implications fit here as well. Even company systems like productivity software fit here.

As ubiquitous as a suite of services like Google Workspace may seem, you won't have 100 percent of your employees using this same set of productivity tools if you have employees in China, who cannot use Google products because of government restrictions. This leads to more complexity and premium incurred. Uber faced a great deal of Admin. Premium due to all the transportation regulations in each municipality they launched in.

Amazon, for example, needed to have a 50/50 joint venture with a local India-based partner for its core retail business to comply with local law. This led to long delays in the launch as the company searched for and negotiated with the right partner, ultimately establishing a very complex partnership deal. When Slack's EMEA HQ office switched locations back-and-forth between Dublin and London, it created Admin. Premium as well.

You can't just send a QuickBooks invoice to customers in many Asian countries, as they likely still have a complex paper-based approach, where contracts may have to be sent via mail to be physically signed and returned.

OFTEN OVERLOOKED

Getting Money In and Out

In previous chapters we made mention of tax considerations when operating in another country and how to be mindful of ways to optimize your operations to minimize tax. Something often overlooked is actually moving funds into and out of the country aside from using envelopes stuffed with cash. In our interviews we heard about difficulties with bringing capital back to the initial market, in particular from China and Brazil. Capital planning, patience, and a clear understanding of regulations are important considerations, and things worth memorializing in the Global Growth Playbook (discussed in chapter seven).

5. Infrastructure Premium

Infrastructure enables the delivery of your product or service and can require more adaptation to fit a new market than is often considered. Infrastructure

Premium depends on whether you are selling a physical product or a digital one. For physical products, Infrastructure Premium includes all aspects of your supply chain (including shipping) in addition to packaging and labeling. This could also factor in the supplier landscape and the process and product changes required to deliver a finished product to customers in a new market. For digital products this includes tech infrastructure, where data is stored, and how it moves. Differences in internet connectivity or the mobile network fit here as well. Payment processing is also part of this category, which can be unique to each country.

For companies selling a physical product, there are set standards like IATA numbers for shipping and specifications set by UPS and FedEx, but intra-country carriers have unique requirements and varying standards.

Software providers have to contend with data storage requirements (as mentioned, countries like Germany, Russia, and Nigeria require citizens' data to stay in-country) and differing levels of Value-Added Taxes (VAT) depending on the location of software running.

6. Organizational Premium

Organizational (Org.) Premium includes the costs associated with bringing on a new team (i.e., training, hiring, and team building), the resources needed to build and manage structures and processes established to support global growth (concepts discussed in chapter seven and labeled as "momentum builders"), differences in local business culture, and the time the team at HQ dedicates to supporting a new region instead of working on their core responsibilities in the initial market.

Org. Premium factors in whether a brand-new team needs to be hired to manage a new market or whether regional resources are able to provide market coverage. Fast-growing companies have limited resources, so directing them to global growth initiatives means that other projects and markets receive fewer resources. Finally, Org. Premium includes how your management tactics may need to shift to be effective in a new market.

Different business cultures merit customized management practices, which can cause complexities in communication, coaching, and motivating teams. Many Asian business cultures, for example, are very hierarchical, which is a very different dynamic than American and European business cultures.

Employees in countries like India and Japan expect more specific instructions around the work they do, including long-form emails spelling out details in the case of Japan. Giving and receiving feedback is also very different. The direct verbal feedback common in American business would be very uncomfortable for employees in some Asian countries who are more accustomed to receiving feedback in writing. These differences not only affect management practices but also the methods for facilitating autonomy and building trust.

Org. Premium, a more nuanced category, also includes the gaps between company and local market culture that arise when building new remote offices. Even time zone differences present an operational challenge as employees who have different working hours must collaborate asynchronously without waiting twenty-four hours to turn around decisions or feedback (and that's in addition to everyday issues of attempting to schedule meetings across time zones).

Moreover, each country has its own unique cultural considerations and ways of doing business that must be adhered to in order to be successful (explored further in chapter ten). Claudia Makadristo, Head of Expansion in Africa for digital trust and reputation platform MetaMap, explains that, in Africa, for example, the amount of regional account management resources you need to support the same-sized customer base may require a different setup compared to other regions because of the plurality of languages spoken throughout the continent (French, English, Portuguese, Arabic, Swahili). These types of complexities can make team building more challenging.

In chapter seven, we will discuss effective team constructs like a Localization Resource Team and other structures that can help you manage localization premium. These teams can be pattern recognizers who connect the dots and fight for resources while also understanding limitations and setting up guardrails for what can and can't be changed in the process of achieving company-market fit in a new market.

Another way to reduce Org. Premium is to hire Interpreneurs, building a strong Global Class Management Model (discussed in chapter nine), a strong company culture, and momentum around global growth initiatives (more in the next chapter).

Org. Premium plays a foundational role in the Three Pillars for Achieving Global Scale (discussed in part three) and is the main enabler of reaching company-market fit. Controlling complexity in this category can mean the difference between success and failure.

OFTEN OVERLOOKED

Organizational Premium's Vast Reach

The Org. Premium category has an outsized impact on other premiums. The way you set up your team, manage that team, create an organizational culture, and implement structures to support communication and alignment with the organization will greatly improve your likelihood for success in localizing, finding product-market fit, achieving company-market fit, and reaching scale, both at the individual country level and across a global footprint.

Your investment in the elements of Org. Premium can help you minimize the other premiums in the LPA. With the right team, management model, and culture, for example, decision-making becomes easier and resources allocated can be optimized, creating a faster path toward traction and scale. These three areas—team, management, and culture—also happen to be the focus of part three of the book.

The creation of structures and processes to support market entry and growth does incur Org. Premium but is the primary tool to creating momentum around global expansion and scaling (as we will discuss in the next chapter). With less friction in operations, the process of localizing a business accelerates because the localizations made in the other premium categories can be scaled to other markets. Org. Premium is the category that organizations often overlook at the beginning of global expansion initiatives until international markets become a significant source of revenue, which can lead to wasted time and money since this organizational scaffolding isn't built soon enough.

Part A: Creating Your Own Localization Premium Analysis (LPA)

Companies differ wildly in how they map out their localization premium. While all categories are important, some will be more crucial than others. In the fintech and pharmaceuticals industries, for example, Admin. Premium from burdensome government regulations and compliance requirements plays an outsized role compared to Org. Premium. The level of importance of each category would be notably different for a consumer internet business compared to an enterprise software company.

In order to create your own LPA:

1. Get a clear understanding of the changes you will likely need to make to your business when entering a new market. You can do this through establishing a set of questions to answer relating to each of the localization premium categories.

2. Conduct research using the localization discovery process discussed in the previous chapter.

3. Identify customer benefits and potential ROI that comes from the change.

4. Measure how different the new market's model will be compared to your initial market (or whatever market you choose as a reference point) for each premium category in localizing and then plot the dots on the LPA chart.

With all the dots plotted, connect them to visualize the size of the total surface area of adaptation required to localize in the new market (i.e., the total amount of complexity incurred). As you can imagine, where you think each dot should be placed (how different that aspect of the business will be in the new market compared to the current one) will change as you gather more information about the market and actually enter the market. The LPA is meant to be dynamic, so you can change a dot's placement whenever merited. You can see a good example of how initial planning and the actual level of localization that the market dictates will differ in the case study of Evernote's entry into India (later in this chapter).

Note: While the default core of the LPA can be the proven model in an initial market, company-market fit in any other markets can serve as the core as well. Since the LPA is also a comparison tool, the core can be changed to the successful model from any market the company is in as a reference point, and then you can see how much change would be required to get company-market fit in a new market.

Filling out the LPA—Talabat's expansion into Oman

As food and grocery delivery platform Talabat looked to expand into Oman, the team recognized that a number of aspects of their business needed to be changed to fit the market. Here is how they evaluated the localizations when entering the market and how it would be mapped out on the LPA:

- **Sales Premium**—Plotted four levels from the center because the processes of selling to restaurants was very different compared to Talabat's initial market. They needed to hire an on-the-ground sales team to go into small towns to talk with individual restaurant owners. They also had a different revenue model for the country.

- **Product Premium**—Plotted two levels from the center because there weren't many changes to the product required. While other markets in the region preferred Quick Service Retail (QSR) restaurants, Omani locals preferred exploring new tastes, so the food images and descriptions in their mobile app and online platform were adapted to fit these preferences. Google Maps was not as reliable in more rural areas and often locals had different definitions of boundaries on a map than Google's categorization. Given the importance of geofencing to Talabat's platform, team members had to drive around in a car and manually draw their own geofencing for each region, stopping to confer with locals along the way.

- **Marketing Premium**—Plotted five levels from the center because the marketing strategies needed to be hyperlocalized for the Omani market. The team uncovered the importance of three key advertising channels that were very different from other markets the company was in. First, in Oman, social media influencers played an outsized role, the same role celebrities play in other markets. Moreover, these social media influencers were an untapped market since brands hadn't engaged much with them. This allowed Talabat to take advantage of an influential advertising strategy at a much lower cost than typical celebrity endorsements in other markets. Second, people in Oman are particularly engaged in social media, so Talabat saw the opportunity to create customized social media strategies. They executed on this by creating SnapChat filters and stickers to be used during the Muslim holy month of Ramadan when the local population fasts during the day. People used these augmented reality filters to share their thirst and hunger throughout the day. Finally, a unique occurrence in the Omani market was a proliferation of micro events that occurred where groups of people go together, often in compounds where different rooms had different themes, very different from other markets that more often had large-scale events. Talabat sponsored these events and got a strong ROI since this was also a low-cost channel.

- **Admin. Premium**—Plotted one level from the center. Oman and Talabat's HQ in the United Arab Emirates (UAE) are both within the Gulf Cooperation Council (GCC) or Cooperation Council for the Arab States of the Gulf countries. These countries share similar political and economic systems, meaning that the amount of premium incurred for this category is minimal.

- **Infrastructure Premium**—Plotted one level from the center. As with Admin. Premium, since Oman and UAE are GCC countries, there is little premium incurred in this category.

- **Org. Premium**—Plotted five levels from the center. Because of the Omanization initiative described in chapter five that mandated certain job functions be filled by locals and a minimum percentage of the employee base be local, it was harder to find the right skill sets, particularly in tier two and tier three cities. The company had to develop different hiring and training practices to build a strong team in the market.

Talabat (Oman)

Part B: Putting the Localization Premium Analysis into Context

After mapping out anticipated localizations on the LPA, the next step is to evaluate the quantitative impact of these changes. Other factors to layer on when evaluating new markets include:

- Level of importance/priority to the business (because some localizations would take priority over others)
- Level of scalability (because localizations can be used in other market expansions)
- Core value and company culture alignment (because some localizations may challenge important tenets of company culture that can't be compromised)
- Implementation Stage (because not all localizations can happen at once and should be planned out over time during market entry)
- Cost (the Total Cost of Entry Formula detailed later in the chapter helps determine the cost associated with each localization, providing a major data point that affects level of priority and implementation stage)

While the level of complexity incurred is of utmost importance, including the information in the list above offers a more complete analysis and serves as a bridge between planning and execution since each of the five items in the list above affects the implementation of the localization strategy for a new market.

It's also important to note that the LPA process must also be a collective effort involving multiple key stakeholders, not just a team with a narrow focus operating in a silo. Making the process collaborative helps reduce bias, as there is a subjective element to determining the degree of complexity in each category. Team members participating in the process can represent the beginnings of the Localization Resource Team (discussed in chapter seven).

TRANSITIONING FROM BMLC TO LPA

Both stages of the global agile process have distinct but interconnected goals and purposes. The main use of the Business Model Localization Canvas (BMLC), discussed in the previous chapter, is to faciliate localization discovery, market identification, and identifying potential localizations for new markets.

The LPA, on the other hand, is meant as more of an implementation, communication, analysis, and prioritization tool. It can assist you in achieving market entry and in finding company-market fit during the market growth stage.

It also provides the extra dimension of comparison, as the model in the initial market (or any other market of choice) can be the center of the LPA and used as a reference point to highlight changes needed to enter a new market. The LPA is a more multifaceted framework compared to being a one-time exercise or a tracking tool like the BMLC and Business Model Canvas, respectively. You can see how the two frameworks integrate together within the diagram on page 123 with insights from the BMLC translating into the premiums in the LPA. As suggested in chapter five, you can use the six localization premiums in place of the nine Business Model Canvas blocks to generate new hypotheses for what the business model could look like in the new market when running the current validated model through the government regulation and culture filters during the BMLC exercise. This can be a more direct route to uncovering what localizations will be required in the new market and can simplify the placement of the dots for each premium category on the LPA.

To put the comparison more simply, the BMLC is focused on iteration and validation while the LPA is focused on bridging between strategic planning and implementing localization strategy while being mindful of complexity.

THE DILEMMA: COMPANY-MARKET FIT AND LOCALIZATION PREMIUM

Possible inconsistency alert! At this point you are probably saying, "Got it. I understand I need to adapt my business to fit a new market, but haven't you just spent a bulk of this chapter talking about how bad localization premium (complexity) is and how it should be consciously avoided?" Yes, we know. Welcome to the challenge of growing a business globally. This is not easy to do.

Therein lies the dilemma. On the one hand, you want to reduce complexities and changes to your product, business, and operating models (i.e., minimize localization premium), but at the same time, if you DON'T make those changes, you are most likely going to fail. Moreover, changing your business to attain company-market fit in your new market makes operating it harder, but making these changes is what leads to traction and success. Ultimately, when done right, the benefits of reaching this traction, and the subsequent scale they unlock, far outweigh the complexities that come from pivoting to meet the needs of a local customer base (in particular if the market is sizable).

The solution is (a) to be aware of the importance of finding the right balance between localization and complexity incurred, and (b) to do your best to minimize the changes you make to your business, both big and small. Recall Jan van Casteren's point that navigating "arbitrary uniqueness" versus imperative changes is essential to finding fit in a market. For example, if you sell direct in your initial market and that is an important part of your value proposition and model, don't rush to lock yourself into a partnership with a local company that says they want to work with you if selling direct is the better strategy long term.

As you are planning to enter a new market, label the various aspects of your business as "hypotheses" (utilizing the global agile methodology outlined in chapter five), but constantly evaluate what changes are essential (e.g., adhering to local regulatory rules) and which are not (e.g., using a different collaboration software for the local team). When you develop solutions to obstacles and changes to your model, find an effective answer that also ties into aspects of the current model, thereby reducing localization premium.

Here are a couple important things to keep in mind:

- Keep your core values front and center as you go through this process. Some things are flexible and can be changed; other things shouldn't be. Slack's culture includes a hyper-sensitivity to focus. You don't have to make *every* change, especially when it conflicts with your core values. Slack sometimes takes three years to build a feature from when it is originally requested by clients. Reaching international scale takes time, and attempting to change everything at once may cause too much chaos to find company-market fit in a new market. Of course, the flip side is that moving too slow means lost opportunity and wasted resources.
- A sometimes-overlooked part of finding company-market fit in a new country is talent. This is the third leg of the tripod, along with localizing the six go-to-market and operational premiums detailed above. Given how important the team is to success, you need to make sure you've assembled the right people to execute on your expansion in the new market.

WHEN LOCALIZATION PREMIUM CAN BE GOOD

Since localization premium cannot be avoided, the point is to be more conscious of the complexity being created during decision-making processes.

Along those lines, there is such a thing as "good" localization premium, meaning that some complexity can have a positive value and worthwhile outcome.

One of the primary (and necessary) areas of *good* premium is localization designed to engage target customers in a new market. If, for example, customers in a new market can't read your website, marketing material, or user guides because they are in a language they don't understand, you will probably find it hard to get them to buy your product.

That being said, you should limit the amount of complexity you label as "good"; never use it as a justification for avoiding efficiencies. Think long term, be aware, and stay attuned to the constant change that occurs after launch.

LOCALIZATION PREMIUM IN PRACTICE

The concept of localization premium, its effects, and its trade-offs are core parts of the internal and external analysis you conduct in the expansion planning processes. Localization premium should be included in the case you build to secure support for an international growth initiative, since it provides a conduit for discussing changes that need to be made to how your business operates in the new market. Understanding the pivots you need to make and the resources needed to successfully make them to recalibrate your company-market fit are fundamental elements of your expansion strategy and plan.

As you launch your business in new countries, you will find there is a constant tension between needing to adapt to reach company-market fit and not wanting to add too much complexity, or localization premium, to your operations. This is natural.

The point is to be conscious of the sources of localization premium while working to control them.

Paul Williamson from Plaid recommends, "Don't get too far away from your core. You should feel like you've exhausted your target customer base, for example, before opening the aperture of the next standard deviation. Don't get dragged off in different directions."

Localization premium will invariably exist in some capacity, just as complexities will arise when you expand your business in other ways. Companies that target large-enterprise customers know that often these big clients require some level of customization to close the sale and implement the solution. But what amount of customization is acceptable in exchange for the revenue that the enterprise customer brings, and what isn't? How applicable is this customization to other clients?

To illustrate practical application of the LPA, here are some case studies of complexities incurred when Global Class Companies successfully localized in new markets.

Apple in Brazil

Here is an example of how Apple incurred localization premium when launching a retail footprint in Brazil, one of the company's early global retail locations back in 2014, which caused the company to move standard deviations away from their core company-market fit in the United States.

Apple needed to change in a number of ways to find traction in Brazil. Chief among them was to change the layout and value proposition of its stores. In Brazil, an iPhone can cost more than two thousand dollars (USD) because of tariffs (Admin. Premium), compared to less than half that in the United States. This led the company to reconfigure its retail locations to focus less on selling devices, especially its mobile products, and more on servicing its products, through support services like its Genius Bar. This required redesigning the back of the store from inventory storage to more stations for servicing devices (Infrastructure Premium). The customer journey was also different, as some Brazilian consumers would travel out of the country or use another channel to purchase Apple devices (Sales Premium). Apple even had to start hiring Portuguese speakers in its stores in parts of Florida to communicate with the Brazilians who would fly to the US to buy devices because that was cheaper than buying in Brazil (even when factoring in travel costs).

Small changes incurred a premium, too. The Brazilian government required paper receipts for all transactions, which had to be printed on a specific type of paper (nota fiscal), an issue for Apple because it could no longer use its paperless purchase transaction process (an Admin. Premium that would have been discovered through the government regulation filter process in the BMLC discussed in chapter five).

Apple (Brazil)

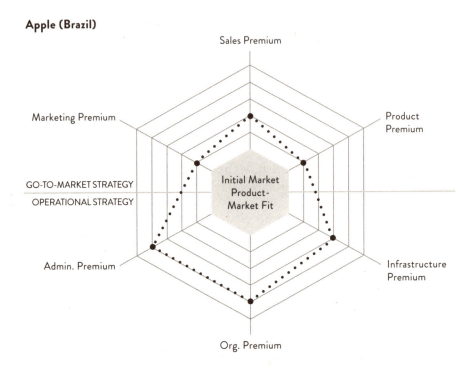

Organizational Premium was particularly high, since the local team had to revamp its hiring and training processes and parameters. While Apple typically trains employees to have deep knowledge in a specific product area, the staff in Brazil needed to have a broader knowledge of the company's whole suite of products. Labor unions also played a much more prominent role in Brazil (and in other Latin American countries), so the company had to build local partnerships and work within these constructs to ensure labor unions could be leveraged as partners instead of fought as foes. Moreover, focusing on service over sales required the company to adapt its ROI calculations and break-even timeline to account for lower sales volume and longer runway required to get to profitability.

OFTEN OVERLOOKED

Don't Underestimate Operational Premium

Notice how much of the premium Apple incurred fell into the operational strategy categories. This is a prime example of how although go-to-market strategy changes are the most visible (language and cultural differences are more at the forefront), they are often just the tip of the iceberg of the total amount of localizations needed to fit traction and scale in a new market (which is why we have used this analogy to compare both sets of premiums). We heard multiple market entry stories where teams underestimated operational strategy and it caused a great deal of delay and increased the cost of expansion.

The Truth About Similar Markets—Familiarity Bias

Teams focused on entering new international markets are likely to assume that a market geographically adjacent to the initial market, or one that speaks the same language, will be a good market to launch in and will require very little adaptation to find company-market fit. This is simply not the case; it's a Familiarity Bias of sorts. This bias causes dangerous assumptions to be made. Countries that primarily speak English may have similar cultures, but they have differences in many of the localization premium categories that require pivots to the core business model. The same can be said when a company from a Spanish-speaking country looks to expand to another Spanish-speaking nation. We call this *Familiarity Bias*, where a market gets prioritized because the same language is spoken there or it's geographically nearby.

Evernote's Expansion to India

Troy Malone recognized that some aspects of the company's go-to-market and operating models would need to change, but didn't realize to what extent, especially in the case of the latter. Like with many companies, a combination of the size of the Indian market and the abundance of English speakers (India is the second largest English-speaking population in the world) led Troy to believe it would be easier to enter the market than other countries being considered. Much of this familiarity bias was based on a perception that the go-to-market premiums (Sales, Marketing, Product) would be small. The go-to-market premiums ended up being the tip of the iceberg in terms of localizations required to get company-market fit in India.

On the go-to-market side, the Evernote team knew that pricing would need to be different (Sales Premium) and that the product would be able to stay pretty much the same (Product Premium), but didn't anticipate needing to sell their business product through partners (Sales Premium). The team expected that personal users would upgrade to business users, as in the US, but instead a local partner was needed to do more of the hand holding required to get adoption of the product by local businesses. Marketing Premium was higher than anticipated because most of the marketing in the US was geared toward desktop users, but since India is a mobile-first country, the marketing had to be changed to mobile.

Despite the notable changes to go-to-market strategy, the operating strategy changes were even more drastic and unexpected. On the infrastructure side, the team expected minimal localizations needed, and that turned out to be the case. Only minimal Org. Premium was expected and this turned out to be untrue. The business culture in India had a norm around not questioning the boss and only doing what you are told without adding to discussion and building on ideas. This conflicted with Evernote's collaborative and open company culture.

The biggest surprises came with the amount of Admin. Premium incurred. All aspects in this category were complex and needed attention. Regulation in India requires that businesses have a local entity with an Indian national as

Evernote (India)

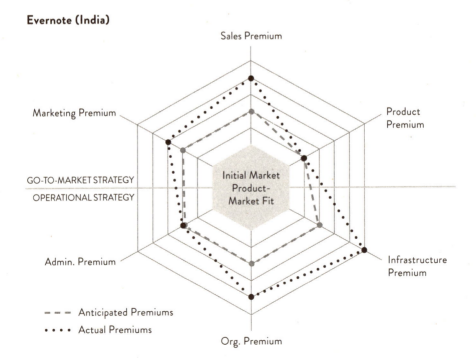

the chairperson of the entity and that the board of directors of the entity meet twice every year, in person (no video conferencing), so company executives were required to fly to India regularly to comply with the local law. Then, after revenue started flowing in, it was difficult to get money out of the country because of paperwork and other red tape. All of this led to an unanticipated amount of Admin. and Org. Premiums.

On the chart you can see a comparison between what Troy and the Evernote team initially thought would be the amount of premium incurred for each category (light-colored line) versus what ended up happening during market entry (dark-colored line).

OFTEN OVERLOOKED

The Risks of Following Organic Growth

Organic growth can misguide global expansion efforts. Many executives see organic growth, customers popping up in global markets with little concerted marketing effort by HQ, as a strong sign of market opportunity. This does not mean these markets should automatically be prioritized. As was the case with Evernote in India, they let organic growth in the country lead to overconfidence in market entry. "We thought that we knew the user and what they wanted," Troy Malone explained. The LPA is a key step in the process so the organization understands the extent of the changes that need to be made to capture this organic growth, and Global Class Companies understand that a combination of organic growth, market dynamics/readiness, and complexity must be considered in the market selection and prioritization process.

Linked Markets

While even adjacent markets have key differences and require pivots, markets can have a linked relationship, meaning that a change made to gain traction in one market may be reused when entering a nearby market. In other words, accumulating localization premium when entering one market may limit the premium in certain categories when entering a related market. Linked markets may have similar cultures and languages, may have similar legal structures, or may be geographically close (or may have neither). The linked nature of certain markets can also affect the order in which certain markets are prioritized.

Airbnb's Expansion to South Korea, China, and Japan

When entering new markets in Asia, Airbnb had three countries at the top of its list (focused first on attracting travelers over local hosts). While China, Japan, and South Korea are all major markets, the travel industry in each was at a different stage of growth and maturity (and different size and scale). South Korean and Chinese consumers—especially young consumers targeted by Airbnb—are more open and adventurous in their travel preferences, while Japan has a more established travel market and more consumers saw Airbnb's new style of travel as riskier.

Despite being the smallest of the three, South Korea was a reference point for Chinese and Japanese consumers, who looked to South Koreans for the latest trends. Because of this, instead of focusing equally on the markets, Airbnb initially focused more marketing resources on South Korea.

To develop traction across the key Asian markets, Airbnb expanded its customer service footprint in these locations and offered Asian language support capabilities (Sales Premium). Text in the app was initially still in English, so they developed and tested a new version of the app that was more image/photo-based to appeal to Asian consumers and bridge language differences (Product Premium). Different marketing strategies were tested with travel trade shows becoming a larger focus, as did partnerships with local travel industry organizations and influencers (Marketing Premium). These travel industry organizations represented additional touchpoints that were not necessary to the company's more direct-to-consumer approach in the United States but were crucial for building momentum in not only South Korea but also in other key Asian markets.

When entering China and Japan, the work done on the app for the South Korean market, the customer care center, and some of the South Korean marketing tactics carried over to these markets, making the new Sales, Product, and Marketing Premiums less than they would have been. Moreover, a proven playbook had been created that could be implemented and adapted, building momentum and speed to market penetration.

Airbnb (Korea)

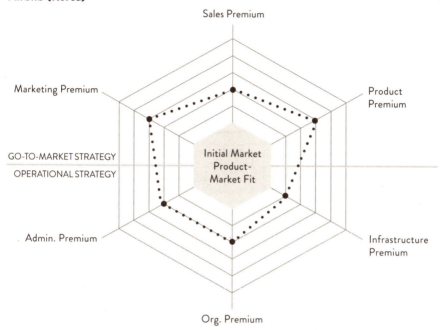

And while Airbnb definitely incurred localization premium, especially Infrastructure and Admin. Premiums in China, the Airbnb team was able to scale faster in these markets because of the groundwork done in South Korea.

Other companies saw the scalability of their localizations as well. Apple found that the work it did in Brazil (especially related to Org. Premium) carried over well when the company expanded to Mexico, where much of the playbook it had developed in Brazil could be reused because of the employee training created and more familiarity with how to partner with local labor unions in the region. Online education platform Platzi found linked markets throughout LATAM, and early in Spotify's global expansion the company had linked markets in Norway and Denmark.

Note: In the following chart, the core represents the adapted company-market fit the company achieved in South Korea to show the smaller changes required to enter China and Japan, creating momentum as they scaled across all three markets.

Airbnb (Japan & China)

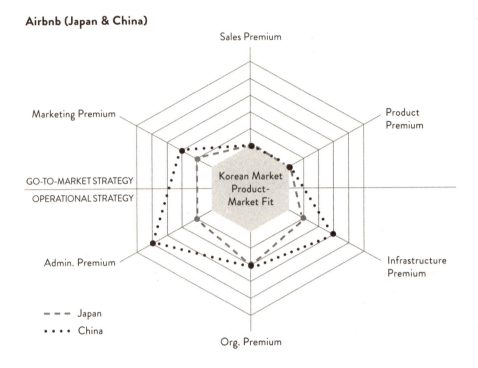

THE INTERPLAY BETWEEN LOCALIZATION PREMIUM CATEGORIES

Which of the localization premium types is most critical for your success when expanding into your target market? You need to decide which areas cannot change (often because they are rooted in one of the company's core values), which can support additional complexity, and the areas where change should be limited.

This ultimately reveals trade-offs you will need to make, such as sacrificing speed to maintain a core value, or allowing for some autonomy at the local market level in exchange for localization premium created by operational or go-to-market changes.

As you analyze potential localization premium sources, you also need to understand how one type of premium influences the others. A change to your product, for instance, may affect your marketing, sales model, and infrastructure.

For example, many companies are coming to grips with changes required to comply with rules outlined in the General Data Protection Regulation (GDPR) legislation from the European Union, since many companies use customer data as part of their business model (either selling it, making it available to outside parties, or using it to generate recommendations and a customized experience). Changes like these can become big sources of localization premium (but also can be scalable across multiple markets). These regulations may require a company to have to build a new technology stack in-country (Infrastructure Premium), which leads to an increased workload for employees (Org. Premium) and, most of all, would require new administrative processes and compliance work (Admin. Premium).

Here are a couple examples of how the subcategories of localization premium affect each other and how leaders are forced to prioritize and choose between conflicting options:

Infrastructure Premium vs. Admin. Premium. Amazon's infrastructure investment in Australia reduces its taxes but creates complexity in data storage and digital service delivery. The company had to consider whether the large investment into new infrastructure outweighed the potential taxes incurred for not doing so.

Product Premium vs. Sales Premium and Marketing Premium. As described earlier in this chapter, LinkedIn created a separate, text-based version of its mobile app that would operate on lower speed mobile networks in India. These changes incurred Product Premium, since the app had to be completely redesigned. On the other hand, if the company hadn't made the change, its product would have delivered a terrible customer experience, or they would have had to change their target customer and severely reduce the number of potential users they could reach, either focusing on higher bandwidth areas or targeting wealthier Indians who had a better phone or a personal computer to access the LinkedIn platform.

TOTAL COST OF ENTRY FORMULA

Simply "doing the math" is an often-overlooked but crucially important step when evaluating the potential changes required to localize in a target market. Creating the Localization Premium Analysis (along with the priority/scalability/core value alignment considerations outlined on page 161) is only step one; it's also necessary to have a more qualitative exercise highlighting *what* needs to be done to localize.

The next step is to put these changes in the context of how much financial commitment is required for each corresponding change to the current model. To help with these, we have developed the Total Cost of Entry Formula, or TCE Formula. You can see it as analogous to the Total Cost of Ownership (TCO) equation often communicated and considered when making a purchasing decision in a number of industries. This equation helps answer key questions, like: What is the cost of localizing the business for a new market? What does success mean?

Completing the LPA exercise is crucial, since it will be difficult to determine the cost of entry if you don't understand how you will have to adapt your current model to successfully launch in a new market.

The TCE Formula maps directly to each of the categories in the LPA. Each change has its corresponding cost. Together, they add up to the total cost of entry for that premium category (Sales Premium, Product Premium, Infrastructure Premium, and so on). All of the premium categories add together to determine the estimated total cost to localize in a new market.

Costs could include estimated marketing costs, administrative costs for setup, required investment in inventory, and salaries and benefits. Manpower costs should incorporate people in the local market and those dedicated to expansion efforts at headquarters. It's worth noting that the up-front costs for market entry are often higher for companies selling a physical product compared to something software based, given the costs typically associated with supply chain and packaging localizations as well as local regulatory requirements, depending on the type of product. The barriers for distribution for software tend to be much lower since many of these types of costs are eliminated.

It is important to look at these costs over a realistic timeline to determine the Total Cost of Entry. While the amount of time will differ depending on your industry and resources, you should account for at least two years of cost. A time factor (Time Multiple) must be considered as well. This is particularly relevant for the human resource cost related to the required change and support of the expansion initiative, and can be listed in terms of months or years. When incorporating the time factor, it is best to separate one-time costs from ongoing/time-variable costs and only factor time into the latter.

Total Cost of Entry Formula Template

[One-Time Entry Costs] + [Ongoing Entry Costs x Time Multiple] = Total Cost of Expansion (TCE)

Or to provide the details of what entry costs consist of (which include the LPA categories):

Entry costs include:

- Sales Premium (SP)
- Product Premium (PP)
- Marketing Premium (MP)
- Administrative Premium (AP)
- Infrastructure Premium (IP)
- Organizational Premium (OP)

Some entry costs are one-time, like making a product feature (software) or packaging (physical product) change, while others are ongoing, like the cost of maintaining a local team. For the ongoing entry costs, a Time Multiple (TM) is factored in (which should account for two to three years of these ongoing costs). Add the one-time and ongoing costs together to get the Total Cost of Entry:

[One-Time SP + PP + AP + OP + MP + IP] + [[Ongoing SP + PP + AP + OP + MP + IP] x TM] = TCE

Total Cost of Entry Formula in Practice

Global Class Companies know that some changes will be more impactful in helping them reach company-market fit. In light of this, Global Class Companies prioritize each localization (or premium category), separating them into different tiers. The TCE Formula adds a cost layer to the analysis, guiding decision-making and helping teams answer the question: What would it cost to implement our highest priority localizations?

Global Class Companies realize that effective localization initiatives don't attempt to make all the required changes at once. The TCE Formula is also useful in determining the costs of each phase of a multi-phase market entry, helping teams answer questions like: How much will it cost to complete the first implementation stage in the new market?

Recalling Apple's expansion in Brazil, the company incurred Infrastructure Premium related to redesigning their retail layout, Org. Premium in hiring and training new employees, and Admin. Premium in navigating the tariffs and other compliance requirements, and so on.

The TCE then needs to be put in the context of market potential, which in turn helps in estimating the return on investment and payback period. Apple, for example, needed to recalibrate its sales metrics and targets to account for the lower sales volume coming from its Brazilian stores, which were more focused on servicing devices than selling new ones.

After you calculate Total Cost of Entry over time, your focus changes to *how* you implement these localization changes.

The combination of effective localization discovery, proper use of the Localization Premium Analysis (LPA), and the Total Cost of Entry (TCE) Formula is effective at directing your efforts at localizing the right things and being conscious of the resources being expended. If these pieces are missing, the success of any global growth initiative is at risk. As Claudia Makadristo from MetaMap puts it, "You don't want to be throwing money around, attempting to disrupt a market you don't know anything about with a strategy that isn't localized."

MITIGATING LOCALIZATION PREMIUM

Since accumulating localization premium is unavoidable (and shouldn't be considered a deal-breaker), it is important to put systems and strategies in place to mitigate the amount of premium you incur and the scale of its effects. Building the right procedural structure around expansion and involving the right HQ stakeholders to provide support to international teams are worth the time and effort. Remember that it's not just about speed to market.

Just making localization premium part of the conversation can limit complexities. When asking for resources from HQ, local teams should provide a high-level view of the complexities/localization premium associated with the request. This will ensure straightforward decision-making and accurate expectations.

Internationalization

One of the most effective strategies for minimizing localization premium is to undertake internationalization efforts. This is the process (often used in the context of software development) where you design centralized processes that can be customized (or localized) to fit each individual market you launch in. This approach helps restrict the areas where complexities can be created, taking a more proactive approach in minimizing localization premium. You do this by standardizing certain parts of your go-to-market or operating model while building in flexibility where localizations can occur. Everything from product functionality or appearance (ability to put a country-specific skin on a software or different color on a physical product) to payment processing to HR processes can be looked at through this lens. In response to the GDPR rules mentioned above, for example, some companies are deciding to comply with them worldwide, using it as the single policy for data in every country where they have customers.

While localization is what Global Class Companies do, internationalization is the mechanism for how they do it at scale.

As an example, one internationalization strategy could be to contract with a business process outsourcing (BPO) or professional employer organization (PEO) provider for the initial launch of each market. This would reduce the complexities of establishing the company in each new market administratively before you have proven there is traction in a market (Admin. Premium). Another example is building a centralized localization team in charge of managing all non-native language content (website, marketing, etc.). Local teams can share key insights with them, and they can help local teams customize to fit their local markets (Marketing Premium). Internationalization could also include choosing a distribution partner with a strong presence in multiple target markets, making the partner the single focal point for channel distribution in a wider international expansion initiative (Sales Premium).

As part of internationalization efforts, Canva created templates and icons for each local market on top of a flexible product foundation that allowed for controlled localization (Product Premium).

Klaus Holse, former CEO of SimCorp, shared an experience he had as an executive in Microsoft's Dynamic Products Division, where he saw a Global Class strategy play out against a legacy one. Microsoft, known at the time for a culture of internal competition, had acquired both the Navision and Great Plains products within six months of each other. The Great Plains product was seemingly superior at the time, but the team had not considered localization premium and ran into problems when needing to adapt to new markets. The Navision team, on the other hand, had a Global Class mindset and built their product to have a fraction of the codebase and had "componentized" aspects of the code, making it easier to adapt. Componentization allows software development teams to reuse components and more easily make changes or replace portions of code to meet the unique requirements of a new market. This led to faster and more effective localization, ultimately leading Microsoft to scale with Navision's product instead of Great Plains's (Product Premium).

You could also adopt an internationalization strategy of having the same launch team members launch in multiple markets so there is a consistency in approach (Org. Premium). Internationalization involves creating uniformity among core elements of the LPA, but can also be a tool used in creating uniformity in structures and resources supporting international growth efforts. *Internationalization can also be thought of as guardrails that limit the standard deviations of changes allowed to be implemented.*

Understand that there are obstacles to internationalization that need to be accepted or overcome. As mentioned earlier in the chapter, what may be a seemingly simple decision, like having the staff use Google Workspace email and productivity tools worldwide, may run into challenges, since employees in China are restricted from using Google products. If you invest in rolling out Google Workspace in your initial market and then need to change to another global platform, it could cost a lot of money and months of time. Simple decisions can have profound impacts. For example, Rakuten changed its official office language to English, even in its Japanese HQ, to better position itself as a global company capable of communicating with global talent and global customers (a process they called "Englishnization").

Traditionally, Workday, which offers SaaS-based human resources and financial management solutions for enterprises, had to pivot and introduce a new pricing model when entering certain markets because of how employment was structured in the country. Workday based pricing on the number of total employees a client had (with designations for full-time employees, full-time equivalents, and hourly workers). This didn't translate to countries that pay monthly or have more seasonal staff or in places where clients were used to being charged by number of active users instead of by company size.

To address these differences, the company went through a difficult process of globalizing price points to be value based, in the process minimizing customization (an internationalization initiative that lowered Sales Premium, defined in the next chapter).

Internationalization efforts don't just have to be implemented worldwide, though. Companies can classify and segment geographic areas based on similarities, aiming to align operational models across multiple countries. It's important, however, not to just lump entire continents together, since there are key differences between the way you'll operate your businesses in countries on a continent as vast and diverse as Asia (the same can be said for all the other continents as well). These multiple-country clusters can be based on any common thread from language—for instance, excluding Brazil when grouping LATAM together to streamline Spanish-language localization efforts—to legal systems and beyond.

OFTEN OVERLOOKED

Doing Things that Don't Scale

While much of your focus is on efficiency and minimizing localization premium, it's fine (and at times good) to do some things that *don't* scale well, like engaging with early adopters in a new market (and the localization discovery process). It is these more direct (and manual) involvements that lead to key learnings and finding company-market fit in new markets.

A core tenet of global agile is that you must account for the cumulative nature of agile when layering on the context of changes for multiple countries. No single localization stands alone; each compounds along with all the others to become a complex mess that is difficult to manage. *Implementing a complexity-conscious agile methodology is essential.*

Effective use of global agile will uncover localizations necessary to find product-market fit in a new market (step one), while effective utilization of the

LPA will help teams control the complexities that come along with localization in multiple countries, keeping the organization on track to build momentum, achieve company-market fit, and reach global scale (step two).

In addition to these tactics, a focused effort on maintaining the Three Pillars for Achieving Global Scale outlined in part three will help you effectively manage localization premium.

Understand the complexities—the localization premium—that operating in multiple countries will create, and balance them with the impact the localizations you implement will have. Be conscious of the process, make complexity part of the conversation, and seek ways to minimize and monitor it.

• • •

The remaining chapters show you how to build on the balance of localization and complexity to reach company-market fit through building organizational capabilities—setting up the right structures, building the right team, managing the organization, and balancing different cultures to support global scale.

With a strong grasp of required localizations needed to succeed in a market, along with the Localization Premium Analysis (LPA) framework to limit complexities, you are ready to take the next step to reach true global scale: establishing processes and operational structures that create momentum and facilitate scale.

CHAPTER 6 SUMMARY

- The output of localization is *complexity*. Through step two of the global agile process, Global Class Companies learn how to balance localization and complexity to gain traction in local markets and manage scale across multiple international markets.
- These complexities (*localization premium*) fall into two categories: Go-to-Market (Sales, Product & Marketing Premiums) and Operational (Administrative, Organizational & Infrastructure Premiums), which can be mitigated through targeted (*internationalization*) efforts.

- The Localization Premium Analysis (LPA) has many uses, including as a new market analysis tool, market prioritizer, communication tool, visualization of risks, road map alignment tool, implementation tracker, and linked markets/pattern identifier.
- The Total Cost of Entry (TCE) Formula can help determine the cost associated with localizations.

CHAPTER 6 REFLECTION & ACTION QUESTIONS

1. How are you balancing localization and complexity?
2. Which premiums are you having the most difficulty with or were unexpected when expanding internationally?
3. What challenges are you facing when it comes to members of your organization's leadership team having myopic views about global growth initiatives?

• 7 •

MOMENTUM

How Global Class Companies Facilitate Rapid Growth

U ber is a unique Global Class Company case study.

Starting in 2012, as Uber began entering multiple international markets, they built a system that made the company incredibly effective at market entry, taking advantage of slow competition and delayed local government action, and wielding enormous financial resources to spur rapid adoption. But then the backlash would come and the company wasn't as adept at managing the disruption they created, at times falling short at localizing the business to fit the nuances of local culture during the fallout.

In a very un–Global Class–like fashion, Uber often prioritized the company way over the local way and didn't build core values with universal appeal. At the same time, Uber's ability to create and leverage processes and structures to facilitate market entry and rapid growth was best in class.

Through a combination of collaborative competition, performance transparency, and best practice sharing, Uber was able to expand to a vast number of markets at breakneck speed.

Uber created a repeatable system that involved launch teams with strong company expertise, playbooks to capture and socialize effective methods for overcoming obstacles, and dashboards to track clear and targeted metrics that focused the team on achieving milestones rapidly.

Each market's performance, measured by clear metrics, was shared with the entire organization globally and actively tracked. The company built a brain trust through both detailed documentation collected and shared by a centralized team, and the knowledge of what did and didn't typically work developed by this centralized team.

Transparent communication was prioritized, and structures were created to identify and reward fast growth while making sure best practices were translated to other teams.

The complexity discussed in the previous chapter was avoided at all costs. As Uber leaned on its universally recognized value proposition and the ubiquity of the problems it was solving, the team attempted to uncover scalable solutions to obstacles that arose during market entry and market growth so all global teams could benefit.

While most companies don't have the luxury of such universality of their value proposition and solution (nor do they have the level of resources), lessons can be gleaned from Uber's ability to create centralized resources and structures that gather and communicate best practices and progress.

Once you have created a balance between localization and complexity, it's about scale. As Global Class Companies transition from planning and market entry to market growth, company leaders must pay specific attention to creating momentum in order to reach global scale.

Having a solid team, product, and company culture isn't enough to be successful globally. Shifting from single-market success to multi-market scale is a pivotal point in a company's growth journey that requires an adaptive support model. Global Class Companies don't set their sights on single market validation; they set them on global penetration. It's not about successful market entry and traction in any one country; it's about operating at global scale. **Effective processes and structures that support and put guardrails on localizations are what enable scale.**

Designing and implementing these structures also give a boost to each of the Four Commitments for Successful Global Growth outlined in chapter four. With effective processes in place, resources can be better aligned and communication more effective, fostering more clarity and alignment across a distributed footprint; trust becomes stronger and HQ feels more comfortable granting autonomy; and iterations that are part of the global agile process can be accelerated.

Switching from market entry to market growth demands the attention of both local market teams and HQ. Adoption of the Four Commitments outlined in chapter four—especially ample resources—is essential. This transition requires processes and structures to support scale and an increasingly distributed team. At the same time, these systems and processes must limit complexity, not create more of it.

Processes are the foundation for scale and help manage the leap between market entry to growth. They become increasingly necessary when a company makes the conscious decision to transition from operating in multiple countries to operating globally, validating whether your solution is universal or only relevant in a limited number of markets. The Autonomy Curve introduced in chapter four provides a guide for the appropriate structures and processes that should be built to match the amount of autonomy merited for that stage of expansion (market entry, market growth, or market maturity). As discussed in the last chapter, an investment in these structures (which falls under the Org. Premium category) helps minimize the overall localization premium (complexity) incurred as a company enters more markets.

In order to create the necessary momentum, it's important to conduct an organizational assessment to better understand what challenges can arise when transitioning from company-market fit in a single new market to truly scaling the organization internationally in multiple markets. It's at this point where complexity can swell to uncontrollable levels and organizational biases become more visible as the organization faces the difficult challenge of aligning people, teams, systems, budgets, and resources.

Global Class Companies establish structures and processes to support localization and scaling efforts, enabling communication, resource allocation, and complexity management. HQ creates processes and structures to facilitate localization through strategy development, implementation support, and tracking, but at the same time gives local teams the freedom to uncover and validate what localizations are required. To better characterize this category of support mechanisms, we will refer to them collectively as *Momentum Builders*.

MARKET ENTRY MOMENTUM BUILDERS

As discussed in chapter five, the goals of market entry are to evaluate target markets, uncover necessary localizations, and gain traction. The main milestone at the end is validating the market by finding product-market fit.

Going through market entry is a bit like running a start-up within the larger organization. Local teams are happy as long as they get the needed resources, leadership buy-in, attention, and autonomy that allow them to focus on the search for required localizations, traction, and ultimately product-market fit. As long as local teams can quickly change and drive local market testing, members stay motivated and engaged. Establishing Momentum Builders takes this one step further.

Structures meant to accelerate market entry include:

- Localization Discovery
- Business Model Localization Canvas (BMLC)
- Global Growth Pitch Deck
- Launch Teams
- Separation of the Initial Market from HQ

Localization Discovery

As outlined in chapter five, localization discovery is the process of doing on-the-ground research in a local market to observe and truly understand the nuances of the market to assist in localizing the go-to-market and operational models.

As we discussed in chapter six, when considering the Localization Premium Analysis, it's important to develop a list of questions in order to fully understand the potential in the new market and the best go-to-market strategy. To answer these questions and capture the voice of the customer, it's important to visit target markets. We found this to be a common ingredient in the analysis conducted by many Global Class Companies that effectively expanded. Some referred to the investigatory trip as a "listening tour" (an apt label, since listening is key), but we refer to it as *localization discovery*. We adopt this label because the whole point is to not just identify market opportunity but to *discover* key insights into how your business would need to *localize* to effectively enter a new market.

In-market localization discovery is essential to truly understand the nuances of the local market. Elise Rubin, Global Head of Program Management, Internationalization, and Product Launch at Google Nest, explained how even "fresh air" can mean something totally different, depending on the local market. While gathering insights in developing new Nest products, Elise learned that, in Japan, the notion of fresh air involved opening up a window and letting outside air in. For South Koreans, on the other hand, "fresh air" means keeping the windows closed and turning the air conditioner on. South Koreans are very concerned about air pollution because of what they call "yellow dust" (also known as "Asian Dust"), which is blown from the deserts of China and Mongolia on strong winds. Because of China's massive industrial development in recent decades, winds carry industrial pollutants from factories and power plants in China to the South Korean Peninsula. Air purifiers are essential appliances there, and South Koreans often wear masks when they are outdoors.

Input from local teams is crucial. Troy Malone, former General Manager of International for Evernote, points out that "getting to the point of understanding a market enough to execute a coherent strategy is the toughest thing about expansion. You can't do it from HQ. The biggest opportunity is taking that front-end analysis you have from your initial research and coupling it with on-the-ground research to create a coherent strategy." Recall the role that Anirban played in influencing Evernote's strategy in India.

OFTEN OVERLOOKED

Getting the Perspectives of Everyday People

We intentionally listed "everyday people" on the list of stakeholders to talk with during localization discovery (on page 125), in part because the category is counterintuitive and often overlooked, but more importantly because it's incredibly valuable. When talking to everyday people during your localization discovery, even at random, you get the most accurate insights about the market you are targeting. No spin like you might get from a government agency attempting to gloss over economic issues in the market, no embellishments from potential partners attempting to sell you on collaborating with them; just honest, unfiltered opinions. Every driver, restaurant server, receptionist, and shop owner you interact with—all of them hold potentially valuable insights. This is particularly true for consumer products and services.

Business Model Localization Canvas (BMLC)

During your preparation and planning stage, you should complete the Business Model Localization Canvas (BMLC) detailed in chapter five. This will enable you to take insights from localization discovery and make them actionable, by incorporating them into a new set of hypotheses to be validated in the new market after running existing operating models through *government regulation* and *culture* filters. You can use the Business Model Canvas blocks, the six localization premiums (Sales, Product, Marketing, Admin., Infrastructure, and Org.), or your own criteria to translate the current validated business model into hypotheses to test for how the new market will operate.

Global Growth Pitch Deck

Similar to the classic start-up investor pitch deck, a Global Growth Pitch Deck is meant to be a simple and easy-to-communicate summary and explanation of your international growth strategy and localization efforts to get company-market fit. The presentation should include insights uncovered throughout your localization discovery. While short and direct by design, it can share detailed research and the voice of the customer. Below you will find a pitch deck outline you can use to better communicate your expansion strategy, the Global Growth Pitch Deck (note that by design you should have a separate deck for each target country):

- **(Slide 1) Why This Market?**—Introduce the country you plan to expand to, including background information about the market, key economic indicators, trends, and details on the local market dynamics.
- **(Slide 2) Localization Discovery Findings**—Share what you uncovered during in-market localization discovery. Highlight insights about the country's culture, the overall market opportunity, and likely localizations needed to be successful in the market.
- **(Slide 3) The Customer**—Outline customer archetypes, the type of value proposition that will resonate with them, and their buying power. Personify your target customer. Incorporate elements of the

local market culture highlighting customer behavior patterns and decision-making criteria.

- **(Slide 4) Localization Premium Analysis**—Plot how much the anticipated local model will deviate from the current go-to-market and operating models to find company-market fit in the new market through the Localization Premium Analysis (LPA) framework. Include details on how you plan to minimize and monitor complexity, as well as its impact on the organization. This slide serves as an overview for the next two slides that detail what is in the LPA.

- **(Slide 5) Pathway to Company-Market Fit: Go-to-Market Strategy**— Outline your planned distribution channel and marketing strategies. Where do your customers "hang out" (aka, get information)? What outlets influence them? What are the demand generators? How will you get marketing messages in front of customers? How will you get your product in the hands of your customers? This maps to the top half of the LPA (Sales Premium, Product Premium, and Marketing Premium). Outline the relevant hypotheses derived from the BMLC, as explained in chapter five.

- **(Slide 6) Pathway to Company-Market Fit: Operational Model**—Outline the legal and regulatory considerations in addition to how operations will work, from payroll and taxes to infrastructure. Include possible public policy threats, risks, and complexities caused by regulations that differ from those in your home market. This maps to the bottom half of the LPA (Admin. Premium, Infrastructure Premium, and Org. Premium). Outline the relevant hypotheses derived from the BMLC that will be tested and iterated on here as well.

- **(Slide 7) Team-Building Strategy**—Explain what team needs to be hired in the local market, the amount of resources required at headquarters, and the organizational structure (describing functional reporting and what is centralized/localized).

- **(Slide 8) Momentum Builders**—Outline the existing structures and processes that this new market entry will utilize and highlight new ones that need to be built to secure support and required resources. This is where the Localization Resource Team and Global Growth Playbook (both discussed in the next section) and other Momentum Builders are discussed.

- **(Slide 9) Total Cost of Entry**—Use the Total Cost of Entry (TOE) Formula to calculate the funds and resources needed to support this initiative. This can be categorized by level of importance or implementation stage, as discussed in chapter six. Highlight the plan's timeline and include when each localization will be created, based on level of priority and/or implementation stage.
- **(Slide 10) Four Commitments for Successful Global Growth**—Highlight the Four Commitments for Successful Global Growth, how each of the commitments applies to this specific country, and plans to ensure executive buy-in for each.

Download an example template from the book website, www.GlobalClassBook.com.

While the exercise of creating a Global Growth Pitch Deck is mainly to gain support within your organization, going through the process of creating it helps formalize your thoughts, build a stronger narrative, and uncover gaps in your analyses. Plus, it is a simple reference point that can be called upon as you formally launch. View the creation of the Global Growth Pitch Deck as an important step to take before entering each new international market, as well as a dynamic document that can be adapted as you pivot and learn from your new market entry. Most importantly, this document (along with the Localization Premium Analysis) offers a great foundation for the creation of a tool crucial to scale, your Global Growth Playbook.

Launch Teams

Although not applicable to every kind of business, creating a launch team whose sole focus is building the foundation for a successful presence in a new market can help speed up market entry and build momentum around global expansion initiatives.

While localization is customized to every market, many of the first steps for launching a market are similar across markets. A targeted team can develop associated skills that can be replicated in many markets, at rapid speeds. In the case of Uber, former Head of Asia Expansion Sam Gellman, the first employee the company hired outside North America, took on the role of launcher and, along with other members of the global expansion team, constituted the first boots on the ground.

For Sam and other launchers at Uber, the largest objective was clear: to hire a team to grow and scale in the market as fast as possible. Other key objectives included securing early adopters (riders and drivers) and reaching a milestone where most rides in a city center were filled through the Uber app in five minutes or less. Then Sam would move on to a new market to do the exact same thing. To ensure focus and increase the likelihood of success, limit metrics measuring local markets during entry to a maximum of three. Uber focused on just two.

The expertise a launch team develops can be incredibly valuable in situations where speed is paramount. This honed skill set, clear objectives, and strong best practice sharing through a dynamic, collaborative playbook are tools that set up launch teams for success.

Separating the Initial Market from HQ

An important (and often overlooked) step that helps companies progress from market entry to market growth, and beyond, is to separate the initial market organizational structure from the HQ organizational structure. During the earlier stages of global expansion, HQ and initial market operations are one and the same. The team members who lead certain functions in the initial market (sales, marketing, engineering, and so on) are the same people charged with leading that whole function globally as a company starts to expand given that, to date, there had only been one market. Continuing this fosters an initial market bias. It's only natural for leaders to favor the initial market that they had been managing and from where a bulk of company revenue is derived. Unfortunately, this bias can become an obstacle to getting local market initiatives the resources they require and can deprioritize the localizations needed to find company-market fit in these new markets.

Global Class Companies know that initial markets and new local markets must be put on equal footing. Instead of HQ and the initial market operating together, the initial market operations must be separated out and structured like any other local market. The initial market should have the same organizational structure as other local markets; so if local markets have a general manager, the initial market should have its own general manager, and if local markets had their own marketing teams and customer service, the initial market should have the same.

This separation accomplishes a number of things, including:

- *Removing the us-versus-them mentality*—In chapter one, we discussed how an us-versus-them mentality is toxic to international expansion initiatives. When HQ favors the initial market (which is natural if the same leadership is leading both HQ and the local market), the needs of local teams in international markets can become subordinated to the needs of the initial market. Separating the initial market from HQ and putting the initial market team at the same level as local teams is a much-needed equalizer.

- *Activating distributed work*—As mentioned earlier in the book, the concept of HQ is different for Global Class Companies today because of the acceleration of distributed work. Separating HQ from the initial market decouples HQ from a specific location, which aligns well with organizations who maintain a distributed workforce; no single location is more important than the other and team members outside of the initial market are at less of a disadvantage. As discussed in the chapter two case study, the act of Canva removing the HQ label from communications channels is a manifestation of this separation, putting the initial market and local teams in international markets on an equal level.

- *Allowing HQ to become an enabler*—With this separation, HQ isn't an operator with staff focused on the initial market. HQ is a separate internal structure whose main goal is to be an enabler and supporter of multiple local operations (the initial market being one of them). After the separation, HQ is no longer an operator of the initial market region but instead a separate group fully focused on global enablement.

It's important to make this transition soon after a company enters multiple markets so as to not entrench the initial market into HQ too much. In fact, it is an important prerequisite of achieving company-market fit. As Jan van Casteren points out, you don't want the (initial market) roots to grow too deep (within HQ).

OFTEN OVERLOOKED

Where Should "International" Sit in the Organizational Structure?

"International" often doesn't have a standard home within a company's organizational structure. Some companies have an international team (like the one Abe Smith runs at Zoom), while others take a more centralized functional approach. The Global Class concept and mindset provide a safe haven and testing ground for success while international transitions into a company-wide commitment, but they still need to be protected until international generates enough revenue to receive resources on its own merit. Before that, global initiatives need a steward of all international growth efforts who can work cross-functionally and has the authority to rally the team; otherwise, it's more difficult for global to capture company-wide buy-in.

MARKET GROWTH MOMENTUM BUILDERS

As an organization begins to find company-market fit in multiple markets, a new set of challenges emerges. The focus shifts from traction to scale. Rapid scaling requires momentum, facilitated by a cross-border organization operating synergistically through effective Feedback Loops and structures that remove friction and complexity. Removing bias, avoiding an us-versus-them mentality, and maintaining balance are all chief considerations to keep in mind.

While finding fit during market entry is the crucial milestone, the momentum sought after during market growth must be sustained.

Entering the market growth phase, the team's mindset changes with more local experience and processes that help local scaling efforts. It is at this stage that local teams are typically happy to take on more responsibility so they can drive things locally without needing permission from HQ. The challenge becomes to what extent autonomy should be granted (in light of the greater goal of reaching global scale and how autonomy contracts for each local market to create momentum, as reflected in the Autonomy Curve). As a company begins reaching the market growth stage in multiple markets, the focus should shift to facilitating global growth over penetration of a single market.

Structures meant to accelerate market growth include the:

- Localization Premium Analysis
- Localization Resource Team
- Global Growth Playbook
- Job Function Pendulum

Localization Premium Analysis

The Localization Premium Analysis (LPA) discussed in chapter six is useful during market entry to map out localizations to bridge between planning and implementation and stay ahead of complexity and properly prioritize markets. It's also valuable during market growth as a way to identify and implement localizations that are scalable to multiple markets.

Tracking mechanisms like the LPA can bring differences and complexities to the forefront, surfacing crucial information. Tracking these at a global level can uncover patterns of localization premium. A specific area of the business, supply chain and inventory (infrastructure premium category), for example, may need to change to successfully launch in new markets. If localizations are being done independently in multiple markets at once, then the company is likely creating more complexity than if there was more of a centralized effort. Utilizing the LPA can make these patterns clearer, leading Global Class Companies to create a common solution (internationalization). This is also a signal for scalability, showing linked markets and uncovering additional criteria to evaluate new markets by, as outlined in the last chapter. During periods of evaluation, return to the LPAs you created during planning so you can compare the actual premium to the forecasted; Evernotes's market entry into India illustrated that what is expected doesn't always match reality.

OFTEN OVERLOOKED

The Role of Global Agile in Momentum Builders

The structures you create to facilitate market entry and growth must put global agile at their center. As discussed in the previous chapter, establishing processes to allow for the testing of localization hypotheses and iteration based on key learnings is crucial to finding company-market fit in a new market. Adoption of the customer development mindset, paired with resources to conduct tests and Feedback Loops to share key learnings, is paramount for finding traction. Validation during market entry transitions into optimization/innovation during market growth. Focus changes, but the mindset stays constant. In doing this, Global Class Companies stay on the lookout for insights and best practices from one market that may have global applicability.

Localization Resource Team

The Localization Resource Team (LRT) is a cross-functional team, ideally with representation from various work functions and departments. It creates momentum by removing obstacles and sharing/implementing best practices. The LRT helps the local team communicate key learnings and implement localizations, aggregating best practices to be used across the organization's growing global footprint. On the HQ side of the diagram (on the next page) each smaller circle within the larger circle on the chart represents a person sitting on the LRT. They are part of their respective departments in the reporting structure but come together with the cross-functional team to represent their department and assist the local teams in their areas of expertise.

The LRT's job is not to tell local teams what to do but instead to serve as a conduit between HQ and local markets. It can be a front door for sharing issues and localization ideas, and a brain trust that intimately understands what does and doesn't work as the organization enters more markets. The team doesn't set direction or make decisions; it facilitates them.

In practice, if a local market lead has a problem best solved by HQ, or needs a certain aspect of the product or operating model localized, they can come to the LRT. Instead of spending their time tracking down how to develop a new feature to localize the product, they can bring the request to the LRT, who can run with the task.

In concept, members of the LRT would know how to get this done faster and more efficiently than the local market lead. Moreover, removing this burden would allow them and their team to focus on more important imperatives, namely uncovering new insights, gaining traction, and achieving company-market fit.

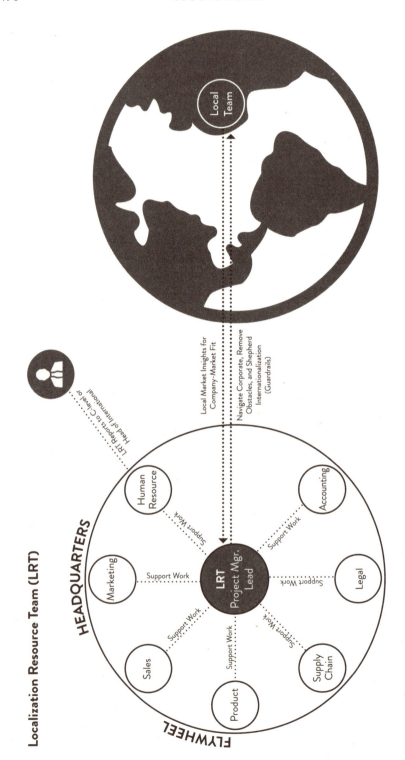

If built early enough, the LRT can spearhead testing and preparation for full-market launch. After launch, the team serves as tactical support, removing obstacles so the team in-market can focus on finding company-market fit and gaining traction. Some organizations refer to this group as a "go-to-market" team or "international" team, but we are intentionally using the word *resource* to best describe the team's core function and purpose.

An effective LRT facilitates Feedback Loops, translating core values from HQ to local teams and decoding key insights from local teams to HQ, navigating cultural nuance. Since they regularly communicate with local teams but also report through HQ, LRT members have strong visibility into competing priorities and possible conflicts that could stifle growth.

The LRT is a catalyst for momentum because it facilitates well-rounded decision-making, understanding trade-offs and the often competing priorities of HQ and local teams. Its members are simultaneously a bridge and buffer between HQ and local teams. The LRT can become both go-between and glue that holds an increasingly distributed organization together, keeping disparate teams focused on the same goal.

Strong LRTs are full of Interpreneurs who have the right balance of cultural curiosity and cultural sensitivity. They have the empathy required to identify the need for localization, but also the agile mindset and resilience to navigate the existing organizational structure to get things done. Members of this team serve as internal salespeople, evangelists, and advocates for global growth initiatives who can secure executive buy-in and cheerleaders to motivate all parties touching international expansion initiatives.

When recruiting members for the LRT, you should look for functional expertise and intrapreneurial skill—in particular, *company-specific* intrapreneurial skill. In other words, it's one thing to have an agile mindset and be able to navigate cross-functional bureaucracy, but to have the familiarity to specifically do it at your company is most important. Team members must have strong communication skills, the ability to influence key stakeholders, and effective project management skills. Strong internal relationships, established trust, and a track record of getting things done at the company make for strong LRT members.

The LRT brings forth the company expertise required to successfully expand. Each member of the team doesn't have to be dedicated to the launch efforts at first, but they all must be engaged and involved in the efforts (either as a shared resource or fully dedicated depending on available company resources). All key functions/departments must be represented to mitigate the opportunity for failure. Moreover, the team can help minimize complexity, as they have a more global perspective of how the company is operating across borders; something not at the forefront of the local team in-market. Through setting up guardrails for what can and cannot be changed, the LRT helps guide localization efforts while maintaining core value alignment and minimizing arbitrary uniqueness.

Depending on your industry, target customer (B2B/B2C), and product (physical or digital), examples of departments represented on the LRT may include: Product, Engineering, Manufacturing, Sales, Marketing, Supply Chain and Logistics, Legal, Accounting, Human Resources, and so on. Each of these members becomes a Single Point of Contact (SPOC) for their specific functional area.

In some ways, the LRT is a bit like Mission Control for a NASA space mission. Mission Control exists to support the astronauts in space, just as the LRT supports team members in-market—empowering them, waiting for vital signs, and solving problems. Just as the Mission Control team figured out how to create an air filter with only the items the Apollo 13 astronauts had on board, LRT members roll up their sleeves to find solutions when obstacles arise.

The most crucial role within the LRT is project manager. This person will steer the team's efforts and serve as a front door, coordinating the engagement of each department and acting as the main conduit between local teams and the executive team. Each department operationalizes the launch plan, and local teams execute on the plan. As outlined in the case study in chapter four, Flexport's version of this (with a more narrow scope) was the technical program manager collecting and tracking product needs and ensuring product localizations were built.

While it is likely that members of HQ won't have the same detailed knowledge as the team on the ground, the LRT can provide a forum for cross-functional collaboration. It's important for the team in-market to use the LPA to highlight localizations, focusing on validating hypotheses (created during the BMLC exercise) and on executing on the Global Growth Playbook. At the same time, the LRT also uses the LPA to track the progress of these localizations in collaboration with the local team.

The primary role of the LRT is to be the connective tissues between international expansion efforts and the rest of the company, rallying together a cross-functional team to address problems and keeping executives up to date.

Executive support is crucial to the success of the LRT. In situations where a company hasn't created an international team or doesn't have a head of international, outside executive sponsorship is necessary. While having an executive-level champion can be helpful, people in this role often raise good questions but don't always champion international growth efforts because they are more focused on their other job responsibilities, according to Kathryn Hymes, former Head of International Product Expansion at Slack. Dedicated executive support is important, preferably with multiple executives engaged.

While not every company has this level of resource or executive support, Slack maintained two cross-functional teams focused on international growth. The first mirrored our concept of an LRT—a working group focused on execution over strategic design.

The second, which at Slack was referred to as the International Council, was a cross-functional group of executives with responsibility for product, marketing, and operations. They determined strategy and delegated responsibility to the (LRT) working group. This executive-level brain trust helped outline and drive action around all the major items on the checklist required for market entry and growth. Functional leads asked key questions, such as, How does Marketing want to describe what Slack does in Japan? They managed the questions going *up* to C-level management and the board of directors, and managed the tasks delegated *down* to the working group (LRT) and local teams.

OFTEN OVERLOOKED

Creating Too Much Process Too Fast Can Slow Growth

When your company is expanding, it's natural to think about all the processes you want to adopt to be globally functional and support worldwide operations. Kathryn Hymes warns, however, that you should be aware that companies can make the mistake of pretending they are bigger than their true size, adding extra layers of bureaucracy and steps to check data when they aren't really needed. Processes for a ten-thousand-person company and a company with two hundred people are different. The former needs much more structure and process than the latter. If you don't keep this in mind, you risk implementing unnecessary processes that add complexity and hinder growth.

When problems surface, the LRT can act as a virtual war room to provide support to teams across the globe. This is important because, as James Sherrett, founding leader of Slack's expansion into Europe, stated, "All big things start small, all small things insignificant." It's important for the LRT to identify and track these issues because (a) the local team is focused on the actual launch, and (b) the local team may not understand what insignificant things could balloon into larger issues later (accumulating localization premium). If the LRT has been engaged in multiple launches, they have a keen eye for potential issues and can address them before they bubble over.

Moreover, LRT members also have insights into areas where there's no room for change. They are guardians of internationalization efforts and know the guardrails for what can be changed and what must not because of operational complexity, core value adherence, or otherwise. For example, Workday has globalized its metrics and pricing; there are certain things the local team might want to change to better serve the market, but this would go against the organization's global strategy. The LRT takes on the function of monitoring localization premium.

Does pricing need to be changed? It would take a lot of focus for a local market lead to go through the formal process to get the change approved and then operationalized with everyone from the product team to marketing to accounting. The LRT can take care of this. Does a local law firm need to be selected to draft new employment contracts? The legal representative from the LRT can be involved in vetting new firms and serve as the company contact to ensure local law compliance while minimizing localization premium. There are many other examples of challenges that would take the local market team's focus away from better understanding customers, building new sales channels, and adapting the product offering to fit the local market.

There are multiple schools of thought when it comes to the permanency of the LRT. In some situations, spinning up a team pre-launch and scaling it down once you find traction in the market is the best plan. In other situations (especially if you are planning a multi-country expansion), it may make more sense to have a permanent team in place. Uber, for example, was conducting such a widespread expansion campaign that there were always more markets for an LRT to focus on, so keeping HQ resources dedicated to supporting new regions would be worthwhile. At Uber, launchers in each market had strong ties with each other early on, peer coaching each other through obstacles in place of a formal LRT.

While we don't intend to be prescriptive about how long the LRT should be kept intact for those not planning to maintain a permanent team, there is strategic value in keeping the team operational to varying degrees until the local team achieves company-market fit. If there are consistently new markets being launched, the LRT would be a fixture within the corporate structure.

The LRT can help diagnose why a company is facing problems finding scale in a new market, tapping into insights and best practices from multiple market entries given the team's global purview. Feedback Loops are a crucial tool that LRTs can leverage in order to identify why the company isn't getting traction or reaching scale. They also assist the team in recalibrating market strategy by providing a channel to highlight key issues and obstacles.

Global Growth Playbook

A Global Growth Playbook is a resource that maps out all the steps required for a successful launch and growth in a new market, capturing best practices for market entry and market growth. It should be a centralized (digital) repository that both LRT and launch team members contribute to in real time as lessons are learned. We are intentionally calling it a Global *Growth* Playbook, as opposed to a Market *Entry* Playbook, because we believe that a playbook should have a wider scope than just launching in a new market; it should help local teams as they continue to scale the business in new markets.

Effective Global Growth Playbooks are both collaborative and dynamic, adapting over time. Multiple teams must have input, and all elements must be iterated and optimized (like your product and company operations) to take into account best practices and key learnings from each market as your global presence matures.

This document accelerates the speed at which local teams can find traction in a market, limit complexities, and ensure mistakes aren't made multiple times in different regions.

Having a centralized playbook that multiple parties contribute to can be a great best practice sharing tool. Uber perfected cross-region sharing, ensuring that best practices were known and implemented by all local offices. From a management perspective, these communication channels can also be solid opportunities to recognize achievement and reinforce company values with a geographically distributed group. Uber's "just do it" style of guiding principles would have created a great deal more localization premium with so many regions being spun up at once if these benchmarks and communication channels hadn't existed.

As Scott Coleman, former Head of Growth and International Product at Pinterest, notes, "One of the easiest ways to demotivate a team in the market is to make it an execution arm. Give them input into the strategy and build procedures and processes in partnership with them. If people are a part of the building process, there is a greater chance for buy-in." Engaging them in the creation and ongoing development of a Global Growth Playbook can be a great channel to gather this input, a hallmark strategy of Global Class Companies.

Flexport didn't have a formal playbook when it launched its first two international offices, which meant the regional founders had to invent and codify the expansion process themselves. While there was also no formal playbook for making sure the Flexport culture would be consistent, regular visits back to HQ and executives visiting the regions made sure those two new offices lived the Flexport culture. Based on those first experiences, the company now has a better playbook system in place. In addition to tactical tips (setting up an office and bank account, for example), it more importantly captures the intricacies of different markets in-depth to develop a braintrust that can be accessed by other people at the company.

For Uber, the playbook represented a head start for all new regions. Former Uber launcher and first employee outside of North America Sam Gellman pointed out that instead of launch teams starting from scratch each time, the playbook codified 80 percent of what they needed to know and do to successfully launch a new market. This enabled them to focus on learning the other 20 percent, most of which was specific to the market being launched. Sam explained, "If you learned something in Bangladesh that didn't work, you added it into the playbook." No matter where the lesson was learned, it was shared with other regions to help them with their launches. There was even a centralized team that managed the playbook, receiving inputs from the field (an LRT of sorts).

Getting 80 percent of the way there through a robust centralized brain trust gave Uber an incredible advantage, enabling them to scale at warp speed.

As with anything that an Interpreneur does in launching a new market, these playbooks are meant to have a level of flexibility and need to be changeable. Because each market is different, the pathway to success will differ as well (this is where the 20 percent that needs to be discovered comes in). As long as the playbook remains an agile document, rather than just a road map that has to be adhered to without revision, it can be a valuable tool for getting traction and scale in a new market.

Whether it was an all-encompassing gospel, as it is with Uber, or a simple centralized checklist against which progress can be measured, a launch and growth strategy document was a key ingredient to the success of many companies we researched.

A WARNING . . .

While setting up these structures can enable momentum and scale, they will have the opposite effect if not implemented properly or if established in excess. Have clear rationale for each process set in place and constantly monitor its effectiveness, otherwise your rapidly growing organization will be attacked by the B-word: *bureaucracy.*

CASE STUDY

CREATING STRUCTURES, PROCESSES, AND NORMS TO SUPPORT RAPID GLOBAL SCALING—SLACK

Slack is a true international success story in every sense of the word. Improving business communication in more than 150 countries through more than ten million users, the company has been effective at creating processes and structures that assist at every stop along the way, from initial planning and market entry to support of rapid global scaling.

Here are actionable ways Slack supported its global growth:

Ask Key Questions and Do Research to Find Answers Utilizing the Global Agile Methodology

When entering new markets, the Slack team asked themselves key questions to direct localization discovery, such as: What does knowledge work look like in X country? What pivots are needed? Deeper questions, like "What is communication in the local market?" (customized for your industry/company model) can provide a lens through which localization can be identified.

Then the team focused on localization discovery, conducting research in partnership with local new hires and outside consultants, going in-country to interview current users and potential customers and observe them using Slack. When entering the Japanese market, insights included both the pervasiveness and importance of work-life to someone's identity, but also how Slack was a liberating and transparent tool amidst the hierarchy and formality of Japanese business culture.

Gather the right volume of feedback and get your product into the right hands

The Slack team established mechanisms to gather product feedback and understand customer requests. At the same time they ensured that this feedback was measured and analyzed differently than feedback from established markets. As Kathryn Hymes explained, customer feedback must be given the right volume. Since the quantity of requests for a specific product localization will always be smaller in new markets than in markets with large customer bases, some amplification is needed, along with foresight to estimate the impact a product change would have as a new market scales. The next important step is to get this information from localization discovery and customer feedback to the people who can act on it.

Build Cross-Functional Teams to Support Internationalization

Next, Slack created two-tiered, cross-functional, internationally focused teams, as outlined earlier in the chapter. The more strategic "International Council" of function leaders and the more execution-focused working group each play an important role, from ensuring executive alignment and resources all the way through implementation.

Build Process Even When the Team Isn't Built

Early in Slack's launch in Japan, they only had one employee in-market, a member of the enterprise sales team. Besides having the necessary agile (customer discovery) mentality, this team member would participate in customer research efforts and even participated in established structures like quarterly business reviews with

HQ despite not having P&L responsibility for the market, so that implementation of these processes wouldn't be delayed before a local market general manager was hired.

One of the biggest benefits Slack had was its own platform. In drinking their own champagne, the Slack team benefited from the visibility and transparency the Slack platform provided, especially relevant when communicating amongst a distributed and virtual workforce.

Foster Internal Relationship Building

A combination of knowledge of how to get things done internally and relationships across the business is a recipe for success in scaling globally. While relationship building should be organic, structure can be put in place to facilitate it. The primary drivers are establishing consistent rituals (like regional monthly customer feedback sessions) and inviting people to participate in these rituals (providing visibility and creating team dynamics).

To facilitate this, Slack uses the mantra "create processes to make the world smaller." In pursuit of this, the Slack local teams created what they called Small Hands meetings. While All Hands meetings were effectively used to get everyone together, Small Hands meetings were regionally focused. These meetings allowed for more dialogue instead of top-down information sharing from HQ. The by-products were closer cross-regional connections and best practice sharing; the meetings also fostered a level of regional ownership and identity.

Create, Maintain, and Adapt Playbooks

Playbooks were an important resource for the Slack team. In fact, the team maintained a playbook on how to launch a new market and a playbook to maintain a market in light of the relative investments made in a specific market. While it is tempting to think you can calculate answers to all the questions you have, at Slack the playbooks made an effort to estimate the necessary investments needed for a market and ROI relative to the investments.

Don't Launch and Leave

Finally, there is a natural tendency to put a great deal of effort into the launch of a market and then taper off the focus on the market in favor of other market launches in the pipeline. To get to scale in new markets, teams have to continue to focus on finding company-market fit and provide support to build the team and operations for sustainable growth. As we quoted Kathryn saying, don't "Launch and Leave." The LPA helps build a path toward sustainable growth by giving the leadership team visibility into what's needed to be successful in the local market and an understanding of the resources required to get there.

OFTEN OVERLOOKED

Inflection Points

Along your pathway to global scale, it's important to be conscious of an inflection point that often changes the mindset surrounding global growth, particularly among the executive team and board. Early on and throughout market entry, many people in the organization will not yet "see the light" around the benefits of focusing resources and energy around global growth. They will identify how current market revenue dwarfs traction in international markets and start valuing that the short-term ROI for resources spent in current markets would be much higher than investing in new market entry.

Once international revenue crosses a certain threshold, however, things change. There is no specific number to target, but from our research, once global markets account for 30 to 40 percent of total company revenue, the tide shifts. At this point, the executive team and board begin to see the importance of growing in global markets as the size of the opportunity and impact on the business become more tangible. This is when resource alignment (one of the Four Commitments for Successful Global Growth) becomes much easier. The struggle is managing expectations and maintaining buy-in before reaching this inflection point, which takes grit and perseverance, something Interpreneurs have in bountiful supply.

There are other inflection points as well. Ramsey Pryor, former Head of International Expansion and Sales at Branch Metrics and founder of Port of Entry Partners, compared the process of global scaling to emulating what a hermit crab does, regularly discarding its current shell for a bigger one to grow into. Autonomy shifts along the Autonomy Curve over time, teams outgrow support structures, and the organizational structure changes between functional and general manager models, among other inflection points that merit a new shell (support structure and processes) for the team.

The Job Function Pendulum

As mentioned, international expansion often doesn't have a specific place within legacy companies. There is often no centralized "international" function, and even when there is a team focused on global growth, its members must contend with cross-functional input and implementation that the team doesn't have control over. International responsibility can fall under a maze of roles from executives with responsibility for *growth* or *revenue* or *operations*, from sales to product and everywhere in between.

There is no magic structure or functional home for the team focused on global growth; much depends on the driving force of the company—whether it's product driven, engineering driven, customer driven, or the like. Instead, it is a matter of best controlling operational overhead and managing what functions are centralized, regionalized, or localized, depending on the dynamics of that specific job function and the level of localization required.

The fact is, when your company reaches market growth in multiple markets, important choices must be made around how to structure your team to support a global footprint. In the process of scaling in new countries, when your presence reaches a certain level of maturity, you will need to change your support model. This tends to lead to a process where the company chooses what to localize, regionalize, or centralize, depending on the business function, available financial resources, human resources, and product or industry type.

We call this the Job Function Pendulum, since things may swing back and forth from localized all the way to centralized as your international growth initiatives mature over time. At its core, the pendulum is driven by distribution or centralization of decision rights, established guidelines by authority divided between HQ and local offices (discussed more in chapter nine), the scale of operations, and which function drives the business. For instance, product-driven companies would tend to centralize product decision-making and resources under a centralized reporting structure at HQ, but they'd be more willing to build a local presence for a functional area considered less core.

Early on, some functions must be local (sales is probably the first that comes to mind), while others can stay centralized (product, for example). As new countries are added, a localized function may serve an entire region until a certain level of traction is reached in the new market, when a new person in-country takes over ownership of that function. Over time, it may not make sense to have different people in each country working on the same functional area, so you may move to centralize. Then, if results lag, having a regionalized or localized function may make sense again. It may be best, for example, to have local administrative support in the initial launch and product-market fit search stages (for speed), while it should be centralized in the stages of market growth. You should conduct a cost-benefit analysis along the way to optimize for this, and everything should consider ROI.

Scott Coleman, formerly of Pinterest and Google, views this as a set of "stacked S curves," where a slow initial period leads to faster growth, then a plateau, then starts all over again. Different support models are best for different levels on the S curve, and different strategies will dictate speed. If the company has raised a large round of venture capital funding, the path to growth will look very different than a company who is growing more organically. In the former scenario, the focus is on validating whether there is a global opportunity quickly, rapidly deploying capital in the process. In the latter scenario, a company from a smaller market must identify the right large market to expand to and test operations in the most agile way possible, since resources are more constrained.

Where the specific local market and company's overall global growth initiative sits on the Autonomy Curve (discussed in chapter four) plays an important role in where on the pendulum certain work functions should sit at a given point in the expansion timeline. It's important to allow local teams to be autonomous in the initial post-launch stages to maximize key learnings and allow them to focus on activities with the highest impact instead of adhering to the way things are done at HQ (localized functions). Over time it can make sense to remove some autonomy in order to limit localization premium and create continuity within regions (centralized functions). In the final stage of scaling, however, a level of autonomy becomes an important tool for empowering local teams as they feel like they are in control of some aspects of the business and not just having to do whatever HQ says an ocean away. A notable consideration is that, in all cases and at all stages, the amount of autonomy granted to local teams must align with company culture.

With the right processes and organizational structures creating positive momentum during both market entry and market growth, you have the scaffolding in place to build an organization at global scale. These hard-coded processes must also be aligned with a set of soft-coded principles that keep fast-moving organizations aligned and moving in the right direction. These three catalysts of successful global growth initiatives are the backbone of Global Class Companies (discussed in part three).

CHAPTER 7 SUMMARY

- The source of momentum as an organization moves from the market entry to the market growth stage are the processes and structures (*Momentum Builders*) built to support global scale. They are essential, since validating that a business has global potential is as make-or-break for the company as finding company-market fit in an initial market.
- Two-way communication links (and all Four Commitments to Successful Global Growth) are essential for local teams to internalize company culture and core values, and for HQ to gain insights from local markets to craft relevant localizations.
- There are a number of Momentum Builders designed to support both the market entry stage of international expansion (*localization discovery, Business Model Localization Canvas, Global Growth Pitch Deck,* and *global agile methodology*) and the market growth stage (*Localization Premium Analysis [LPA], Localization Resource Team [LRT], Global Growth Playbook,* and *the Job Function Pendulum*).

CHAPTER 7 REFLECTION & ACTION QUESTIONS

1. How are you creating processes and structures to generate momentum? Which of the Momentum Builders discussed in the chapter most resonated with you?
2. Who owns international within your company?
3. How are you giving executive visibility into your global expansion initiatives?

PART 3

EMPOWER

The Three Pillars for Achieving Global Scale

Global Class Companies are built on three critical tenets. The most important ingredient in any company's quest to reach global scale is its PEOPLE. A globally minded MANAGEMENT strategy ensures alignment of a distributed organization, with HQ taking on the role of enabler, while a balanced approach to CULTURE provides a North Star for a rapidly expanding organization.

THE THREE PILLARS FOR ACHIEVING GLOBAL SCALE

1. **Global Class Team Building.** As all top business leaders know, it's the team members that are the biggest factor in determining the success or failure of any global growth initiative or company in general. Chapter eight builds off of the concept of interpreneurship and details how to create the right team for achieving global scale through focusing on the key characteristics required within local teams.

2. **The Global Class Management Model.** Global Class leaders realize that success on a global scale doesn't come purely from the right mindset or strategy, but must be paired with effective implementation. Chapter nine brings together concepts discussed throughout the book into an actionable framework that can be used both to structure and effectively communicate the best model to manage a global organization.

3. **Balancing Culture.** Interpreneurs understand that culture eclipses almost any other aspect of running a global business, from striving for a consistent company culture across a distributed footprint to navigating the unique norms and beliefs in a local market; culture is king. Chapter ten addresses the importance of the three distinct types of culture and offers insights into how to create a sustainable balance between all three, while introducing a new emerging culture (Community Culture) that companies scaling globally should be mindful of and tap into.

• 8 •

PEOPLE
Building Global Class Teams

Kamlesh Talreja was the perfect candidate for the job.

After growing up in India and graduating from the University of Mumbai, Kamlesh began his career at Tata Consultancy Services, developing a strong understanding of Indian business culture. Although already on a good career track, he realized he wanted more and saw that opportunity lay beyond his home borders. This desire led him to earn a master's degree from UC San Diego, where he experienced local American culture.

After a brief stint at RealNetworks, he landed an engineering manager role at Amazon's Seattle headquarters. Over the next five and a half years, Kamlesh got a better understanding of American business culture, but more importantly learned the inner workings of Amazon. Through working in engineering management positions in both the Retail and Prime Video Division, he solidified his alignment with Amazon's culture, learned how to get things done across departments internally, honed his leadership and people management skills, and ultimately built a strong reputation, gaining the trust of leaders across the business.

Upon learning about a leadership position on the Amazon Appstore team located in Bangalore, Kamlesh saw the next big opportunity. At the same time, the Amazon leadership saw the ideal balance needed to successfully lead a team in an international market.

Kamlesh had the agile/scrum foundational experience to lead a fast-growing development team still solidifying its role, the company knowledge needed to navigate internal obstacles and secure buy-in, and the local knowledge to understand the nuances of building and managing a team of engineers in his native India. His knowledge of the local market wasn't just from his youth; he had, in his words, a continuous "connection to the goings-on of India and how it has been changing" through established relationships. Finally, he had the desire to move back to his home country. He checked all the boxes (and more), and got the job.

Six months into the new role, Kamlesh faced a problem. His team was revolting against him; actually, they were revolting against some of Amazon's American-centric policies. Kamlesh's team felt a lack of empathy and respect from HQ. HQ had unrealistic timelines for the team in India and would also set up meetings during American business hours, expecting the Indian team to meet late at night or early in the morning local time. In addition, the team in India struggled with the direct nature of the American communication style, something not typical in Indian business culture. This led many team members to quit.

In response, Kamlesh jumped into action. He tapped into his knowledge of the Indian workplace, empathizing with his team and seeking to understand their issues. Shortly after, he called on his network at HQ in Seattle—especially on, in Kamlesh's words, an "extreme advocate" he'd built a relationship with—to influence some of the policies to better suit his team in India. He then advocated for his team's local culture and ensured they knew that he was their local champion who would work hard to secure support from HQ.

Kamlesh was able to get the team at HQ to meet them halfway, scheduling some meetings during Indian business hours and others during American business hours. Kamlesh also set up stronger communications processes with more regular cadence meetings, coaching his team in India to overcommunicate and be more transparent than is typical, to better fit the American business culture. In response, morale, performance, and retention increased. Moreover, the teams in India and HQ built mutual trust and a stronger relationship leading to more autonomy. By year three, the team in India was given ownership of a new product line and their own S-Team goal (one of Amazon's most critical goal levels).

Kamlesh represents an ideal that most companies would fight to have when building out teams in new markets—company and local knowledge combined with the leadership skills to get things done. Kamlesh's international experiences helped nurture his interpreneurial mindset, and his reflective leadership style and abilities to influence authority and remove obstacles gave him the right skill set to effectively lead a remote organization. While most companies don't have a pipeline of Kamleshes as they build international teams, there are strategies and a framework they can use to build Global Class teams that collectively possess Kamlesh's skills.

When interviewing executives for this book, we asked them what the most *important* and most *challenging* aspects of international growth were. The number-one aspect for both categories was building the right team of people. **This is why the first pillar of effective global scaling is Global Class team building.**

In our interviews, Sankar Venkatraman from LinkedIn characterized the hardest part of scaling globally as "finding the right people, for the right role, at the right time, which is multiple times harder internationally." Polly Sumner, Salesforce's Chief Adoption Officer, affirmed the importance of the team when she said, "You have to have a talent differentiator." All of this contributes to the outsized role Org. Premium plays in the Localization Premium Analysis (LPA); hiring the right team and dealing with the operational aspects of having team members in a local market can be complex and affects most other aspects of a business.

While local laws dictate employment terms such as severance, it is really physical distance, as well as differences in culture and mindset, that creates difficulty. It is more difficult to build trust from far away, even more so when language and cultural translations stand in the middle.

The human side of international business has changed.

The romanticized image of an expat trailblazing in a new land with their driver and expense account, inking new partnership deals and unlocking the vast potential in a new market, is a thing of the past and happens to be a far cry from reality in the new global business environment.

The new reality is that teams are distributed across the globe and companies have begun to understand the importance of having team members with native knowledge of local markets. Global Class Companies see that having a centralized or even clustered hiring strategy limits the pool of talented job candidates they have access to.

The old criteria companies used to build local teams is becoming obsolete. Nicole Sahin, founder and CEO, Globalization Partners, highlights how many American companies expanding to new markets would choose candidates with the best English-speaking skills instead of finding someone with all the other skills germane to the job they were hiring for.

To succeed in this new global talent market, you'll need a new strategy that takes into account all aspects of what is required to accelerate through the market entry and market growth stages. Enter the Global Class Team Building Framework.

GLOBAL CLASS TEAM BUILDING FRAMEWORK OVERVIEW

Every company has their own hiring mantra. LinkedIn, for example, looks for people with the Three Cs:

- **Connect the dots**—understanding what's happening in one area of the business and bringing those best practices to other parts
- **Communicate**—communicating persuasively in written and verbal forms across time zones while maintaining a strong point of view and empathy for others
- **Collaborate**—working with others to influence authority even without direct authority of one's own

For other companies, it's a completely different formula.

Regardless of a company's current hiring practices, global leaders need to consider a unique set of factors when building an international team.

Global Class teams possess the following traits, which we call the Global Class Team Building Framework:

1. *Interpreneur Mindset* is the combination of agile, company, and cultural mindsets outlined in chapter three.
2. *Local Knowledge* conveys an understanding of local culture (and business practices) and experience within the local market.

3. *Company Knowledge* indicates understanding of, and alignment with, company culture and trust built with HQ.

4. *Leadership Skills for Distributed Organizations* specifically relate to the requirements for effectively operating distributed teams outside of HQ.

A particularly unique aspect of the framework is that the criteria are used to evaluate a cohesive team, not just individual candidates. As you will see, it is not easy to find someone who is able to fully cover all four key categories in the framework, but it is crucial that all categories are covered to reach Global Class status. In fact, for most companies, someone who covers all these bases is *a unicorn who probably doesn't exist* (although as Interpreneurs become more prominent in the talent pool, more of these leaders will emerge).

It's rare for companies to have people with traits that cover all four categories as Kamlesh does. That is why it is often most effective to build Global Class teams that collectively have all of these traits amongst an entire team.

Global Class teams are able to identify required localizations and market opportunity, iterate through the customer development process to reach company-market fit, and build and utilize processes and structures to build momentum and achieve scale, doing all this while maintaining strong

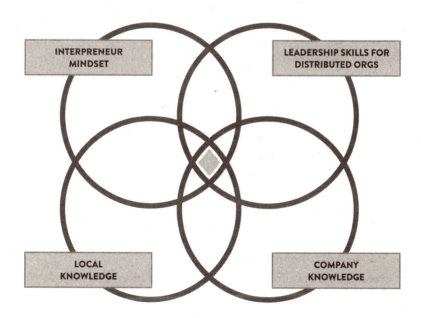

communication channels and alignment with HQ and company leadership—a set of tasks not for the faint of heart.

Interpreneur Mindset

As discussed throughout the book, Interpreneurs are the secret sauce of Global Class Companies. Their agile mindset helps navigate the customer development process, their company mindset helps them navigate HQ to get things done, and their cultural mindset helps them navigate the local market and identify the localization required to find fit and scale there.

Interpreneurial traits include:

Agile Mindset—Entrepreneurial
- **Grit**—Persistent and stubborn, leaves no stone unturned, overcomes obstacles, and never gives up
- **Comfort with Ambiguity**—Forges ahead in the face of uncertainty
- **Openness to Failure**—Knows failure is part of the process, takes educated risks
- **Problem Solving**—Creative-solution oriented
- **Customer Development Mindset**—Able to wear many hats while working cross-functionally to implement the global agile methodology

Company Mindset—Intrapreneurial
- **Strong Collaboration**—Cross-border, cross-function, cross-culture; gets buy-in and drives results through others
- **Navigate Bureaucracy**—Overcomes the complexities of getting buy-in within an established organization with set processes
- **Builder's Mentality**—Creates lasting impact, builds blocks to something bigger

Cultural Mindset—Cultural EQ
- **Global Scope**—Sees opportunities everywhere, a Global Citizen
- **Values Diversity & Inclusion**—Seeks different perspectives
- **Holds Bias**—Suspends beliefs, assumptions, and judgment
- **Cultural Curiosity**—Open to cultural learning, cross-cultural translator
- **Empathy**—Sees (and acts on) new perspectives

As Jennifer Cornelius, Chief People Officer at Ritual and former Head of Organization Design for Apple's Retail Division, shared with us, it is important to allow experimentation between HQ and the local team; this is at the core of honing the entrepreneurial mindset and intrapreneurial skills that are part of being an effective Interpreneur. As Emil Michael, formerly of Uber, stated, "You have to hone an ethic of problem solving within the whole company." This starts with putting the right team in place and then setting up processes and training to foster this behavior.

While these interpreneurial skills are crucial during market entry, they are also important during market growth. Local teams need to continually work to optimize processes and challenge themselves to be better, constantly iterating. This interpreneurial skill is needed to optimize operations while having the cultural framing to understand what will work in the market.

It may take time to find someone who thinks this way in countries with highly structured business cultures. As Jan van Casteren, founder of Flexport's European business and former Head of Europe, points out, "If your team doesn't have an interpreneurial mindset, you will be disappointed, and finding people with this mindset in some countries is very difficult. In Germany, for example, the more rigid and hierarchical traditional business culture may make it harder to find people that fit."

One way to uncover whether a potential hire has the right global mindset is by creating proof points for international exposure. John Brandon, former Vice President of International at Apple, for example, said he would look for "fat passport people." In other words, people who had a great deal of business travel experience were more likely to be Interpreneurs.

Local Knowledge

Knowledge of the local market (ideally native understanding) is crucial for success in any new market. Being able to identify changes to the operating model and leverage relationships with potential partners and customers to gain traction is an important one-two punch required during most market launches.

Local knowledge traits include:

- **Local Business Experience**—Understands Local Business Culture (ideally) at a native level

- **Local Language Skills**—Multilingual, for Local and HQ
- **Local Network**—Strong relationships with influencers and stakeholder groups in the local market
- **Pride in Local Culture**—Passion to drive value in the local market

Local knowledge is absolutely essential to connecting with customers in the new market, navigating local laws, and adapting the solution and operating model to work profitably at scale. Local knowledge traits don't come from *visiting* a market but from being a *native* or having *deep* experience working there. In many countries, local relationships are paramount and can take years to build, not something that can come from a localization discovery visit. Local knowledge also helps translate the company culture and value proposition to local market customers and employees alike.

As Manas Mainrai, Head of Enterprise Business APAC for online education platform Emeritus, explained, the best candidates have the right framing for the market, a strong network of relationships, experience in the market, and relevant expertise. Depending on the market, each of these will carry a different weight. In Singapore, for example, expertise is highly valued, while in Japan the most valued attribute is relationships because of the local business culture. Even knowing these nuances in and of itself is a key indication of the level of local knowledge.

One interesting finding from our research was the pattern of the final trait in this category, Pride in Local Culture. While not entirely universal, most business professionals who gravitated toward working for fast-growing international businesses had a desire to bring innovation to their home country to solve problems and improve lives. They saw Global Class Companies as vehicles to improve their local communities and had a passion to accelerate their impact. Kamlesh from Amazon is a great example of this mindset.

Company Knowledge

Since teams growing in new markets have to tap into the resources and structures of HQ, it is crucial for the team to know how to navigate the bureaucracy of the organization to get things done (secure resources, enact changes to the local operating model, and beyond).

Company knowledge traits include:

- **Company Values and Principles Alignment**—Core value and vision buy-in
- **Culture Fit**—Embraces the type of environment teams operate in
- **Ability to get things done internally**—An understanding of the inner workings of the company and how to get things done
- **Trust**—Established reputation with leadership and/or key stakeholders fostering autonomy

The traits in the company knowledge category translate to the ability to get things done, whether that is gaining buy-in for a necessary localization or securing additional resources for the local market.

The ability to get things done internally is not predicated on having previous company experience at HQ, but that is extremely helpful. However, while it's a valuable area of expertise, company knowledge does NOT equal tenure. Company knowledge doesn't supersede local knowledge or an interpreneurial spirit. In other words, it's easier to hire for/teach someone to internalize *company* culture than it is to master *local* culture.

While the complete collection of skills outlined in the Global Class Team Building Framework creates a well-rounded team capable of dealing with the challenges of running a local office, one trait in the company knowledge category plays a more prominent role and directly affects many of the other traits: cultural fit. In some ways, culture fit supersedes skill-set fit when an interpreneurial mindset is present. At the company level, it is more important to ensure continuity in company culture across geographies than to bring in a rock star who doesn't buy into core values. At the individual level, a deep connection with company values can generate the passion to develop some of the skill sets needed for success, something that doesn't work the other way around.

Culture and core values can also drive companies to be more prescriptive about the skills they want to encourage in all employees, especially the leadership team. This can be specifically designed for distributed teams, like at Zendesk, which outlined four "guideposts" to drive the development of targeted employee traits:

- Drives productivity through access to knowledge
- Cultivates cross-team collaboration
- Overcommunicates—and finds new communication channels
- Automates essential workflows

These principles are a filter that potential team members can be evaluated through and can be used to select the processes and structures that the company invests resources in. These guideposts also fit well with an international footprint and make an effort to minimize localization premium (complexity), Org. Premium in particular.

Finding a leader who has overlapping company and local knowledge is the goal, but building a team where multiple people cover these bases works as well. As John Brandon from Apple put it, when it comes to company culture, you want people who are "smart enough to know what is and what isn't negotiable." The same can apply to local culture as well.

Leadership Skills for Distributed Organizations

Given that teams focused on global growth are almost always distributed between local markets and HQ, it is important that the team has the necessary skills to communicate effectively with HQ, interfacing with and influencing leadership while removing barriers on the path to growth. Many of these are addressed with the Momentum Builders discussed in chapter seven.

Leadership skills for distributed organizations include:

- **Strong Communication Skills**—Fosters two-way translation between local team and HQ
- **Autonomous Decision-Making**—Acts independently, tapping into core values, knowing what to get HQ's input on
- **Ability to Influence Authority**—Drives change through others by managing up
- **High Integrity**—Regards truth over self-preservation
- **Reflective Leadership**—Understands gaps within team and fills them, emotional intelligence (EQ)
- **Removal of Obstacles**—Removes distractions and roadblocks to focus the team on traction and growth
- **Building of High-Trust Culture**—Fosters honesty, transparency, and support
- **Culturally Conscious Management**—Creates a contingency approach to management that takes local culture into account (described further in the next chapter)
- **Partnership Building**—Builds strong, culturally aligned relationships with local team and HQ

The traits outlined above are particularly important. Local teams operate remote from HQ but still must influence HQ decision-making while being afforded the autonomy to adapt the product and operations to fit local market culture and business culture. The team must also have the wherewithal to push past obstacles and take advantage of the structures and processes HQ puts in place to support the global team.

As highlighted in the story of John Brandon managing Apple's team in China (chapter four), integrity is important, but local business culture may conflict in some scenarios. Creating a high-trust culture can help navigate these nuances and more stark cultural conflicts alike.

Not every company has someone who hits the diamond in the center of the Global Class Team Building Framework like Kamlesh for Amazon, but with skills from these four categories, any company can assemble a team that possesses all of the traits outlined in the framework.

OFTEN OVERLOOKED

Lacking Both Functional and Cultural Expertise

While finding the overlap in these categories is ideal, having little to no overlap can be a recipe for disaster. As Scott Coleman, formerly of Pinterest and Google, puts it, if you hire someone who is new to the role AND to the country, you are putting your global growth efforts at a disadvantage. Someone in this situation doesn't have a bearing on how to fulfill their job responsibilities AND doesn't understand the nuances of the local market. Don't hire someone with gaps in both *functional* expertise AND *cultural* expertise. Uber mitigated this risk by having individuals on its launch teams who traveled from country to country. While they often didn't have deep local knowledge, they were clear on how to implement their strategy in a new market based on repetition. Our example of Amazon sits on the other end of the spectrum, where native understanding of a local market and experience working at company HQ were often prerequisites for being hired to take on a new role.

The Importance of Local Team Leadership

While the Global Class Team Building Framework is meant as a guide for hiring an entire team that collectively has the traits to implement a successful global growth initiative, the local team leader still plays an important role in the team's success.

As Dawn Sharifan, SVP, People, at Slack, puts it, "The leader is key in 'island offices' [referring to offices apart from HQ]. That leader is more important than the market's total addressable market size. With the wrong leader the culture falls apart and you can't accomplish what needs to be accomplished on the business side."

The local lead has to develop strategies with HQ while making the necessary changes to ensure successful execution in the local market. They need to be able to identify new opportunities and inspire the team at HQ and in-country to rally around these opportunities. Most paramount, they need to serve as a conduit and translator between HQ and their team in-country, setting expectations and mending cultural divides. They have to be all of this, plus be the person who sets up bank accounts, works with local attorneys to make sure everything is being operated legally, and serves as the face of the company in the new market.

A more apt image for this local leader, as shared by Jan van Casteren, is that of a kitchen sink. The place where all the dirty dishes get stacked, the place everything flows through.

The local team leader has to shape the identity of the local office and local presence and position where the local office sits in relation to HQ and the local market. As Ethan Evans, formerly of Amazon, puts it, the local lead must be the "culture keeper and culture evangelist, and there it's important to hire someone who is willing to be reprogrammed to not only fit the local market but the company culture as well."

One important note: While having local leadership who can "hustle" with an autonomous entrepreneurial spirit is important for navigating the ambiguity of a new market launch, there must be a balance with some of the other traits and company culture. As Jennifer Yuen, former Head of Americas Marketing for Airbnb, put it, "You don't want too much of a cowboy. Cowboys may have short-term success but can burn bridges internally. You want someone who is entrepreneurial but internalizes company core values to direct decision-making and strategy." As a member of the local team, the local lead must still be a *team* player and must have the company mindset discussed in chapter three.

EFFECTIVE GLOBAL CLASS TEAM BUILDING STRATEGIES

Global Class Companies use the following four strategies to build world-class teams:

- Facilitate company-local knowledge overlap
- Select, nurture, and create Interpreneurs
- Enable decentralized talent strategy
- Create the right system for success

Facilitate Company-Local Knowledge Overlap

The overlap of local and company knowledge has the largest impact on international growth initiatives. Local teams must have local knowledge to understand how the business must be localized and the know-how and trust built with HQ to get things done to support the new market.

Ideally, the team leading the global growth hiring efforts can find a "unicorn" who has it all. Someone who has experience working at the company in a leadership role, with a strong track record, established trust, tight cross-functional relationships, practiced people management skills, a broad functional understanding, experience successfully launching companies with similar cultures and products in the markets being targeted, who is well aligned with company core values, and, of course, is a native speaker with a keen understanding of local business culture, with existing local contacts and experience working in the local market . . . oh, and they need to not be magically tied to one location but be able to travel wherever is needed. It is nearly impossible to find someone within your current ranks that checks all of these boxes.

The larger the cultural differences between the company's initial market and target market, the more local knowledge is needed. Additionally, the more momentum-building structures and processes are in place, the more gaps in company knowledge and internal relationships can be filled.

When faced with a choice, most executives we spoke with said that local experience was more important than company experience. A deep understanding of local business culture and the target customer was more important than knowing how to get an internal process problem fixed. Company knowledge can always be taught through process and exposure.

At the same time, be cognizant of the fact that candidates from a local market who don't have international expertise or experience may not possess the interpreneurial skills essential to forging a strong partnership between the local team and HQ.

When a Global Class Company lacks overlap between local and company knowledge, the team builds it by implementing strategies that bring a local team member to HQ to work there for a few months. This is a great way to strengthen bonds between local team members and HQ while also increasing company knowledge.

BlaBlaCar did this effectively prior to launching in new markets, hiring locals to manage the market pre-launch, and having them work out of HQ. This served two purposes. First, it allowed employees with local knowledge of the target market to influence the product and operating model so they would more easily work in the new market. Second, these employees were able to develop strong company knowledge that paired well with their local market knowledge. When they returned to their native market, the combination of company and market knowledge led to success as these employees understood how to localize the product for the market and how to get things done from afar through HQ.

In referencing expansion readiness, Jennifer Cornelius of Ritual, formerly of Apple, suggests that key local team members should be part of the process from the beginning, when the team is mapping out the product and other elements.

To facilitate the overlap between local and company knowledge, it often makes sense to incorporate these local market team members into the planning stages of a launch, not just the execution. Remember that hiring can start with interviews of job candidates during localization discovery, so if you discover some good candidates, it may be worth bringing them on sooner rather than later (and it's not just to lock them in before they take another job opportunity). Their perspective can be helpful in creating the Global Growth Playbook and going through the Business Model Localization Canvas exercise, along with creating tools and processes to support the local market.

One other strategy, which has been used effectively at Plaid, is a "Send One, Hire One" structure. The local lead role can be tag-teamed, held by one leader coming in from HQ and another being hired locally. While this definitely covers the overlap of local and company knowledge and provides an additional senior resource, note that it can cause some issues when it comes to decision-making and separation of responsibility.

Select, Nurture, and Create Interpreneurs

As discussed in this chapter and throughout the book, Interpreneurs are the catalysts for global growth. Global Class Companies know how to identify, hire, and activate these candidates to build their businesses globally.

"Hire people where no projects are below or above them," experienced former Uber launcher Sam Gellman explained when talking about building the right team. Team members need to be able to accomplish any tasks thrown their way, but most importantly, they must be able to handle it without having to go check with HQ to get guidance and permission at every turn. These needs align well with the interpreneurial skill set.

Along similar lines, Jennifer Yuen, formerly of Airbnb and Facebook, said the toughest thing about global growth is "getting the right team that can take you from zero to one to put you on the path to deliver on the full potential of that market. Getting people with the right skill sets, and traits such as honesty and transparency, is crucial. The right team is the key to understanding the company culture and translating it to resonate with consumers."

To assist in identifying Interpreneurs, companies often build their own archetypes to better uncover solid candidates.

Zoom targets hiring people who worked in Silicon Valley (or at least for a Silicon Valley company but in a satellite office) and then went back to their home country to build a career (a set of experiences that is probably more likely today with distributed teams and the move to virtual work). Similarly, DocuSign looks for people who have led expansion efforts before, representing an American company in their market and knowing how to serve as a bridge to HQ. In other words, they don't hire someone to grow into a role but someone whose experience would allow for the role to grow into that person.

Some companies are more prescriptive, adhering to an archetype of a local market lead, much as you can do with target customers. Gonzalo Begazo would look for young professionals seeking an experience that would build their resume and help them get into a top business school to launch new markets for Chazki. For Uber, this archetype was someone who was a former Bain consultant in their late twenties who graduated from a top US business school and had the capacity to be analytical and dive into the numbers. Uber's focus on Bain consultants was intentional, since Uber had seen that Bain employees were in their opinion "grittier" than their McKinsey counterparts and had a fierceness that paired well with company culture and an ability to take direct feedback without hurt feelings.

What not to do when building teams: Japan has a tenure-based ("next in line") culture, which can set up companies headquartered there to fail internationally. Rewards, status, and promotions are given to those who have been at the company a long time and have the right internal connections, something that bears no resemblance to the skills of effective international leaders outlined above. Another layer of complexity in the Japanese model is their approach of creating generalists by having employees change roles every third year, switching from accounting, for example, to business development. Although being a generalist can be a positive trait, a lack of foundation in functional areas and a lack of merit-based career progression can put the wrong leaders in key roles, especially if local knowledge isn't prioritized for international teams.

Conversely, Global Class Companies prioritize interpreneurial mindset over seniority. It may very well be that the right candidate doesn't have the longest tenure with the company or isn't as far along in their career. The story we heard of the account manager from Zoom who took the initiative to start building a customer base in LATAM early in the company's international expansion efforts is a great example of this. He took it upon himself to build a lead list of top prospects in the region to target and, after getting leadership approval, began building the foundation of Zoom's enterprise customer base in the region. Often more senior employees will be a poor fit for the local market lead role because they are used to having ample resources at their disposal at HQ, keeping them in their comfort zone. Local market leads have more to do with fewer resources and are constantly on the edge of or outside their comfort zones, which is why having an agile mindset is so important.

When building a team, it's also important to look at the team holistically, finding the right people to play key roles on the team that are best for that stage of growth. As Mads Faurholt, former Global Managing Director and Partner at incubator and company builder Rocket Internet, puts it, "We tend to try to find a person who can do every job function, but the truth is that selecting the right people is a bit like a football [soccer] team. You don't want a person that's good at everything. You want the best attacker, the best goalkeeper, and the best defender."

Enable Decentralized Talent Strategy

Legacy companies build clusters of talent focusing on building whole offices of people in specific geographic areas. If the company needs software engineering resources, for example, the strategy is to hire a whole development team centered in Bangalore, known as the Silicon Valley of India. Global Class Companies see a different path.

Far from rejecting the recent acceleration of distributed work, Global Class Companies see this change as an opportunity. They fully embrace the new distributed team-building world we now live in.

Global Class Companies hire talented individuals wherever they happen to be. They understand that talent no longer needs to be centralized at a single HQ location, nor does it need to be clustered in specific locations due to an abundance of a certain skill set in that area. They realize that it is liberating to be able to identify and onboard talent anywhere in the world. Since they aren't restricting themselves geographically, Global Class Companies are able to take advantage of the growth of knowledge workers across the globe, in developed and emerging markets, and find the best individuals.

Global Class Companies then leverage team members' local knowledge of their home country to better understand and ultimately gain entry into that market.

Moreover, Global Class Companies believe it is important to hire a diverse team that buys into company culture in order to build interconnectedness and avoid silos. This can lead to innovation (from having a more diverse way of looking at problems), fostering two-way innovation in particular, where local teams have as much influence as HQ.

Create the Right System for Success

Once the right team is in place, Global Class Companies activate their talent by providing them with processes and structures that create momentum and support scale.

This support can come in many forms. Thoughtworks was designed as a global-first organization. Key leadership principles and employee evaluations align with this viewpoint. More specifically, the company aims at having 20 percent of the employees in any given office work outside their home countries. Thoughtworks specifically sends employees on project-based assignments in other countries to gain international exposure. Team members enter a new country with a cross-cultural team to form a pod and find local leaders on the ground to be the foundational team at the office. After a year or two, the international group moves on to other assignments, being brought back to their respective home offices.

In creating these systems, HQ levels the playing field for all markets. In an organization where relationships exist, some markets are given an outsized voice because of local leadership's internal reputation and their knowledge of the inner workings of the company. Global Class HQs work hard to eliminate any bias for certain markets (including the market where HQ is located), creating systems to put all teams on equal footing.

OFTEN OVERLOOKED

Invest in Quality Local Resources

For knowledge workers, the time of cheap labor is waning fast. You need to realize that you get what you pay for. When entering a new market, don't get too caught up in the reduced cost of living and lower wages it might offer if you are headquartered in a market with a higher cost of living. You don't need to drastically overpay local resources, but providing competitive compensation is better than attempting to minimize cost. This applies to staff but especially applies to service providers like law-yers. Generally you pay a premium for a great attorney, which is more than worth it.

CASE STUDY

INTERPRENEURIAL RESILIENCE—SLACK

Every business, whether in a single country or worldwide, is, at its core, all about one thing: people. And not just related to their productivity as employees, but everything that comes along with it: the whole person. In this context, the most important trait for any Interpreneur to possess, especially those working away from their home country, is *resilience*. Global Class Companies recognize this and look for people who possess a fair share of resilience to overcome the obstacles on the road to expanding a business in new markets. At the same time, the Global Class understands that their people driving expansion in new markets aren't machines but are people with preexisting relationships and needs, and that they must support both the professional and personal lives of team members who are away from HQ growing the business.

As James Sherrett, Slack's first employee in EMEA and former head of the region, can attest, it is difficult to hire and manage a team, find traction, and achieve company-market fit; all of these come with failures that require grit to overcome. But personal resilience is also necessary.

Life didn't stop for James when he uprooted his life in North America to move to Europe, but the change in scenery and lifestyle didn't just affect him.

Keep in mind that some members of the team are disrupting their lives and moving away from family to be part of a company's global growth. While more tactical things like living arrangements and health care coverage need to be consid-ered, it is also essential to be conscious of the mental health of the people involved (both the employees and their families). It is difficult enough to navigate a new country to find company-market fit for the company, but this compounds when you are also dealing with the culture shock of being far from home and away from the familiar.

James's wife and young kids moved with him, but there were times when it was very hard to be so far away from home and extended family. At one point, James's dad was in poor health and James was an ocean away, having to plan Slack's regional strategy and make plans for his dad's health care coverage. There were similar feelings when his stepfather passed away while he was still living abroad.

As James points out, "We're all humans, and those [things related to family] are the things we remember when we look back. No one is going to have their involvement in [the company's] expansion initiative written on a tombstone."

The key is to help create an environment that supports the team in local markets, especially those far from home, and nurtures a sense of resilience to help the individual and whole team succeed. It is important for the local team to be resilient because without it, the momentum of the whole team would swing in the wrong direction, as failures would distract and decrease morale instead of exemplifying grit and using a tough situation to improve bonds within the team.

Global Class Companies have the right hiring frameworks to put the right people in the right roles and equip them with the right structures, tools, and mindset to be successful.

Once the right (interpreneurial) team is in place, the organization must be able to manage this distributed team through the market entry and market growth stages, navigating the complexities of localizing the business. The Global Class Management Model outlined in the next chapter is designed to provide the right framing so that organizations know just how to do it.

CHAPTER 8 SUMMARY

- People are the most important ingredient of successful global growth initiatives and must possess a combination of *Interpreneur mindset* and *leadership skills for distributed organization*, as well as *local knowledge* and *company knowledge*, an overlap of the latter two being most crucial.
- Since all traits may not be represented in one person, the *Global Class Team Building Framework* can help ensure that the collective local team has the skills and mindset to succeed in finding traction and then scale.
- Global Class Companies do the following to build world-class teams: *facilitate company/local knowledge overlap; select, nurture, and create Interpreneurs; enable decentralized talent; and create the right system for success.*

CHAPTER 8 REFLECTION & ACTION QUESTIONS

1. How are you ensuring your local teams have a strong overlap of company knowledge and local knowledge?
2. How are you identifying and developing diamond/unicorn people who fit all four team-building trait categories?
3. For those team members who don't have company knowledge, how are you instilling the company culture in them?

· 9 ·

MANAGEMENT
The Global Class Management Model

"T he key is to create an environment where ideas are exchanged without borders," Polly Sumner, Chief Adoption Officer of Salesforce, explained. "That goes for internal communications and connecting with customers."

Global Class Leaders at Salesforce understand the importance of effective two-way communication in building Trust (the company's #1 value). They also understand how setting up a management system that is conscious of culture allows for two-way innovation, putting everyone on equal footing—whether they are part of a local team or at HQ. With the proliferation of distributed work and digitally enabled workers, Global Class Companies understand that the traditional definition of HQ is a thing of the past.

To address this, the role of HQ must change to be more of an enabler that supports a federation of connected teams instead of a nexus that centralizes authority and control. Salesforce has codified the Global Class mindset in the form of what it calls its Digital HQ. The concept of enabling a virtual HQ manifests itself in the form of beliefs, norms, and processes that foster momentum (as discussed in chapter seven). Salesforce's values, culture, and structures allow the company to act quickly, identify innovation at the edges of the organization (in local markets), and act.

As Salesforce began to focus on building a stronger global presence, leadership saw the need to ensure the voice of the local market was heard by HQ, since innovation at the local market level was key to Customer Success (the company's #2 value). To amplify the local voice, Salesforce created a "Cultural Ambassador" program, calling on leaders across the business to help remove boundaries between HQ and local markets.

Leaders within Salesforce were assigned to key international countries to serve as a bridge to HQ. This closely matches the Global Class mindset on team building outlined in the previous chapter (in particular, the need for overlapping company knowledge and local knowledge).

In Japan, the cultural ambassador was an American executive who had lived in Japan as a young girl, nurturing the ability to bridge language and cultural gaps. With her help, the HQ Engineering team deepened their understanding of the needs of Japanese customers, and bridged both the language and cultural gaps.

In 2008, Salesforce acquired Instranet, a French software company led by Alex Dayon. Alex and Polly "swapped locations." Alex moved to San Francisco to lead the Salesforce Product team, and Polly took the role of cultural ambassador to France. She worked side by side with the newly formed sales and success teams in France. Polly combined her knowledge of the inner workings of Salesforce HQ with her experience in the Salesforce way of sales and customer success to accelerate the growth of the business in France.

Meanwhile, Alex brought international perspective and insight to Salesforce's engineering, delivery, and marketing teams located in San Francisco, and Innovation (the company's #3 value) flourished.

Salesforce's French customers received the same level of access/intimacy as a customer located in San Francisco, 7,500+ miles away, ensuring their success.

These bridges between HQ and local markets are paramount for companies to operate at the speed needed to meet ever-changing customer demand. They must also operate at scale and not create complexity by leading to additional localizations in every market.

As Salesforce illustrates, effective management at global scale involves balancing the core values set forth by HQ with the needs of the local market, establishing two-way communication and innovation through Feedback Loops, transparency, and empowering all employees and customers in local markets to improve the company worldwide.

In addition to building a strong team of globally minded Interpreneurs, Global Class Companies effectively implement a management model that is cognizant of culture and supports global scale while striking the right balance between influence from local markets and HQ.

This is why the second pillar of effective global scaling is implementing a system of management that facilitates international growth: the Global Class Management Model.

MANAGEMENT IN THE CONTEXT OF GLOBAL AGILE

For the agile methodology to thrive across a global organization, company leadership and management teams in local markets must create an iterative environment accepting continuous testing, failure, and pivoting away from established plans. While norms and decision rights (how decision-making is split between HQ and local teams) are agreed upon, there is a level of flexibility in each to account for the uniqueness of local culture, the demands of the local market, and corresponding autonomy merited given the stage of the global growth initiative, since each merits its own contingent approach.

A balanced management approach is required to effectively localize and create momentum without incurring too much complexity. Managing a distributed global team therefore requires a model that motivates and empowers local teams while still maintaining visibility and influence for HQ. Effective implementation of this management model is a catalyst for companies achieving company-market fit and global scale.

BUILDING A BRIDGE—THE GLOBAL CLASS MANAGEMENT MODEL (GCM MODEL)

In chapter two and throughout the book, we have discussed the importance of the Global Class mindset. Through the following management model, we outline a system for how to operationalize this Global Class mindset and turn leadership principles and strategy into an actionable process that can be used across a global footprint.

The metaphor of a bridge best encapsulates the details and spirit of how Global Class Companies manage a global footprint.

Gaps in culture and geography exist between HQ and the local office. When growing internationally, Global Class Companies are literally building bridges: between their brand and customers in another country; between their team at HQ and the local teams managing their presence with boots on the ground; between company culture and the culture of the local market.

In building these bridges, agile is the common language between HQ and local teams for Global Class Companies, which utilize strong channels of communication (Feedback Loops) and processes like the Localization Resource Team (LRT) and Global Growth Playbook outlined in chapter seven. Agile cuts across language and cultural divides to connect all parties with common goals and accepted processes.

The Bridge Framework

To better orient you, imagine a suspension bridge with shore on each end. The shore on the left is HQ, the support functions enabling a global organization that is becoming increasingly distributed/virtual. The shore on the right is the local market and its customers. A roadway with towers and suspension cables sits in between, connecting the two sides.

The Towers

The bridge in the model has two towers; the one on the left represents the structures and processes HQ establishes (Momentum Builders) to support the local team and create momentum. As outlined in chapter seven, this includes the Global Growth Playbook and the LRT, among other tools and resources that accelerate achieving product-market fit during market entry and achieving company-market fit and scale in market growth. The strength of the connection between these towers has a direct impact on the effectiveness of localization initiatives for that market.

The tower on the right represents the team supporting the local market (either in-market, regionally, or at HQ). Their local knowledge, paired with resources from corporate (the left tower), drives implementation of growth initiatives and localizations. The strength of the team's local market knowledge has a direct impact on the ability to find company-market fit and the effectiveness of growth initiatives.

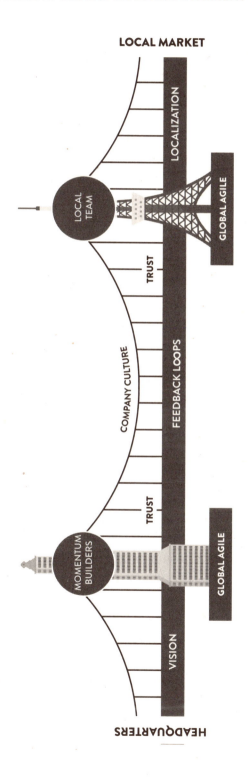

The global agile methodology serves as the cement foundation for the left and right towers, enabling the organization to find company-market fit and scale. The depth of the pylons under the towers represent how deep agile is rooted into the culture, processes, and norms of the organization. The deeper the foundation of agile, the more effective the organization will be in achieving global scale. You can build many structures and Feedback Loops, but without a fundamental understanding of the importance (as well as buy-in) of agile methodology in a global context, failure is more likely.

Just as with a real structure, if one tower is too weak, the bridge won't stand. That is why it is crucial to build a strong local team (right tower) who can effectively localize the business. HQ must dedicate ample resources, setting up structures (left tower) that are aligned with core values and strong communication collaboration between both parties (the roadway). This all must be aligned on common work principles, such as agile, to support the global growth efforts. At Salesforce, trust is number one and customer service is number two on the matrix, so company decision-making criteria have been built to align with both of these core values ahead of profitability. Establishing strong core values is paramount in international locations because the risk is higher. When issues arise in making key decisions, employees are taught to find solutions where these core values and profitability intersect. As Ernest Ng, Vice President of Employee Success Strategy and People Analytics at Salesforce, puts it, "If your customers are across different regions around the world, it is best to have a consistent culture and way of doing things."

The Roadway

The roadway in this model is where collaboration between HQ and local teams happens and where work gets done.

The portion of the roadway on the left that connects to HQ is the Company Vision and Core Values (which facilitates the structures represented in the left tower). All members of the organization, both at HQ and on local teams, need to truly understand the company vision and keep it as a North Star in all business activities. HQ sets this vision and is responsible for making sure the local teams understand and internalize its gravity and principles.

As Abe Smith from Zoom stated, "During busy and stressful times, a clear vision and core principles bring people together." Strong core values create a fertile environment for reflective leadership. Zoom's philanthropic values led the company's CEO, Eric Yuan, to offer millions of students free Zoom accounts so they could participate in school during the pandemic. He did so after mentally projecting himself twenty years into the future and asking himself whether at that point he would feel that doing this now was the right decision.

At the same time, you should recognize that there are both global and local values that may differ and this should be proactively managed. That is why it is important for Global Class Companies to universalize their core values, something that legacy companies don't do at their own peril and one of the top ten reasons why global businesses fail, as outlined in the first chapter.

Connecting the local *team* to the local *market* are the localizations (changes to the go-to-market or operating model) implemented to address market requirements. A strong team that has both company and local market knowledge facilitates effective localization, fostering deeper market penetration.

The span of road that connects both towers is the two-way communication and translation that occurs between HQ and local teams. This includes communication of key objectives and translation of the company vision from HQ to the local team, as well as results and insights relevant to the localization process from the local team to HQ. Translation includes navigating language and cultural differences between HQ and the local office, as well as differing points of view.

Effective Feedback Loops facilitate communication and translating, providing transparency and accelerating the company from market entry to market maturity. These loops sit at various points along the roadway connecting HQ and the local team. They help solve problems in a structured way and are an effective tool for building trust, rooted in regular communication. In reference to the need for a strong communication link between HQ and local offices, Scott Coleman, former Head of Growth and International Product at Pinterest, says that local teams will "die on the vine without access to [the] core." Formalized Feedback Loops can effectively facilitate this two-way communication.

The roadway part of the model is particularly important because it is where authority and responsibilities meet. This authority and responsibility for the continuous communication and translation must be shared between HQ and the local office; hence, communication must be two-way.

The multi-directional nature of feedback, communication, and translation is crucial, since HQ needs to understand the key learnings and progress being made in the new market, and the local team needs direction, resources, and feedback from HQ to support scaling. The roadway (and its Feedback Loops established by both parties) is also where localization work is done and complexity is created, and therefore must be actively monitored.

The goal of this collaboration along the roadway is the validated model for the new market, product-market fit during market entry, and then momentum and scale that lead to company-market fit through the market growth phase. In the process, HQ translates company culture into a form that resonates with the local market, and the local team translates the changes required to meet local market needs back to HQ.

The translation that must occur isn't just about the words used but also the processes set in place. For example, in some Asian countries that have a heavy reporting culture, a great deal of time and focus are spent on building formal reports to be sent up the chain of command. Whether they are reviewed in detail or not, these communication structures take focus away from the core goal of finding company-market fit and then scaling in the new country. This becomes a source of Admin. Premium. A team with a presence in the United States or another market with a different business culture must find a middle ground between these different communication styles and business cultures. The depth and extent of the structures to facilitate balance will depend on the organization's stage of growth. Start minimally (as Kathryn Hymes recommends in the chapter seven cash study) and then build more formality as you grow, without setting up obstacles and unnecessary bureaucracy for local teams that distracts them from achieving company-market fit. Effective communication is also key for maintaining a coalition of support at HQ. Christina Lee from Chegg points out that maintaining these coalitions is key to her success; because of this, she spends approximately 10 to 15 percent of her time on maintaining communication links with HQ to support her international teams' efforts to scale the business in new markets.

This is also true for maintaining support throughout an entire organization scattered across the globe. Not adapting communication to fit a distributed workforce is a mistake that leads companies aspiring to scale globally to failure.

That said, communication must be clear and concise. Zendesk has 200+ senior leaders, who can interpret a message in a variety of ways, depending on the lens they are viewing it through. This is why the company ensures that communications are focused and that the entire leadership team is aligned so that they can engage the rest of the company's 6,000+ person team around the same goals. Slack also does this through what James Sherrett referred to as "Summarizers and Simplifiers," which control the volume of information shared and highlight what is most important.

OFTEN OVERLOOKED

Navigating Time Zones

On a related note, just handling time zone differences for a global organization can be difficult. Finding a single time for team members scattered across the whole world to meet is a challenge in itself and can eventually create fatigue for local offices and HQ leadership alike. Be conscious of this and find ways to accommodate via meeting scheduling and team alignments. One of Microsoft's business units aligned local offices by time zone, not just region. Slack navigated the issue of time zones through its Small Hands Meetings system, where members from local teams in nearby regions met to share best practices without relying on HQ to facilitate communications, as referenced in the chapter seven case study (page 203).

The Cables

In this bridge analogy, the main horizontal cable holding up the bridge is company culture. As with a suspension bridge, the towers (Momentum Builders and the local team) uphold the cables (company culture), and the cables uphold the roadway. Like the cable on a bridge, culture is a common thread that holds everything together and bears the weight of all other elements of the management model. If the cable/company culture is not strong enough (or breaks), the bridge and model fall apart; you can visualize the famous collapse of the Tacoma Narrows Bridge last century. When a strong wind comes along (i.e., challenges), weak cables can snap and cause catastrophe. This merits repeating: *without a strong (and consistent) company culture, the whole structure falls apart.*

Suspension bridges like the famous San Francisco Golden Gate Bridge also have a system of smaller vertical cables that connect the main cable to the roadway. Related to international management, these smaller cables represent trust points.

Trust is a powerful extension of a strong culture and hence is one of the Four Commitments for Successful Global Growth. The presence of trust supports each part of the roadway from one end of the bridge to the other, as visualized by the vertical cables connecting the "culture cable" to the roadway and towers. While the main "culture cable" is singular, running through all parts of the model, these "trust cables" are numerous and exist over the entire span of the bridge.

Each local market lead must trust their team to execute; the local team must trust the LRT that supports their launch efforts; and so on. If any one point of trust (cable) breaks, the entire bridge can be destabilized, leading to other breaks and ultimately ending in collapse. Relationship-building rituals, along with strong Feedback Loops, build trust, support core values adoption, and further the alignment of the local market team with company culture.

As we learned from our conversations with former Airbnb executive Jennifer Yuen, physical distance makes it more difficult to create trust, leading to work being done in silos. It's important to create connections and a bridge back to HQ as well as directly among local teams and a distributed employee base. As Berkeley Haas faculty member Dan Himelstein puts it, "People want to work with people they like and respect. That is universal." This, along with structures to cultivate company culture, serves as the foundation for connections to be made.

Recall how the small cables running from the main cable to the roadway in our bridge diagram represent trust. As with a suspension bridge, the points of trust must exist all over the organization, between HQ and the local office and within the local office itself.

The trust points between the local market lead and the rest of the local staff are incredibly important as well. Depending on the office location, the level of comfort with transparency and trust will differ, as these are not typical in every business culture. Hiring the right local market lead is crucial so that these can be properly translated to the local market. High trust facilitates collaboration and the sharing of challenges, so problems can be addressed instead of brushed under the rug. As detailed in the chapter four case study about Flexport, the strong trust between COO Sanne Mander and Head of Europe Jan van Casteren was a catalyst for the company's success in entering European markets, finding initial product-market fit, and scaling to reach company-market fit.

That said, it's important to understand that there will be different levels of trust in each local market across the company's footprint because of preexisting relationships or performance. This can affect the power dynamic, giving more of a voice to those with stronger ties to HQ or those performing better. Make sure to monitor this so it doesn't hinder decision-making and resource allocation.

The strength of the bridge comes from commitments made by HQ and local market stakeholders. This includes commitments to transparent two-way communication, utilizing structures and processes established by HQ, upholding company culture, building trust (the cables of the bridge), and localizing for the market.

BUILDING THE BRIDGE BETWEEN HQ AND THE LOCAL MARKET

The Four Commitments for Successful Global Growth are the beginning of your expansion process, where both HQ and the local market can align on core operating principles. Ensuring support of these commitments confirms alignment on vision and resources while building trust and educating the local team on organizational culture.

Confirming alignment on the Four Commitments allows HQ to take on the new role of *enabler*, avoiding any of the issues that come from the legacy command-and-control management strategy and setting the foundation for future success.

The entire bridge structure in the GCM Model is built on the team's adherence to the Four Commitments.

For example, when HQ grants the appropriate level of autonomy to the local office, and it's paired with strong communications efforts by the local office, trust develops. Clarity and communication around the importance of performance metrics increase the likelihood that established goals are met. Communication around obstacles in local markets and necessary localizations fosters traction in new markets. The balance of localization and complexity through the global agile methodology leads to company-market fit. Strong resource alignment accelerates growth, and so on. The Global Class mindset facilitates the creation of a bridge between HQ and local teams, and through this mindset HQ understands its most effective role is to be an enabler and supporter of local teams instead of a command-and-control force lording over local teams. HQ's adoption of this enabler role and a management style that recognizes and adapts to differences between company and local cultures is a key driver for successfully managing a global organization.

The New Role of HQ

Global Class Companies are building a different dynamic between HQ and local teams, with management playing a different role. Legacy companies have maintained a command-and-control strategy where HQ acts more like a general giving marching orders to the local team. Global Class Companies understand that local teams are much more than just execution arms and that managers must engage and empower these teams in planning and strategy creation.

As mentioned in chapter one, the acceleration of distributed work has forever changed the notion of what "headquarters" is. HQ is now decoupled from a geographic home base. No more is it a single building or corporate campus where the entire power structure of a company physically sits. Employees of all levels, including company executives, now sit everywhere because of the acceptance of distributed and virtual work. Distributed workforces make communication more challenging but also potentially more equitable, especially for those not physically working out of a company office space.

This trend, in fact, makes it easier for companies to turn the role of HQ into an enabler and supporter of the localization and traction efforts being driven by the local team, as outlined in chapter two. No longer are team members in remote locations the only ones who have to adapt to better communicate and influence decision-making. HQ still sets the vision and core values (as referenced by the far-left span of roadway on the GCM Model bridge) but serves more as a coach removing obstacles and providing observations and insights that help the team sustain peak performance. HQ still must hire well, putting the right Interpreneurs in the best roles, but they also have to become stewards of the levers of autonomy.

Culturally Conscious Management

In the context of market entry and scaling in new global markets, management must be culturally conscious, and management tactics must consider norms in local markets. Whitney Bouck, former COO of Dropbox's HelloSign business unit, observes that Global Class Companies have a much more global management strategy by nature when HQ is no longer a single building in one geography and the initial market operations/functions are formally separated from HQ. Instead, the management model is shifting to a more distributed model, which necessitates more consideration of culture.

The third of the Four Commitments—Trust and Autonomy—is consistent with a culturally conscious management mindset. A core purpose of this mindset is to recognize and reinforce the value that local teams have in understanding the nuances of their market. Building trust and granting autonomy are the best ways to do this. Local knowledge is key to successful localization. Granting local teams autonomy not only empowers local teams but also better facilitates localization initiatives. Granting trust and autonomy also puts HQ in more of an enabler and supporter role where local practice adoption balances any command-and-control measures. Interpreneurs at HQ must be stewards of culturally conscious management, including translating management best practices into the local best practices.

Wrapped into this concept is the contingency approach to management, whereby management tactics differ depending on the situation the team is facing and the people involved. For example, established, high-performing teams in growth situations need to be managed differently than underperforming, newly formed teams. Culturally conscious management builds on this contingency approach and incorporates cultural factors.

Overall management techniques need to fit the local style. In some European countries like the Netherlands or Denmark, it is normal to be more direct with feedback, hitting problems head-on, while in Japan, employees are more comfortable with written feedback. Different cultures are used to certain business structures. Employees in many LATAM countries are more used to hierarchical management structures, compared to the flat organizational structure in Silicon Valley.

HQ-centric tendencies can be illuminated when culturally oblivious decisions are made, like grouping three wildly different regions—Europe, Africa, and the Middle East—together under centralized management and a singular grouping, EMEA. The culturally conscious management style of the Global Class builds a company culture and organizational structures that consider local nuances and don't wrap diverse regions together, treating them as homogenous. Klaus Holse, former CEO of SimCorp, shared a story about an experience he'd had with a former company working with a team in Japan. Klaus had to work with a local general manager (GM) who didn't agree with the way HQ wanted projects completed, but given that saving face and respecting authority are core tenets of Japanese business culture, the local GM couldn't openly argue with Klaus (who represented HQ). Instead, Klaus explained how, when he expressed any concern, the local GM, in a very public manner, would commit to fixing the problem. Unfortunately, when Klaus came back later to confirm resolution, the problems had only become worse.

The local team, under the guidance of the GM, intentionally made things worse to prove that their idea was better than HQ's, since openly disagreeing with HQ would be against local business culture. The experienced local market GM was fired because the company's senior executives didn't understand this cultural dynamic.

Afterwards, a young local GM was brought in, and he subsequently explained this cultural dynamic to Klaus and then offered a culturally acceptable solution: HQ and the local market lead (GM) would decide together on the best strategy and path forward, the local market lead would make sure the team would get things done, and then executives from HQ would come in and praise the local market lead. This worked well. Bottom line: the management model utilized in a company's headquarters market can't be successfully applied universally across a global footprint.

This story is a great example of the benefits of making the right hire (an Interpreneur who can translate both cultures) who can align with a strategy (the Four Commitments for Successful Global Growth) and localize the Global Class management style.

Global Class Companies then pair this culturally conscious management mindset with effective delineation of roles, responsibilities, and decision rights between HQ and local offices.

DECISION RIGHTS

One of the fundamental elements of any international management strategy is the process by which decisions are made; what decisions can the local team make independently, what requires joint agreement, and what should be controlled and dictated by HQ?

There is a logical rationale for placing certain decisions in the hands of either party, from minimizing localization premium through centralizing, to localizing to reach company-market fit through decentralizing; from having expertise to remove obstacles and see the global picture, to empowering local teams.

It is not for us to prescribe who should decide on pricing, performance review procedures, or marketing campaigns. Each company should decide what is best. The important point is to address the topic head-on. In our research, we heard this topic, packaged under the label of "decision rights" or "decision authority," mentioned over and over again. Regardless of where decisions are made, being transparent is important, since it will foster strong communication, trust, and engagement.

Developing a plan for decision rights brings transparency around what is often an opaque process. It helps bring structure to core values and makes it easier for both HQ and local teams to know when to take the lead and when to consult.

As one of the Four Commitments, trust and autonomy is important to many aspects of global growth. It is particularly necessary in delegating decision-making. Empowerment is a by-product of pushing decision authority to the local level, paired with a willingness at HQ to accept failure (which is in line with the global agile mindset). Trust is core to empowerment, as is creating a sense of meaning and purpose within the local team. More than anything, local team empowerment is a by-product of HQ forgoing command-and-control styles in favor of an enabler and supporter role. Local team engagement doesn't come from complete autonomy, however. Even when HQ creates boundaries, people tend to feel empowered when given a container to move fluidly in, versus not having clarity on who decides what.

Along the way, HQ and local teams meet at different points on the roadway of the bridge in the GCM Model. Depending on company stage and maturity of a local market presence, decisions are made closer to HQ or the local market. Teams need to adapt decision rights along the way, swinging back and forth along the road depending on market stage (entry, growth, or maturity), company culture, and other factors—all of which should be aligned with the Autonomy Curve discussed in chapter four

Companies that always defer to HQ can be less effective at localizing. At the same time, deferring too much to the local team will incur too much complexity. A balance is needed. Companies must find a local way of doing things instead of relying on the company way. At the same time, they must set up guardrails to ensure continuity with HQ, which has a global purview.

The Pendulum Revisited

Just as with the Job Function Pendulum, a pendulum exists in the realm of decision rights. Where you place decision rights is a strategic decision that drives the pendulum, and favoring these rights toward HQ or the local team changes over time.

You can grant varying levels of autonomy to international teams for many aspects of your business; there is no right answer. Uber and Apple were at opposite ends of the spectrum in terms of international management during early expansion, the former granting near full autonomy to local offices, the latter maintaining a more centralized control structure. Both can work. Keep in mind, though, as Scott Coleman put it: "There is little empowerment for the local team if they are told exactly what to do by HQ."

As Jose Chapa, former Director of Product for Amazon's Home Innovation Program in Europe, points out, there is often a complex network of internal organizations gathering inputs to create their outputs, which then travel to other teams and become their inputs. In other words, organizations within a company are interconnected and information flows organically. If there is no centralized visibility or process, then bureaucracy, complexity, and silos lead to issues. It's important to centralize things that need scale. This applies to decision rights, among other processes and structures designed to build momentum (as discussed in chapter seven).

Centralizing some of these decisions can level the playing field, since, as mentioned, it is typical for a company in multiple geographies to favor some markets over others and give the teams in favored markets an outsized voice because of the trust developed with HQ.

At the same time, a case can be made for moving responsibility to local markets, since, as Jorn Lyseggen, CEO and founder of Meltwater, puts it, "The farther from the problem, the dumber the solution," and HQ is often farther from the problem than the local team, especially as it relates to changes that need to be made to scale in a local market.

That said, HQ should be an enabler instead of a commander. As Chang Wen Lai, CEO and co-founder of Singapore-based Ninja Van, puts it, "Headquarters is not a control tower; it's the underground cables helping the company run."

Mapping Out Decision Rights

The distribution of responsibilities is very particular to a company's industry, customer base, target markets, and stage of growth. The only thing we do urge, based on insights from our research, is that the distribution of control and decision-making authority should be driven by (and aligned with) your company culture and core values. This, and that decision rights should be transparent and openly communicated across the organization.

Time and time again we have been reminded about the importance of culture (as discussed in the next chapter). Whatever your culture may consist of, it is (and should be) a driving force behind how you manage your global presence.

Allowing autonomy can also generate momentum and build morale. As long as you have the right support structure, such as a Localization Resource Team, autonomy in targeted areas of operations can create quick wins that serve as oxygen for the engagement and commitment of a nascent local team.

Jennifer Cornelius, Chief People Officer at Ritual and former Head of Organization Design for Apple's Retail Division, says, "The more often you can delegate your team to make the more significant decisions, the greater the learning is, and the greater the engagement is in the long term."

As we quoted Tiffany Stevenson saying earlier, "Autonomy allows for scale to happen," not only early on but over a longer period of time. Autonomy does not give complete freedom to the local team, but it keeps HQ from getting bogged down in the details, taking focus away from more strategic initiatives across the company.

HQ may also need to fight cultural norms to get local teams to accept and utilize autonomy. While hopefully this is mitigated by hiring local leaders with the traits outlined in the last chapter, some cultures resist speed by nature.

In Japan, decision-making is often group-based. In the context of managing a local team in Japan, it may mean that the local team is less inclined to make decisions on its own without guidance or approval from HQ. This cultural norm can benefit organizations during market growth when alignment and managing complexity are important for creating momentum, but this mindset may slow down momentum during market entry. To overcome a local nuance like this, HQ must communicate the importance of using autonomy, showing support when local leadership takes ownership, even if mistakes are made.

To answer a question that Scott Coleman, formerly of Pinterest and Google, posed ("How do you create some level of control?")—for the local office, being granted autonomy creates control. For HQ, providing clarity around core values and guardrails around internationalization and uniformity balances control.

A balance is needed. Maintaining a command-and-control, HQ-centric viewpoint will hinder effective localization in the same way that favoring local offices will force companies to manage a plethora of disparate models that are both hard to manage and scale. Companies must find a local way of doing things instead of relying on the company way, but at the same time they must set up guardrails to ensure continuity with HQ.

CASE STUDY

MANAGEMENT FAMILIARITY BIAS—MICROSOFT

The Familiarity Bias mentioned in the LPA case studies not only can affect market selection but can impact management as well. This is especially true when managing a distributed team spread across the globe. Such was the case for Scott van Vliet, former Corporate Vice President of Intelligent Communications at Microsoft.

Sitting in Microsoft's Redmond, Washington, HQ, Scott managed teams in the EMEA and APAC regions, as well as a team less than 150 miles away in Vancouver, Canada. In managing a virtual team, Scott understood the importance of face time and exposure to leadership in managing a distributed team. Teams in local markets don't have the same visibility into what is happening at HQ as the leadership team at HQ does.

He understood that the best way to deal with the asymmetric visibility into company operations and decision-making between HQ and remote teams is to level the playing field and foster an environment of fairness. Scott did this effectively by building an inclusive culture. He also spent a significant amount of time visiting his teams on other continents, ensuring they were getting the kind of face time that was not typical for teams so far away.

There was only one problem. In all of his efforts to bring together teams from the far reaches of the globe, he neglected the team right under his nose, less than 150 miles away in Vancouver. Companies entering new markets often give proximity an outsized bias, but the opposite can happen when managing teams. As it was with Scott, there is a tendency to think that distributed team members nearby (geographically, culturally, and in spoken language) don't need as much support or guidance in reaching team goals. This is not the case.

As Scott points out, "Proximity can make you complacent or ignorant to differences." Given how close the Vancouver office was, he skipped visiting the office when doing quarterly visits everywhere else. Overlooking the differences and not treating the office as distinct hurt the relationship with the team there. They spoke the same language, but in fact there were many differences between the two nearby locales.

Scott was able to eventually right the ship and get his local team back on track. He would never again forget that they still needed the same attention and guidance as someone half a world away.

GLOBAL CLASS MANAGEMENT BEST PRACTICES

As the Chinese proverb goes, "The mountains are high, and the emperor is far away." Managing a global organization is difficult, and not just because of long distances and time zone differences. Effectively managing a multinational organization takes a certain set of skills and management principles to best fit the complexities of the management use case.

Here are the top ten best practices effective managers at Global Class Companies use to establish and maintain a strong bridge across borders.

Best Practices for Building Bridges to Manage Across Borders Include:
- Vision and Core Value Alignment
- Culturally Conscious Management
- Balance Localization and Complexity
- Building a Team of Interpreneurs
- Effective Communication
- Balancing Autonomy and Speed
- Transparency and Trust
- Localized Empowerment
- Prioritization and Focus
- Removing Obstacles

Vision and Core Value Alignment

While important in any management scenario, vision and core value alignment are paramount when managing an international organization because leaders have to navigate both physical distance and cultural differences. It is important that managers constantly repeat core values and tie them into decision-making. Creating a clear set of leadership principles helps international staff members understand appropriate behavior and form good habits.

OFTEN OVERLOOKED

First-Line Managers Are the True Drivers of Company Culture

Remember that first-line managers are the most important translators of company culture. Core value alignment needs to be present for hiring at all levels (not just at the executive level), and these lower-level managers must have the support they need to communicate the culture and ensure adherence.

Culturally Conscious Management

As discussed earlier in the chapter, culturally conscious management is a style rooted in the interpreneurial mindset. It allows leaders to navigate cultural differences and nuances to make adjustments that respect culture and drive better results. Empathy is at the core of this management style. This is in stark contrast to the classic image of a self-confident American company coming in and deciding that things can only be done the company way (like the way Walmart made German shoppers uncomfortable by insisting that a friendly and smiling staff did things the Walmart way). The core ingredient of culturally conscious management is found where cultural intelligence and emotional intelligence intersect—Cultural EQ. It means leading with empathy and understanding while also being able to navigate differences. Moreover, this management style can reduce Org. Premium as the organization grows.

Balance Localization and Complexity

As discussed in a number of chapters, balancing the localizations implemented in new markets with the complexity each creates is a cornerstone of global agile and a skill of Global Class Companies. Not creating this balance will lead to a difficult management scenario when the company is operating in multiple countries and managing multiple models, hindering momentum and scale.

Building a Team of Interpreneurs

As discussed in the last chapter, team building is the most difficult task companies scaling globally face. Effective teams hire based on characteristics and company culture fit over experience (guided by the Global Class Team Building Framework). Remember that companies that build the wrong team of people often fail at implementing global growth strategies and lose time and money along the way.

Effective Communication

Communication can be a catalyst for success or an obstacle that creates failure (which is why communication and clarity is one of the Four Commitments and a key function in the GCM Model). This is true for any domestic organization but is even more so with international organizations because of the extra layer of translation that exists; not only language translation but cultural translation as well. Successful interpreneurial leaders are able to facilitate effective communication.

CASE STUDY

MANAGING A DISTRIBUTED TEAM—APPLE

Once Feedback Loops are established, it is important for leaders to hone their skills from the right side of the Global Class Team Building Framework—company knowledge and leadership skills.

Whether you are leading a local team in-market or overseeing team members from afar, company knowledge is crucial to your ability to be a conduit to HQ, securing resources and buy-in, navigating internal bureaucracy to get things done, or communicating changes necessary to scale in a local market.

The next important elements are the leadership skills listed in the Global Class Teambuilding Framework, none more important than the one listed at the top of the Leadership Skills for Distributed Organizations list (on page 222). Effective communication is one of the most important tools for harnessing a distributed team and empowering them to reach lofty goals.

Leadership (both at the HQ level and local office level) sets the tone for communication. Besides a clear message, one of the other ways effective managers set the right tone is by being visible.

When overseeing Apple's worldwide market presence, former Vice President of International John Brandon facilitated distributed communications through various virtual channels, but he also included in-person communications.

John's strategy included the following four touchpoint methods, which helped him run a global organization that drove more than $100 billion in annual revenue.

1. **Quarterly visits**—As John puts it, it's important to "get mud on your boots." He made an effort to schedule in-person visits in every major market on a quarterly basis.

2. **Team-led business reviews**—With a member of the sales finance team at his side, he would have the local teams present their updates, specifically mandating that all members of the team be present, not just the general managers (GMs), so that he could build a relationship with all levels of the local team.

3. **Annual all-hands meeting**—When getting the entire organization together, he would make sure that key messages were being heard directly from the top and not translated through the reporting structure.

4. **Weekly one-on-ones with GMs**—John established a set meeting time each week with every one of his GMs. No matter what time zone he was in, the meetings would occur at the same time each week and would allow for a cadence between him and his direct reports. Through these regular touchpoints, which generally had an open agenda that gave the GM the floor to ask for help in running their business, he was able to develop a deep knowledge of local office issues and build trust through offering advice and transparency.

This strong communication plan accomplished a few productive things:

- Allowed John to confirm culture and core value alignment within each market.
- Gave local employees a sense that they were important and valued.
- Provided reminders to employees about "how we are going to think and behave," as John puts it.
- Presented early indications of challenges and obstacles.
- Showed him what was happening in the market and allowed him to connect directly with employees below his GM direct reports.

Digital tools help engage a distributed workforce, but being physically present is still an effective management strategy for a global footprint. Global Class Companies effectively leverage digital tools to connect and engage distributed teams; however, there continues to be a value in face-to-face human interactions (especially in helping local teams develop company knowledge and in HQ gaining local knowledge). Even with many effective technology tools that allow virtual distributed teams to thrive, some things should be done in person.

Maintaining a globally distributed team creates disparities in face time with employees at HQ or in more convenient time zones getting more of a chance to interact with the company's leadership team. It's important to be mindful of the advantage some employees have being at HQ versus those at a local office. Differences in business culture and respect for hierarchy can make these disparities even more pronounced. Heini Zachariassen, Vivino's founder and former CEO, ensures that virtual face-time sessions are facilitated between the global leadership team and local teams, allowing distributed workers to have direct communication with HQ leaders.

The regular cadence referenced in the Apple case study above applies to all levels of the organization: from the LRT to the local market lead, then to the rest of the local team and between themselves. Efforts should be made to ensure communication channels and Feedback Loops exist at all levels, both virtually and face-to-face.

Balancing Autonomy and Speed

As we've said throughout this chapter, one of the main elements to balance between HQ and the local office is autonomy. The topic elicited different responses in our conversations with executives. Those with personal experience in a local office tended toward more autonomy, while those who only had experience working on international expansion at HQ went for less. Nevertheless, all agreed it is an important factor that needs to be proactively managed with intentionally built processes to support the chosen level of autonomy. In practice, autonomy, which is directly correlated with control, is a lever that can be shifted depending on the stage of global growth, as illustrated through the Autonomy Curve concept outlined in chapter four. The topic of how much autonomy to grant to local teams is best characterized as answering the question, What should the local office have the ability to drive?

A related factor is speed of execution, which is often directly proportional to autonomy. The more autonomy given by HQ, the faster the local team can act on local market dynamics, unless alignment between HQ and the local team is lacking, leading to a breakdown in communication.

Transparency and Trust

Transparency about how and why decisions are made can foster trust between HQ and a local office, even when there is no local team input. Effective communication is the main vehicle that enables this. Trust points throughout the organization allow for effective implementation of operational and go-to-market strategy (the two-halves of the LPA), and help facilitate customer engagement and how the brand is viewed in the local market.

Localized Empowerment

Ignited by trust and autonomy, empowerment leads teams to take action and achieve results. From a management practice perspective, empowerment starts with motivation. As Aaron highlighted in his book *The Young Professional's Guide to Managing,* "At its core, motivation comes from belief . . . Generally motivation comes from external sources. Empowerment, on the other hand, is self-generated. It develops when someone believes deeply in what she is doing." Moreover, "When you empower people you give *them* the power and authority to achieve."

Along those lines, he provides the following formula to translate an employee's internal motivation into empowerment: Start with impact. If you allow an employee to have impact, they will be more engaged. That engagement leads to fulfillment, which in turn generates empowerment. Finally, in a circular fashion, this empowerment generates more self-initiated impact.

Prioritization and Focus

Given that there are limited resources and much to do, it is important to direct the local team's efforts toward the most impactful areas. Prioritization and focus facilitate this and provide the most likely path for success, which is why they were highlighted as core tenets of the Global Class mindset (see chapter two). Strong planning and prescriptive communications, like the strategies outlined above, as well as tools like the Global Growth Playbook, can create and remind the team of the areas of focus. The resource alignment commitment should support the main areas of focus and set guardrails, facilitated by the Localization Resource Team (LRT).

Removing Obstacles

As Aaron also highlights in his book *The Young Professional's Guide to Managing*, one of the often-overlooked roles of management is to remove obstacles. Other roles of management, like setting a vision and motivation, get much more airtime, but removing obstacles is a hidden tool that the best managers use. Doing this keeps the team focused, creates momentum, increases job satisfaction (and ultimately retention), and helps the team overcome adversity. Feedback Loops are one of the most effective tools for uncovering the obstacles and providing status on how they are being removed.

In the international context, these obstacles can take many forms, ranging from HQ bureaucracy (processes that hinder local autonomy), a shortage of adequate resources, or some cultural conflict with the current operating model that must be adapted to gain traction.

When they have the right team in place, effective managers know they should just get out of the way and let their team perform. Removing operational challenges allows the organization to achieve its potential. This is well aligned with the Global Class school of thought that HQ is an enabler and supporter, not a command-and-control dictator.

• • •

The goal of the GCM Model is to facilitate effective localization during market entry and effective momentum and scale in market growth and maturity phases, built on a foundation of global agile, all while controlling complexity along the way.

Through the use of the GCM Model (a strong bridge between HQ and local markets) and the effective use of the management best practices outlined in this chapter, Global Class Companies can develop a robust communication and feedback structure, control localization premium, create momentum, and, most importantly, drive results and scale, all while balancing core tenets like autonomy, trust, direction setting, and upholding company culture and core values.

Effective localization leads the way to company-market fit in a new market. Effective team building puts the right team in place to succeed at localizing and finding company-market fit. Effective management further facilitates company-market fit through creating empowerment within the team. Then, there is the final facilitator of company-market fit, the pillar that holds all of these other elements (and the whole company) together: culture.

CHAPTER 9 SUMMARY

- Global Class Companies utilize a management model (the *Global Class Management Model, GCM Model*) that builds a bridge between HQ and local teams, facilitating each stage of global scaling: market entry, market growth, and market maturity.
- The sharing of decision rights is an important indicator of the balance between HQ and local teams and dictates the role each plays.
- Global Class Companies build these bridges through a set of ten best practices that help them manage a distributed global organization: Vision and Core Value Alignment, Culturally Conscious Management, Balance Localization and Complexity, Building a Team of Interpreneurs, Effective Communication, Balancing Autonomy and Speed, Transparency and Trust, Localized Empowerment, Prioritization and Focus, and Removing Obstacles.

CHAPTER 9 REFLECTION & ACTION QUESTIONS

1. How is your organization managing decision rights between HQ and local teams? How have you mapped them out?

2. How have you built trust points throughout your organization?

3. What management best practice resonates most with you? Which do you/your organization need to work on? Which are you/your organization the best at?

· 10 ·

CULTURE
Balancing the Three Layers of Culture

After DocuSign validated and scaled its business in the United States, the team set its sights on international markets, seeing that the value proposition of its e-signature platform also resonated across borders as the company gained traction in multiple markets.

Japan, however, presented a challenge in DocuSign's quest to convince the world to stop using handwritten signatures, primarily because as a society the Japanese never really handwrote signatures in the first place. For centuries, Japan maintained a non-written signature system with *hankos*, carved stamps unique to each person.

Besides maneuvering the complexities of a different signature system, DocuSign also had to navigate the distinct cultural norms in Japanese society. Japan is a good example of a unique local culture, and companies attempting to penetrate the economically mature market have to localize more there than in many other places.

While localization for many companies centers on Org., Admin., Infrastructure, Sales and Marketing Premium, DocuSign's localization in Japan was clearly Product Premium driven.

If DocuSign had maintained a legacy (company way) mindset, their approach would have involved positioning e-signature as a way of the future, prioritizing disruption over cultural consciousness in an attempt to overcome the inertia of a system they labeled as archaic and in need of change.

Instead, DocuSign did something that many business leaders today would think illogical. Former Chairman and CEO Keith Krach decided to partner with Japanese physical hanko-maker Shachihata to make a digitized version of the hanko.

Why would a company with a digital product pay to partner with a physical stamp manufacturer? Because Keith, a savvy Interpreneur who had previous business experience in Japan, understood the importance of establishing cultural credibility and honoring trading in the market.

The deal itself was sealed on a cultural connection. After an evening of dinner and drinks with a key executive decision-maker at Shachihata who barely spoke English, a spontaneous decision on the taxi ride back to the hotel led the group to a karaoke box. The DocuSign team's version of Kyu Sakamoto's world-renowned song "Sukiyaki," followed by Shachihata's rendition of Tony Bennett's "I Left My Heart in San Francisco" (where DocuSign's HQ is located), solidified the partnership (and proved the importance of localizing your karaoke skills).

The results were clear and immediate. In a short period of time, Japan became one of DocuSign's top international markets. Because of their cultural sensitivity, DocuSign was well positioned to continue its growth as the Japanese government launched digital transformation initiatives that included a war on paper in order to create efficiencies combating the country's shrinking workforce due to its aging population.

Many business leaders would agree that company culture is the secret sauce that drives a company and all of its employees in global growth initiatives and beyond. **This is why the third, and arguably the most important, pillar of effective global scaling is balancing culture.**

While the hundreds of companies we researched had many differences in their products, target markets, and pathways to international growth, all of them, without exception, believed in the power of culture. Every single one had a strong and unique company culture that guided the organization on its journey to global success. Culture quite literally permeates every corner of this book. In fact, at its core, this entire book is about culture.

All of these companies translated their culture into core values and principles that were understood by all employees across geographies. These values were repeated often and became internalized by all levels of the organization. Culture serves as a common language, allowing HQ and local teams to communicate without the need for translation.

WHY CULTURE MATTERS

Each Interpreneur had their own way of saying it:

"Culture fit trumps skill set fit," stated Tiffany Apczynski, former Vice President of Public Policy and Social Impact at Zendesk. "You can put lawyers on legal issues, but you can't pay yourself out of cultural issues," explained Hiro Rodriguez, formerly of DocuSign.

"Culture eats strategy for breakfast," Peter Drucker, father of modern management, famously stated.

Former Apple executive John Brandon explains that the combination of core values, culture, and priorities, along with Cultural EQ, is a great guide because it "tells you what is and isn't important."

No matter how you say it, it all translates to the primacy of culture. **Effective global growth starts and ends with culture.**

Culture affects everything within an organization. Company culture materializes in a company's product, its brand, employee behavior, and how the business operates. That is why company culture runs from end to end in our Global Class Management Model (GCM Model); it is the main suspension cable between Momentum Builders and the local team (the bridge's towers) supporting the entire bridge. Company culture drives the level of localizations you implement to reach company-market fit in new markets and how you build your local team and create guardrails for decision-making. Without this strong culture running throughout, the whole effort to scale would fail, much as a bridge would fall.

The same goes for culture in local markets. Local culture affects everything from how to communicate with customers, what appeals to them, and how they make decisions. Culture reveals itself in many ways: in customs and traditions, in food and in laws, in habits and in mindsets. Thoughtworks CEO, North America, Chris Murphy even goes as far as to say, "Language is a manifestation of culture and cultural norms," with vocabulary, formality, and cadence providing a window into the thought process, values, and culture of those speaking it.

"Culture is dynamic," former Head of Airbnb's Americas and APAC Marketing Jennifer Yuen exclaims, keying in on how culture isn't a static thing to be mastered once. Global Class Companies study culture (their own and those in local markets) to ensure ongoing alignment. Troy Malone, who has extensive experience expanding businesses in Asia, still conducted localization discovery in South Korea recently, although he previously lived and launched businesses there. When questioned, he explained that while he understood the market from past experience, it had been five years since he last launched a business there, so he needed to understand how the local culture and market dynamics had changed since; such is the Interpreneur's mindset.

To be successful in reaching company-market fit and building a global organization, you must understand and balance the various types of culture at play.

Important Disclaimer About Culture

We are far from experts on culture (there is extensive research done by others on the topic), but in our own research we saw time and time again how important culture was to running a global business and to properly localizing. With that in mind, our discussion of culture isn't meant to be a deep analysis, and our intention is to provide a way to frame the topic of culture to help you approach it in the context of running a global organization. We recognize there are many viewpoints and sensitivities around culture and don't mean to prescribe any specific way of thinking beyond making two key points: (1) the importance of culture can't be overstated, and (2) we believe that diversity of thought, opinion, and experience is like oxygen for Global Class Companies, essential for reaching global scale. We hope that this chapter provides some insights and framing for how to think about the topic.

THE THREE LAYERS OF CULTURE

Companies understand their initial market and its culture well. Laws are more familiar; attitudes and beliefs are understood, if not aligned. This makes the leap to achieving company-market fit much more straightforward, if not easier.

When you add in other unfamiliar layers, go-to assumptions must be thrown out the window, requiring a different reference point. This is the case when scaling in international markets. While important at every stage, the importance of culture grows as your company enters the market growth stage, when the organization grows in local markets as you move past product-market fit toward company-market fit and must build the structures to support a multi-country operation at scale.

When growing globally, the three layers of culture that should both coexist and balance each other are:

- **Local Market Culture**—the shared beliefs, behaviors, and norms of the local population in a specific target country or region
- **Local Business Culture**—the shared beliefs, behaviors, and norms of a specific country or region that affect how business is conducted and how the local team operates in a professional environment. Local business culture is one of a number of subsets within local market culture
- **Company Culture**— the shared beliefs, behaviors, and norms of an organization that guide how employees communicate, make decisions, and create and implement strategy

In this chapter we will discuss all three, as well as a fourth later on that has recently emerged. The goal is to balance all three of these culture types and find a way to make your company's culture fit within the local market.

When Local Market Culture Conflicts

Local market culture is the key driver behind how people in a local market think, act, and make decisions. It's the powerful engine that necessitates most of the changes a business must make to its model (incurring every type of localization premium—Marketing, Sales, and Product Premiums in particular) when seeking traction and company-market fit in a new market. In some respects, local market culture also drives the laws and regulations within a country (affecting Admin. Premium), as local market culture has a strong effect on a country's social institutions.

Global Class Companies seek to understand how buying decisions are made, what the decision-making criteria is, the most important benefits, relevant use cases for target audiences in the market, and habits of your target customer. In the process of uncovering this information, they gain many insights about the local culture and how it may differ from other markets the company is in. For example, the concept of getting "fresh air" is very different in Japan versus South Korea, as described in chapter seven.

Global Class Companies also take the time to understand local market culture and what is important to local people. Showing respect for local market culture through adopting local cultural practices and communication styles with current and potential customers, versus clinging to the company way, will go a long way in building local connections to your brand.

The practice of physically being in the market (as during the localization discovery) and interacting with everyday people provides a rich look into what life is really like there. The nuances of local market culture necessitate having local knowledge expertise within the team, as discussed in chapter eight.

Global Class Companies pay particular attention to local trends and government interventions that drive behavior in a market, creating opportunities to tap into. Recall how DocuSign saw the aging workforce and corporate digital transformation (zero paper policy) as a catalyst for getting adoption in the Japanese market (the first being a shift in local market culture and the second being a shift in business culture).

Some Global Class Companies take the process of connecting with the local market culture one step further by building personality behind their brands and finding ways to integrate their products into the cultural zeitgeist. In Vietnam, Heineken connected its beers to the country's most popular holiday, Tết (its lunar new year), by creating a cultural ritual where people from urban areas would bring beer to relatives in rural areas. The practice became so ingrained that Vietnamese people embraced Heine*ken* as their own and even nicknamed the Dutch brand "Ken."

CASE STUDY

FINDING CULTURAL UNDERSTANDING AT THE BATTING CAGES—DAN HIMELSTEIN

Dan Himelstein, lecturer in global business and former Executive Director of the undergraduate program at UC Berkeley's Haas School of Business, was on his interpreneurial journey in the late 1980s, working in sales for a semiconductor distribution start-up when he landed a role in Japan. He was living in the Shinjuku district of Tokyo and, as a former baseball player, found solace and a slice of home by frequenting a 24-hour batting cage nearby. His days would consist of a full workday, followed by dinner, drinks, and karaoke sessions. At around 3 AM he would find himself being the only non-Japanese native at the batting cages, along with hospitality and food service workers who had finished a long night of work.

While this might seem unlikely, it was there at the batting cages where Dan ended up learning more about Japanese business culture than in the boardroom. Through broken Japanese and nonverbal communication, Dan was able to not only immerse himself more in the culture of Japanese people but also get feedback on mistakes he made in certain work situations. He learned proper business etiquette from the locals, who would give him advice on how to eliminate faux pas and help him solve some of the problems he was having due to differences in business cultures.

One thing he learned from the batting cages was how many of the Japanese executives at the time were World War II veterans. They harbored animosity toward the United States because of the emotional scars they carried, often causing them to be standoffish. This understanding informed Dan's behavior and gave him perspective in some of the situations he experienced at work, helping him improve his abilities to sell to Japanese executives.

In B2B sales situations, cultural curiosity and expertise are differentiators that help when you have less leverage or are on equal footing with a competitor. It is the soft skills—relationships, nonverbal nuances, and insights into a culture— that make a difference. People want to work with people they like and respect, and people who immerse themselves in all aspects of a culture (as successful Interpreneurs do).

As Dan puts it, "Talking to the everyday person is critical to effectively working with the CEO."

When Local Business Culture Conflicts

Local business culture is a manifestation of local market culture and the beliefs and mindset of the local population. The unique way business is conducted can present challenges and opportunities for companies planning to build a local presence. It drives decision-making and strategy and dictates how team members interact with each other and customers.

Differences in how business is done in various countries range from the small and customary to the broad and mindset related. There can be small nuances in processes or larger core value conflicts. Having a keen understanding of how business is done locally is helpful for building relationships with key stakeholders and showcasing cultural sensitivity can be an effective way to attract local talent to join your team.

The examples of these differences are plentiful. In some parts of Europe, it's typical for employees to know each other's salaries, while salary transparency is not as common in the United States. There is a hierarchy of Turkish businesses, with eight families controlling many local industries, and if you are accepted by one of them you are often accepted by the entire business community by and large. As previously referenced, the Thoughtworks team learned that in China it is customary for the final invoice not to be paid as an investment in the business relationship for future deals.

Meetings have their own set of norms and rituals. Many business professionals with experience working in Asia are familiar with the two-handed business card passing as a custom, as is providing a small gift from home when traveling to meet with someone. Mirroring these practices is often appreciated, which is why we often travel with a suitcase full of San Francisco Ghirardelli chocolates when visiting international clients. Communicating understanding by adopting these and other traditions shows commitment to the market and tends to strengthen business relationships.

OFTEN OVERLOOKED

There's No One-Size-Fits-All Relationship-Building Strategy

The effective approach to building a business relationship varies by region and country. In some parts of Europe, there can be a tendency to get right down to business, while in some Latin American countries, relationships often start with more personal sharing and "getting to know you" conversations. Regardless of the timeline of relationship-building, it's important to note that while it may seem that a formal meeting is where relationships are made and where deals get done, get-togethers outside of the office are where the deeper business and relationship building happen in many business cultures, as seen in the DocuSign/Deutsche Telekom partnership case study in chapter five.

Work hours can also differ drastically from country to country, something that needs to be clearly understood when selecting markets, building out a team, and forecasting future results. Ethan Evans, formerly of Amazon, found that different local business cultures upheld different sets of values and work ethics. While Amazon's US-based culture resembles a "holy quest" that requires endless hours of work per week, some countries have a culture where everyone goes home at 5 PM. This difference in business cultures could lead to brutal clashes between HQ and local teams. For many American employees, your work is your identity, pride, and priority, which doesn't always align with other local business cultures, making it harder to build a team globally that fits with the company culture. Conversely, in Scandinavia, having a balance between work and family is core to the local culture.

Referencing the Global Class Management Model (GCM Model) shared in the last chapter, Ethan explained that when the local business culture and company culture don't align, that weakens the cables (company culture and trust points) supporting the entire international company structure. He also warned that these differences in work culture often don't surface right away and may eventually surface in year two, when problems are harder to fix.

Bosses and management play various roles in different business cultures. Dawn Sharifan from Slack had to learn through experience how intimidating it could be for Indian employees when an executive comes to visit, putting the team on edge given the local business culture. Dawn learned that being present in local markets unlocks trust and that it's important to build a relationship and rapport before visiting a local office with this kind of business culture to be seen as accessible.

While growing Apple's retail presence in China, Jennifer Cornelius saw how differently feedback was shared there than in the United States. She identified that the cultural norm of "saving face" and protecting the boss impacted the feedback process. The culture of saving face often leads employees to withhold their true opinions in order to respect hierarchy.

China's business culture is void of any "gray area" around certain decisions. Priority is given to plan execution and listening to authority. Similarly, getting employees to share feedback, speak up, and feel "empowered" are US-centric constructs, as is the concept of employee "engagement," which doesn't translate well in some business cultures.

To gauge engagement, the Apple team had Chinese employees complete anonymous surveys. Results showed high engagement and satisfaction, but this didn't align with the fact that turnover was extremely high. The local business culture around feedback was the reason why. Even though team leaders said the survey was anonymous, it didn't make a difference as employees were concerned about even anonymously sharing negative feedback. In answering a question about whether they would recommend friends and family to work at Apple, they always said yes to protect the boss instead of telling the truth. To address this, Jennifer and the team began asking different types of questions, such as about happiness, to navigate this element of local business culture and improve employee retention. She learned that to succeed in global markets, companies have to build balance and processes to allow for differences in local culture while still making sure to align employees with company values.

OFTEN OVERLOOKED

Job Titles

Local differences in job titles can cause confusion around decision-making authority and role, which are very relevant in building relationships in new local markets. This is why we have attempted to avoid titles in our frameworks. Getting titles right is so important in some cultures that we have helped the local office of a government client of ours get approval from their home country to adapt their titles to better fit with titles used in Silicon Valley. Moreover, if you are hiring for a position with the local team and you don't choose the appropriate title, you won't attract the right job candidates.

The general manager (GM) title, for example, is very important in many Asian countries. It is well understood and helps communicate the authority of the person in that role. If people in the local business environment don't understand your role, responsibility, and decision power by just looking at your title, it can cause confusion. Make it simple and easy for people to understand positions within the team as best as possible.

Moreover, when it comes to highly traditional business cultures, you can't be as creative as some tech companies in Silicon Valley that have titles like "chief evangelist." Sometimes it is better to avoid being too original. In Japan, the business culture discourages being a "bent nail." Fitting in is valued more than standing out there, while in other markets it is completely okay to let your creativity show.

When Company Culture Conflicts

Mastering company culture mainly involves finding a way to maintain company core values and principles in new local (market/business) cultures. While it is true that companies and their leaders should never attempt to be anything they aren't and should always be authentic, trustworthy, and straightforward, they will have to morph elements of your company culture to fit in the local market. In adapting, it is important to retain a strong foundation to keep some level of consistency and continuity in decision-making and behaviors. Your company culture provides the clear reference points needed.

For Rakuten, it's "Speed, Speed, Speed." For Plaid, it's "Learn and Grow, Together." At Chegg, it includes "Dream Big, Debate, Decide and Do." At Zoom, it's "Community, Customers, Company, Teammates, Selves." While the companies' core values (principles) differ, they each serve as the North Star for their respective companies worldwide. Core values guide the effort of all aspects of the organization, both internal and external facing.

Company culture directs and focuses team effort and brings people together. It goes beyond policy to include nonnegotiables and elements that make up the core of the company's DNA. Along with core values, it can guide you in setting goals and help you judge what success is. Company culture even gives the team a sense of identity that builds trust.

Company culture and core values are indeed a guiding light for so many reasons: they tell employees how to treat others, they highlight what matters, they provide an indication of how well employees are performing, and they provide a connection to other employees and the company itself, generating a sense of identity, trust, and true meaning. They also can facilitate a connection with customers when they have shared values.

Using company culture and core values as a first filter in making tough decisions can provide clarity in times of high stress (which is why it is a factor in step two of the LPA process). It can also help you determine the areas where you are open to failure and key learnings, and where compromises shouldn't be made.

Company culture and core values are increasingly important with a distributed workforce as they provide a unified identity that brings people together across borders. They are also an important driver of social bonds within the team, given that face-to-face interactions are limited, bolstering the feeling that the organization is still a team even with people working in decentralized locations.

A deep understanding of all three types of culture allows you to understand how to navigate a local market and also prevent problems ahead of time, using processes and safeguards to limit cultural tendencies that conflict with company values.

With cultural differences, you can see why it's beneficial to have someone on the team with knowledge of how local business is conducted so that an HQ team that lacks this local market experience doesn't have to learn these lessons the hard way, wasting time and money and burning opportunities in the process.

STRATEGIES FOR STAYING AHEAD OF CULTURAL CONFLICT

Invariably, there will be times when company culture conflicts with local market and local business cultures. There are times when the decision of which to prioritize is clear to a certain audience, like for an American audience when

John Brandon of Apple prioritized company culture by firing much of the team in China for reporting fraudulent financials. This same situation may be less clear to another audience, like how a Chinese audience may agree with the local team's actions given the importance of protecting the boss in local business culture.

As Claudia Makadristo, Head of Expansion in Africa for MetaMap, points out, the Nigerian business culture is more confrontational than some East African countries, so a basis of understanding and a conscious effort to tailor communication to the audience is needed for teams distributed in both locations. These types of cultural conflicts may occur regularly, making it essential that companies find a way to build a bridge between different cultures.

Considering culture and core values within the constructs of decision-making is an effective exercise to understand where there is and isn't flexibility in prioritizing local market culture or company culture. As Jan van Casteren says, "Values should spark a conversation." Further, Tiffany Stevenson of Patreon asks, "What are the decisions that a team is making that put values to the test?"

There are also other strategies that Global Class Companies utilize to mitigate conflicts before they arise and to balance conflicts between local and company cultures, each with key benefits for fast-growing global organizations:

- Universalize Core Values
- Hire the Right Team
- Practice Culturally Conscious Management
- Integrate Cultures

Universalize Core Values

When establishing core values, most companies think of their relationship with key stakeholders, including employees, partners, and, most importantly, customers. More recently, environmental and societal impacts have made their way into company core values as well.

The main difference between the core values developed by Global Class and legacy companies is scope. For most legacy companies, the customer archetype and halo of impact is limited to their initial market, while Global Class Companies consider a global audience.

Concepts like liberty may appeal to an American audience, as would a core value like Walmart's "Respect for the individual." However, this could conflict with the support of collectivism in many Asian cultures.

If a company's core values are too specific to their initial market, then they will not resonate with stakeholders in other markets, leading to less engagement with customers and less empowerment of employees, which hinders achieving company-market fit. Rakuten, in the story we previously shared, would not have run into as many issues with employee morale in the European office early on if their core values had been more understandable to a non-Japanese audience up front.

Differences in local business culture can lead to different interpretations of core values and strategies. One of Amazon's more difficult to understand core values, "are right, a lot," means that it's a leader's duty to make the right decisions by getting diverse perspectives and working hard to do things with good judgment. In India, there is a high respect for authority, so local employees interpreted this core value to mean, "the boss is right, don't question them," through their cultural lens. It's important to make sure core values translate through differences in local market and business cultures.

Global Class Companies create and uphold core values that are universal and are understood by people all over the world. Universalizing their core values attracts top talent and better connects with customers across the globe, transcending borders.

The agile mindset comes into play here as well, with organizations making culturally conscious iterations to find the right balance between company and local cultures. This point is particularly germane because, as Gabriel Engel, co-founder and CEO of Rocket.Chat, explains, "Company values need to be discovered, not created"—something that Global Class Companies with global aspirations inherently understand. We have seen how companies change elements of their core values as they scale, incorporating the influences from an increasingly global operation. Flexport, for example, had a core value, "fill the gap," that empowered employees to find solutions to challenges as they arose to facilitate rapid growth unhindered by bureaucratic processes. As the company began to scale in multiple markets, however, this core value ran the risk of creating additional complexity, as local teams could use this mandate to figure out their own ways of operating without coordinating with HQ. Ultimately, the Flexport team determined that this core value was valuable early on as they validated their business model in their initial market, but needed to be changed to reach global scale.

The LinkedIn team made sure its mission and vision were simple enough for people in every part of the world to understand and connect with and simple enough to internalize and to articulate. This core message is about creating economic opportunities for anybody in the world. This simplicity and universality directly led to business success and access to new markets. This is one of the key reasons why LinkedIn was the only non-Chinese social media platform allowed to operate in the country for a time.

When companies find it hard to universalize core values, the next best thing is to bridge company culture and local market culture, as Rakuten did in Europe. Beyond local cultural awareness, any effort to operate local offices according to principles familiar to the local teams can be effective at gaining buy-in. Slack made an effort to connect its core values (courtesy, craftsmanship, empathy, and playfulness) with local culture. One of Slack's core values, craftsmanship, resonates with Japanese people since they value quality work. Another core value, empathy (with an effort made to understand through listening), was more difficult to understand, since in Japan people don't talk about their feelings as openly, especially in a professional setting. It's often better to lean into the core values that do have local counterpoints instead of attempting to get adoption of every core value.

As Jennifer Cornelius puts it, "Universal core values create an equity of experience" that can cross borders. She continues, "You know when you feel it, but you have to purposely think about how to break it down and use it as part of mechanisms within the organization." With internalized core values that resonate with all employees, especially those on local teams, company culture can be a differentiator and engine for growth, particularly when supporting processes and norms are in place. Universalized core values break down any sense of an us-versus-them mentality between HQ and local offices, fostering more local market buy-in.

Hire the Right Team

The best way to balance the three types of culture is to hire the right people. Interpreneurs who understand that part of their role is to bridge the gap between cultures are incredibly valuable to any international growth initiative.

They happen to be more effective at localizing and engaging communities as well. Moreover, since the local team members are stewards of company culture to local markets, the alignment of local team members with company culture and core values is extremely important.

Culture fit should be one of the highest criteria by which you evaluate job candidates during the recruitment process. While culture fit can't stand alone as the only criterion, when mixed with the traits listed under Interpreneur mindset and local knowledge (pages 218–220), someone who fits all of these categories has a much higher likelihood of making a positive impact in the local market. Having the right people is key to a company's collective cultural consistency.

Hiring the wrong team can have catastrophic effects. As Jan from Flexport explained, "It's risky entering into a new market with a business that is disrupting a highly traditional industry. If you hire an experienced local market lead with a traditional mindset, you will likely fail—they need 200 percent buy-in into the company vision and core values, and to be able to experiment and adapt." To use Jan's analogy from chapter eight, this balanced mindset is what keeps the kitchen sink clean.

In order to properly establish your company culture in a new market, you have to hire the right people who understand and buy into company values. If you hire someone with strong local market knowledge and experience working in-country but no commitment to a common company culture, you risk accumulating Org. Premium as the hire may not adhere to company core values. On the other hand, if you hire someone with a strong connection to company culture but no understanding of local business culture or local market culture, then they would be more likely to be ineffective at adapting the business to find company-market fit and navigating the local team environment. In either case, the result is an increased chance of failure for an international growth initiative.

When you hire employees with traits that match the Global Class Team Building Framework (in particular, interpreneurial skills), you will gain a competitive advantage in your global scaling efforts.

Practice Culturally Conscious Management

The Culturally Conscious Management mindset outlined in the last chapter (page 246) is also very effective at achieving balance when the three types of culture conflict. The contingency approach explained in the last chapter, factoring the culture context into decision-making, can play a big role in helping leadership foster engagement and empowerment within local teams that have different local business cultures than the culture at HQ.

The Global Class mindset factors into this process as well. The command-and-control leadership style is incongruent with HQ taking on the role of enabler and supporter of local teams. Culturally conscious management leads HQ to adapt to support local teams and their local cultures, adopting local customs, communication styles, and feedback practices.

Integrate Cultures

The most effective way to balance between each of the culture types is to integrate them. While this is meant to be more directional than scientific, the 80/20 principle can fit when it comes to company culture. Eighty percent needs to stay the same (including core values), but 20 percent can shift for the local market.

There are specific steps you can take to integrate cultures. Ethan Evans, formerly of Amazon, suggests the following practical tactics:

- Incentivize people to work out of different offices and get international experience beyond HQ and the home country.
- Create organic communication about what is happening in each place. Evans describes this as "a good way to decontaminate the us-versus-them dynamic."
- Establish an ambassador/liaison role that empowers peers to say things they would never say to the boss, leading to more realistic feedback.
- Conduct formal training around core values and specifically explain cultural differences.
- Travel—encourage employees to do company-sponsored "micro-moves," where they work out of another office for a few weeks. People see the experience as an adventure to learn from instead of as a big life change.
- Ask yourself, *What can I do to ensure that culture can be discussed and analyzed?*

Building off of this tactical list, we see three higher-level strategies to assist with cultural integration: leveraging Feedback Loops, supporting rituals from the local culture, and celebrating diversity.

Leveraging (Small) Feedback Loops

Feedback Loops allow team members at HQ and in local offices to keep a pulse on any conflicts in culture to address them head-on. Moreover, these Feedback Loops are also channels for two-way learning and innovation, allowing HQ to take cultural best practices from local offices and implement them across a global footprint, and individual team members to learn from each other.

These Feedback Loops shouldn't just connect HQ and local teams, but should also work within local teams ("small loops" referenced in chapter four), facilitating the integration of company culture with the local business culture at the individual office level with the goal of finding the optimal balance. These small loops can be a great way to connect the members of the local team who are from HQ or another part of the world with the local team members who are native. These small loops can also serve as an effective tool for ensuring a local team is maintaining a balance of local knowledge and company knowledge and influence global growth initiatives from the ground up.

Supporting Rituals from the Local Culture

While core values may not change, letting local teams maintain rituals important to the local community can be a useful tool in empowering remote teams. Slack holds an annual celebration to commemorate when the company was founded, but let the local team in Dublin also have a Christmas party because it was important within the local culture even though this wasn't part of the schedule at HQ. As long as there is not a conflict with company culture, local teams should have more freedom to add elements of local culture to the company's local presence, which in turn increases employee commitment and engagement.

Celebrating Diversity

Finding ways to share cultural norms across distributed teams helps with balancing culture and improves trust and camaraderie while facilitating relationship building. Something as simple as employees on a local team sharing culture celebrations from their market with the global team can be a bonding experience. NetApp Vice President Lori Harmon launched a local cultural activities and awareness campaign showcasing traditions from different offices within her organization. In October, her organization held a virtual Oktober-fest event where the German local team shared background about the festival and everyone enjoyed a beer (prost!). Even doing something as simple as listing international holidays on all company calendars, as Roku does, brings cultural awareness. At 10X Innovation Lab, during holidays throughout the year, each team member shares how that holiday is celebrated in their home country, allowing us to learn how certain holidays are celebrated across the four continents we hail from.

As Chris Murphy, CEO of Thoughtworks, North America, aptly explained, fast-growing global companies tend to be multicultural by default. They test and learn the culture of prospective markets. Their organizations are built to be more mobile and built to accept and adapt to diversity (even when they are starting in their initial market). This openness to diversity applies to the mechanics of scaling a business globally as Global Class Companies are adept at adapting their products to fit new markets and are willing to pivot based on a data-driven, test-based approach. They also recognize how diversity helps with the development of new ideas.

OFTEN OVERLOOKED

Showing Appreciation for Local Culture Is a Powerful Differentiator

"Food is the organizing principle in international business," explained Dan Himelstein from Berkeley Haas; it connects people and builds bridges. As a culturally curious Interpreneur, Dan worked hard to learn new skills and build his cultural acumen for the markets he did business in. He shared a story about how his ability to pick up a single salt peanut with chopsticks after being given the challenge by a Taiwanese client during a business meal helped build what became a successful long-term business relationship. "Ninety-five percent of what you offer to potential clients will be the same as the competition, but it's that five percent, much of which relates to cultural understanding, that makes the difference." This level of cultural awareness inherent in Interpreneurs is a key differentiator.

THE RISE OF THE COMMUNITY CULTURE

The world has gone from dispersed to interconnected. Increasingly, national identity doesn't hold a singular place of importance for people. While nationalism has recently grown in some countries, Interpreneurs are accelerating the rise of global citizenship in parallel; cross-border connections are getting stronger. Shared values and common interests don't end at the edge of the shore. That is why a new type of culture, a culture defined by countless smaller communities that transcend borders, is on the rise because of communication and social media platforms that provide more channels for people to connect over common interest. We refer to this as *Community Culture*.

Airbnb recognized this and used it as a tool to not only help with targeting niche groups for market entry but also building a cross-border community paradigm into the company's very fabric.

More tactically, Airbnb creates target customer groups based on mindset instead of geography, which they refer to as "tribes." This analysis structure focuses much more on customer archetypes and identifying niches. In some respects, this is more actionable at the beginning of market entry, since it paints a much clearer path to who your target customer is and how to get a marketing message in front of them. Instead of basing segmentation on demographics, it is based on beliefs or a mindset within the group that transcends borders.

This framing also bridges part of the cultural divide. Instead of making the cultural paradigm rooted in language and local customs, it is based on common vernacular and beliefs within a group, bonded through a hobby or passion, for example. Peloton Interactive, the exercise platform, has built a cross-border community around a common interest in health and wellness, developing a set of beliefs, vocabulary, and cultural norms that appeal to its community members from all over the world.

When you have identified customer archetypes that already use your product in your initial market, the job of translating a message to members of this same archetype in a new country becomes easier. It more closely taps into the psychology of human storytelling. According to Jennifer Yuen, Airbnb found great early traction with marathon runners. The company was able to build a bridge to the customer and help them understand that Airbnb "gets" them through their shared behaviors around their passion for running (and adventure).

What Airbnb does on a tactical level for market entry and growth permeates the whole business and supports the concept of Community Culture. Even the company's mission, to "create a world where anyone can belong anywhere," is built on a concept of cross-border global community and helps universalize the company's core values. Through the Global Class movement we are attempting to build a Community Culture around the concepts of Interpreneurs and Global Class Companies, connecting internationally minded people across the globe.

This framing around community embodies a concept of culturally conscious global business where a company has to be mindful of local markets and a cross-border network of people. The notion also fosters a company's commitment to global citizenship. This mindset aligns well with the core tenets of the interpreneurial mindset as well (global-mindedness and cultural sensitivity).

At the same time, that doesn't mean you should ignore local market culture to solely prioritize Community Culture. The former is still crucially important. Global Class Companies know that understanding local culture shows a commitment to the local market and its people, but they also don't ignore how the human condition goes beyond local borders.

It's a balance of local consciousness and global context. As mentioned in chapter two, Global Class Companies seek a consistent experience for employees and customers alike, anywhere across the globe.

In support of the local and global nature of culture, Scott Coleman, formerly of Pinterest and Google, succinctly points out, "People are the same, but their tastes are different." So the goal becomes connecting with someone's innate humanity and then layering on a message that matches their unique tastes. This calls to the idea of an individual's culture that is an integration of local culture and the culture of their chosen (cross-border) communities.

Along these lines, Global Class Companies understand these multiple layers of culture, from individual to local to community of common interest, and find ways to connect with each layer (a challenge that is difficult to overcome, to say the least).

Focus on Community Culture comes in different forms. In addition to customer bases, Global Class Companies also understand that this mindset includes community engagement and sustainability. Finding ways to engage with the community outside of delivering your product or service to customers is an important part of the playbook. Many Global Class Companies understand this and build it into their ways of doing business, as Zendesk has done in addressing local issues where it has a physical presence through its Zendesk Foundation.

Finally, and most practically, the concept of aligning to this Community Culture makes sense from an operational perspective. Framing your business purely by national borders will lead to more localizations, complexity, and "arbitrary uniqueness." Finding cross-border communities will increase efficiency as the work you do to adapt go-to-market elements (Marketing, Sales, and Product Premiums) becomes more scalable. This cross-border approach taps into the concept of linked markets, which enable localizations done for one market to create momentum across multiple markets (as discussed in chapter six).

Ultimately, a great way to build local market engagement, as validated by Airbnb's strong traction in the APAC, is to take Jennifer Yuen's advice and focus on the humanity of people in your new market, searching for ways to connect and communicate the common ground that exists between your brand and them. The primary way to do this is to take the time to understand their culture and what is important to them. Show respect for the local culture through how you operate your business and communicate with current and potential customers. Then find ways to transcend local borders to create momentum around your efforts to target cross-border communities, creating global scale.

With this new type of culture on the rise, the role of Interpreneurs becomes even more important for companies looking to accelerate achieving global scale. The cultural mindset, empathy, cultural curiosity, and community-mindedness Interpreneurs embody allow Global Class Companies to tap into this new Community Culture and build cross-border connections.

Assembling teams of Interpreneurs, building a bridge to manage globally distributed teams, and delicately balancing company and local cultures help Global Class Companies localize, connect with the local community, and achieve scale, leading to company-market fit. It is why these are the Three Pillars of Effective Global Scaling. They are the differentiators that, when paired with global agile methodology, effective localization, and complexity management, make companies Global Class.

CHAPTER 10 SUMMARY

- There are three types of culture to be understood and consciously managed to be successful reaching company-market fit in new markets and achieving global scale: local market culture, local business culture, and company culture.
- When these types of cultures conflict, Global Class Companies use the following strategies to find balance and achieve company-market fit:
  a. **Universalize Core Values**—Establish core values that resonate across a global audience.
  b. **Hire the Right Team**—Hire Interpreneurs with strong culture fit.
  c. **Practice Culturally Conscious Management**—Use the contingency approach to support and empower local teams.
  d. **Integrate Cultures**—Balance and share cultures (company and local) through leveraging Feedback Loops, supporting rituals from local cultures, and celebrating diversity.
- A new type of culture that transcends borders, *Community Culture*, is beginning to emerge, forcing companies to look at culture in a new way

CHAPTER 10 REFLECTION & ACTION QUESTIONS

1. Have you experienced a clash between company and local cultures? How did you navigate it and create balance? How are you creating the right environments for local team success?
2. How have you universalized company core values to appeal to a global audience (employees and customers)?
3. How is your company tapping into emerging cross-border Community Culture to grow your business globally?

• 11 •

CONCLUSION

The Global Class Company,
Interpreneurs, and You

We have finally reached the end of our journey investigating how the world's fastest-growing companies—the Global Class—find traction and scale in international markets. Hopefully our insights and frameworks make you feel more equipped to continue on to the next destination of your quest as an Interpreneur.

We have gone through a journey together—across continents, industries, and stages of growth. In the process, we have learned about the mindset of the Global Class Companies that are leading the way in this new era of business and the Interpreneurs who are the catalysts behind their companies' successes (part one). We outlined the commitments Global Class companies must make to support international growth initiatives, the importance of leveraging a global version of the agile methodology to localize go-to-market and operations strategies, and how managing complexity and creating organizational structures can facilitate achieving company-market fit (part two). Finally, we explored the major pillars that support growth: effective team building, a management model that empowers local teams, and strategies to balance culture as you reach global scale (part three). In the process, we have shared a playbook for how to build and manage a successful global organization. Now it's your turn to apply these concepts to elevate your organization to join the Global Class.

It has also been an exciting journey for us personally. At the outset, we took a bold step. Not seeing a definitive book on the topic, we went on a quest to find the answers to what makes the most successful companies able to find traction in new countries and then operate at global scale. In the process, we were inspired by the many stories we heard, intrigued by the similarities we found, and interested in the different growth paths each company took.

We were so ecstatic (and frankly surprised) at the open arms we were greeted with from hundreds of leaders from some of the most successful companies in the world, and we are so grateful for their insights and ongoing support with spreading the message of Global Class.

Depending on your role, the journey can be both lonely and frustrating, especially if you're the first employee opening a new international office. Whether in a local market or at HQ, Interpreneurs we interviewed often had to contend with limited resources while fighting to get company leadership to understand the differences and opportunities in a new market, endlessly translating culture and core values in both directions.

Despite these challenges, the leaders we interviewed thrived (as any true Interpreneur would). All the hard work never seemed like work, or, at least, it was well worth it because of the calling many of them had to cross cultures and learn new things in the process.

While they have much more to share with us than we could share back with them, we want to let them know that they are in good company and that this is just the beginning. They are trailblazers, illuminating the path for a growing group of professionals who see the role global business can play in building connections and improving societies. Whether selling to businesses or consumers, offering a solution in the form of a physical product or a digital one, at its core, building a successful business at global scale comes down to people and connecting with them to help solve problems and make things better.

In the process of presenting this material, we invented some new concepts, built on others, and made an effort to create tangible frameworks and universal lessons, not just a collection of vignettes and situations that didn't relate to each other.

In our work with organizations across the globe, we found that many couldn't put their finger on the mindset needed to successfully scale an organization globally. That's why we wanted to give the combination of a cultural curiosity, global mindset, and empathy a formal moniker (the Interpreneur).

We did this so that the lessons would be practical, but more importantly, translatable to non-Interpreneurs who need to approve of and support global growth initiatives.

We hope that what we presented is actionable. Our intention was to provide insights in a way that could help everyone interested in global business, from team members at HQ to those in local markets, from those with vast international experience to those who aspire to have global careers. Hopefully our effort for a well-rounded view shone through.

We want to reframe and reset the tendency for companies to tout the company way of doing things. We also believe that in the future the interpreneurial mindset and cultural considerations will be both more common and more important to an organization's success.

For those who connected with the stories of Lee, Isabel, and Samantha (in the introduction), here's a message for each of you:

For all you Lees out there . . .

We hope that this book serves as affirmation for all the hard work you have done up until now and motivation to get the alignment and resources you need to take your company's international growth initiatives to the next level. Through this playbook, we look forward to joining you on your company's journey to global scale.

For all you Isabels out there . . .

We hope that this book has helped unlock the Interpreneur that has been inside of you all along and that you take the next step in building an international career; there is an exciting path that lies ahead. We are confident that you are now equipped with the vocabulary and strategies to show how you will be a catalyst for global growth (to help you get the job), and with the tool kit to call upon to be successful (once you get down to work).

For all you Samanthas out there . . .

We hope that through the frameworks herein you now have the clarity needed to have a positive impact on your organization, regardless of the obstacles and bureaucracy that stand in the way. Be resilient; we support you in driving change to transform your organization from legacy to Global Class.

For all of them and you, too . . .

Pass along the message of Global Class. Help create more Interpreneurs like you (the world needs more of us). Our goal is to make global business a shared experience, not a solitary one.

Don't forget to check out the resources available at www.GlobalClassBook .com (including electronic versions of the frameworks we covered in the book). Connect with us (email us at hello@globalclasscompany.com); we would love to help your company on its journey to becoming Global Class. No matter where you are on your career journey, we hope that our message inspires you to build a global career and be a catalyst for Global Class Companies.

• • •

To sum it all up, remember: if you seek first to learn and understand, nothing will ever be *foreign*.

· EPILOGUE ·

IMPACT: The Role of the
Global Class in Society

As we look back on the two years this book has been in development, we have become more convinced of the unique inflection point we are at in global business. In interacting with business leaders who have scaled some of the most successful companies of our time and with leaders from fast-growing companies earlier in their global growth journeys, we see the principles outlined in this book emerging in the mindsets and strategies of the Global Class Companies of the future.

THESE ARE EXCITING TIMES

The acceleration of distributed work is a paradigm shift (like the onset of the internet and emergence of software-driven business originating during the dot-com boom); Global Class Companies are learning how to tap into a global workforce, finding the best talent everywhere, and leveraging the diversity of opinion this creates to connect with a global customer base. Access to new forms of education stemming from the adoption of technology means that communities of knowledge workers can bloom everywhere.

Besides the benefits the expanding global talent pool provides for Global Class Companies, we are particularly excited about how this will help further develop economies and provide fulfillment to people who want to participate in the global community. We see how emerging countries are implementing systems that leapfrog legacy infrastructures of more mature economies, such as through the adoption of mobile-first technology and fintech solutions. We look forward to how this can help improve these societies and avoid some of the negative entrenchments that exist in more mature economies. Business leaders in these emerging economies have the flexibility to build better solutions from the ground up.

The scale is enormous. Companies are reaching a scale that is larger than the GDPs of many nations. Platforms exist that connect over one billion people and provide shared identities (and create Community Culture). The emergence of groups of people who cross borders, linked by common passions, allows for communities to transcend national boundaries and conflicts, finding new ways to create a shared purpose and strive for the lives they desire without limiting themselves to confinement within their local borders.

THE RISE OF THE GLOBAL CLASS COMPANY AND INTERPRENEURS

Even though many of the companies profiled in this book have been around for years, they represent the very infancy of the Global Class Company concept detailed in this book, and the impact the Global Class will have is only just starting to be seen. With global as the new agile, companies' views on global growth will transform, and soon new companies will see the principles in this book applied as ubiquitously as we now see agile methodology. They will adopt the global flavor of agile and practice culturally conscious management, with company-wide buy-in and adoption of these principles from day one.

As seen throughout the book, everything starts and ends with culture: company culture, local market culture, the local business culture, and even emerging Community Culture. The themes of empathy, localization, and the need for business to *integrate* with society, in addition to *contributing* to (a new view on disruption), are all core tenets. Communication and the rest of the Four Commitments for Successful Global Growth will be increasingly important as Global Class Companies seek ways to connect with a distributed workforce and customer base.

These changes and opportunities go beyond the team level to the individual. Probably the most fascinating part of the work we did in developing this book came through the discovery of the unique brand of business leader, who has been there for a long time but has yet to be recognized, profiled, or lauded. These Interpreneurs are catalysts, not only for the global growth of the companies they work for and the Global Class concept, but also for the positive change in society that can come from the value companies deliver to customers worldwide. We feel honored to put them on a pedestal and hope that this book will create many more Interpreneurs who will have both global and local impact.

THE PIECES ARE FALLING INTO PLACE

Tools to take advantage of the opportunities in front of us are developing. Platforms for marketing, operations, distribution, delivery, and education are in place. Technology and company processes that allow employees to work from anywhere and for companies to tap into a global talent pool have arrived.

Hierarchies are beginning to be challenged. As seasoned Silicon Valley executive and Salesforce Chief Adoption Officer Polly Sumner points out, "When people connect via virtual tools, you can't tell who is rich or poor; you can't see how fancy the room or house someone else lives in [is] by their virtual background or wall behind them. There is more equity. What matters more is how you think, how you listen, and how you communicate."

The fourth type of culture we discussed, the concept of emerging Community Culture that transcends borders, can be an effective catalyst Global Class Companies use to rapidly build engaged cross-border customer bases.

The next necessary ingredients are frameworks and a mindset to have an impact at global scale. We hope that the resources we have created don't just serve executives looking to reach a target or maximize a metric but positively impact communities and help companies fulfill community-minded missions.

The notion of balancing localization and complexity, the foundation of global agile, and the structures and processes that can be used to create momentum and accelerate scale can be used as a force for the collective good.

THE ROLE OF GLOBAL CLASS COMPANIES

Despite all these positive trends, we recognize that nations are fighting these uniting forces by creating fragmentation. Nationalism and an us-versus-them mentality are reassembling the barriers that technology has been toppling.

In response, Global Class Companies can stitch people together, transcending these borders. Worldwide customer bases and distributed workforces fight this negative wave and can have more collective strength than national control.

It is the duty of Global Class Companies to enable and empower global economies, communities, and individuals. Through culturally conscious disruption, the Global Class can elevate the local economies they are in. Through a devotion to distributed work, they can help distribute access to wealth and knowledge. This doesn't mean giving profits away; rather, it means being global in mindset and spreading out the financial impact the company has to include the local communities where customers and employees live and work.

As Marc Benioff wrote in a 2019 *New York Times* opinion column, "Profit and purpose go hand in hand, and business can be the greatest platform for change."

Beyond business and beyond transactions, Global Class Companies can create lasting connections with, and uplifting impacts on, communities. These companies are not only *creating* communities but are also *part of* the community.

Both Global Class Companies and the Interpreneurs that drive them must be role models who maintain a culturally conscious mindset.

THE GLOBAL CLASS MOVEMENT HAS ALREADY BEGUN

The shift has already begun. We are seeing the role Global Class Companies already have in the communities they serve today. Global virtues that resonate across borders are enhancing core values, bridging gaps, and bringing people together. Business is now going beyond engaging with customers and providing purpose and livelihood for employees; it is shaping society. Global Class Companies have the opportunity to shape it for the better.

Each Global Class Company has its own flavor of how to create relationships with and contribute to society, selecting areas of impact that fit with the organization's DNA and focusing on areas where they can leave a mark. As we heard Prezi co-founder and Executive Chairman Peter Arvai say, it's important that a contributor mindset "run all the way through the company." This is why he is a big proponent of companies paying taxes to support the local economies (and thereby their customers) in places where they make money, instead of avoiding tax at all costs.

Zendesk targets hiring from underserved communities to tap into a diversity of backgrounds, in addition to its community impact program through the Zendesk Foundation and beyond. Eric Yuan, Zoom's founder and CEO, gave the company's service away to millions of schoolchildren across the world as teachers and administrators struggled to figure out how to teach remotely during the pandemic. Salesforce's equal pay and diversity initiatives provide a blueprint for how all companies should operate in the global business world.

Amazon recently added a new leadership principle: "success and scale bring broad responsibility." In the announcement of this core value change, the company self-consciously stated, "We are big, we impact the world, and we are far from perfect. We must be humble and thoughtful about even the secondary effects of our actions. Our local communities, planet, and future generations need us to be better every day."

Platzi, an online business education platform founded in Colombia, is opening a world of career opportunities to more than three million people across Latin America who are joining a rising middle class. Airbnb built a sense of belonging into its mission and facilitates sharing of the uniqueness of individual perspectives and openness of community in every corner of the world.

These Global Class Companies are not always perfect, but they recognize that there is an opportunity for all companies to contribute to humanity, and they aspire to play a positive role in society. These companies don't bring people together at just a local community level; they can bring us together as a global community.

CONCLUSION AND CALL TO ACTION

The Global Class concept applies at the individual level (through Interpreneurs), at a company level, and at a community level, both locally and globally.

We are passionate about cultivating Global Class Companies and Interpreneurs and we love to roll up our sleeves and engage with global communities on every continent to elevate economies that support community-minded organizations.

We call upon other businesses and their leaders to look beyond their backyards and take advantage of the role society is offering you. Whether you are an executive running an organization at global scale, an entrepreneur launching your business in a new market, or an employee or student aspiring to build a global career, you have the opportunity (with the Global Class/Interpreneur's mindset as your guide) to achieve success and positive impact at global scale.

Utilize the tools we have designed to help your company grow globally (learn more at www.GlobalClassBook.com). The frameworks and resources we present in this book are meant to help you through your international expansion journey.

Remember that it's all about culture. Be conscious of it. Be sensitive to it. Be eager to learn it. Share it. Celebrate it. Your company culture is what engages customers, employees, and the community; your acknowledgment and acceptance of local culture are what leads to traction and scale.

Be part of the interpreneurial community. Connect with other Interpreneurs. Share best practices. There is a small but growing group of globally minded Interpreneurs that you can join; strive to make global business a shared experience instead of a solitary one.

We are putting our Interpreneur hats on, a tool kit of Global Class resources on our backs, and are heading off on our mission. Will you join us?

To put a "Global Class" spin on the Mark Twain quote about travel mentioned earlier in the book:

Engaging with global communities is fatal to prejudice, bigotry, and narrow-mindedness . . . Global scale can only be achieved through cultural curiosity, and diversity of thought and experience, not by clinging to the company way.

• ACKNOWLEDGMENTS •

This book is a manifestation of our mission to make global business expansion a shared experience instead of a solitary one. It is not the output of two authors sitting and pondering, but of a concerted effort by an entire community of supporters who have guided us and supported us through a long journey of questions, iterations, and requests. This book would have been very different without our many collaborators (and not in a good way). So many people contributed to this book, from sharing stories and insights of their interpreneurial careers to book strategy/positioning/development ideas and beyond. It's been a two-year-long project that started in the early parts of the pandemic and has finally come to fruition after countless hours of research, writing, and continued iteration.

There are two people who have been incredible mentors throughout the entire publication process from initial idea to printed book. First, Jonas Koffler. You have been a true ambassador of *Global Class*, helping us in so many ways, from book proposal development to securing a deal with our publisher to being there the whole way to answer an endless amount of questions and to hop on impromptu FaceTime calls to help us overcome the latest challenges. Your ongoing encouragement helped motivate us to make the book and platform surrounding *Global Class* better and better. You started as our agent and ended up as a friend, being an advisor, marketing consultant, and editor along the way.

Second, Patrick Vlaskovits. This book would have never come to be without your guidance and willingness to open your network to help us achieve each milestone along the way, taking *Global Class* from an idea to a finished book. More than that, your sage advice as someone who has successfully navigated the journey to being a best seller (twice) helped us focus on what was important, ignore what wasn't, and has empowered us to put in the work to give our best shot at following in your footsteps.

To the team at BenBella: You are the ideal partner for *Global Class* and a chief supporter of our goal to get the concepts within the book out into the world. It takes a team that is OK with iterating and pivoting as lessons are learned to make a book like this work. Matt Holt, you believed in our idea (and us) and have been a tremendous advocate for the book, always open to considering one more "slight" change and being flexible when new ideas come to light. Your agile way of collaborating with authors is rare and much appreciated. Katie Dickman, your stewardship of our manuscript helped ensure our message could resonate with a broad audience; we appreciate you helping us take our words to the next level (thanks to Lydia Choi for your help, too). Special shout-out to Judy Gelman Myers, our copyeditor: We wouldn't have been able to communicate our ideas effectively without you smoothing out the edges and correcting an endless number of little mistakes. Brigid Pearson, thank you for iterating with us to create a truly iconic cover design that captures the attention and makes readers want to see what's inside. Jessika Rieck, the interior design elements (and, in particular, the graphics) of this book were particularly important to clearly communicate our ideas and framework, and you did an amazing job helping our ideas jump off the page. Mallory Hyde, thank you for your hard work to get the messages of *Global Class* out in the world in ways that get people to see the value of what we have to say (and actually want to read it).

To our 10X Innovation Lab team, thank you for all you do to make our organization Global Class! In particular, Jo-Anne Loquellano-Cruz, Victor Barbosa, and Crystal Faith Neri, thank you for being there every step of the way as we developed this book and for supporting our mission to make international growth a shared experience through building our global community of Interpreneurs.

As mentioned in the introduction of the book, we interviewed over three hundred people from more than fifty countries (almost all of whom we have yet to meet face-to-face) in the process of developing the concepts and frameworks detailed in this book. We are truly indebted to all of the *Interpreneurs* who took time out of their busy schedules scaling the world's fastest-growing companies to collaborate with us. It's your ideas, stories, lessons, and best practices that made *Global Class* the valuable playbook it has become. We appreciate your enthusiasm to make sure that others didn't have to reinvent the wheel and learn global business the hard way. You are the catalysts of Global Class Companies and your efforts will inspire the next generation of global business leaders (check out the separate list of these awesome *Interpreneurs*).

In particular, we want to thank a core group of *Interpreneurs* who were advisors and advocates through much of the research process and continue to be huge supporters of us today. Abe Smith, Jennifer Yuen, Troy Malone, Elise Rubin, Jan van Casteren, Kathryn Hymes, John Brandon, Paul Williamson, Jennifer Cornelius, Chang Wen Lai, Tiffany Stevenson, Zach Kitschke, Polly Sumner, Scott Coleman, James Sherrett, Christina Lee, Freddy Vega, Mike Jozwik, Heini Zachariassen, Frédéric Mazzella, Gabriel Engel, Muhammed ("Mo") Yildirim, Dan Himelstein, Sankar Venkatraman, Ethan Evans, Chris Murphy, and Daniel Sullivan—we cannot thank you enough for being ambassadors for both *Global Class* and our efforts to spread the word to the world.

We would also like to extend a special thank-you to leading agile thinkers Steve Blank, Alex Osterwalder, and Eric Ries for asking us challenging questions, sharing sagacious insights, and offering pertinent advice on the topic of agile in a global context and on how to socialize Global Class concepts.

Aaron: A rallying cry when going through tough times is to point out that you are not the *first* person to go through the situation you are facing. Equally as important, but more often forgotten, is that you also won't be the *last*. That is why teaching is so important. It's also why I am so grateful for the many, many people who contributed insights, stories, and feedback in the making of this work. Without your efforts to pay it forward, this book would never have been written. This sense that we won't be the last has energized me in my teaching at Berkeley Haas, as it has pushed many who teach. Thanks to all the teachers (both formal and informal) who taught me and who seize the opportunity to help others through sharing their lived experiences.

To Klaus Wehage, it's been quite the journey in getting this thing published, huh? Thanks for the countless brainstorming sessions, constant iterations as you always looked for ways to make our concepts richer, and for really bringing our frameworks to life through approachable graphics. Your fostering and stewardship of the network of Interpreneurs who contributed to this book have truly made it Global Class.

I want to thank my parents for a lifetime of constant support and encouragement. To my mom, Dawn Sunday, thank you for instilling a global mindset in me from a young age. I remember as a kid filing brochures at your travel agency and learning that there were an almost limitless number of places to explore and people with different perspectives to meet across the world. Thanks for the creative ways you taught me lessons and the gentle nudges you have given me over the years to step outside of my comfort zone. To my dad, Jerry McDaniel, thank you for giving me a behind-the-curtain look at what makes some of the world's most accomplished people successful through stories from your work, and for always keeping an eye out for ways to help my career. To my brother, Marc McDaniel, thank you for inspiring me through your culinary creations and your openness to always help others. I'm proud of your successes in bringing people joy through food and how you are carving your own path. To my godmother, Jill Wakeman, thank you for taking the role of godmother way more seriously than almost anyone ever has, for building a bond and kindred spirit connection with me, and for teaching me the importance of empathy and the necessity to fight for equality of all people. To my daughters, Quinn and Shay, thank you for giving me a reason for being and for the lessons you continue to teach me daily. Watching you grow has become one of the joys of my life.

Finally, and most importantly, to my wife, Leona Ma—this book would not have come across nearly as well without the questions you asked and how you challenged me to write things better. From the day we met you have always been your authentic self (whom I love more and more every day). I love the life we are building together. You serve as an amazing example for our daughters and give them so much to aspire to.

Klaus: A career is not a constant, nor linear, by design. Instead, embrace new influences along your journey and allow for personal change to happen. Change can be refreshing, energizing, and become a catalyst for growth. I've felt it in my own skin, body, and soul (*with career pivots and many miles traveled along the way*). Hence, the reason why I love standing by the front door of Silicon Valley, welcoming students, business leaders, and policy makers, evangelizing entrepreneurship and innovation. Formative experiences, as proven through this book, build flexibility in mindsets, unlock empathy toward others, and inspire people to make an impact on the communities around them. The interviewees in this book exemplify this mindset, and without their support in sharing hard-learned lessons, life experiences, and global business advice, *Global Class* wouldn't have become what it is today.

To Aaron McDaniel, with almost two years of deep collaboration, I have gained a deeper insight into your incredible work ethic and passionate commitment. We have been on a journey that's been the foundation to shaping this project to become an evergreen and globally recognized business book. Your ability to take an initial idea and wield it into literary art and a beautiful narrative has been a joy to witness, co-write, and now publish with.

I owe a tremendous amount of gratitude to many people who have helped me along the way. First and foremost are the people who supported me in the moments when life threw challenging curveballs that could have derailed my personal development and shifted my life path. I'm grateful to my college, Niels Brock; their President, Anya Eskildsen; and my professor Max Johannison, who all showed incredible empathy and understanding toward my situation when my brother passed away. Also, a special shout-out to my friend Casey Armstrong, who graciously invited me to stay with him in California when I needed a moment to breathe and reset after my brother's passing. Life is not always pretty but with the right people and community, you find strength and inspiration to carry on. Additionally, love and appreciation goes to my Chilean family—Jose Ramos, Silva Aranda, Javiera Ramos, and Sebastián Ramos—who took me under their wings and showed me that love has no borders. Culture should connect people, not divide them.

To my wonderful family in Denmark: thank you for making me feel close to home despite being 5,500 miles away. To my mom, Anne Børme, thank you for embracing my life decisions and visiting me around the globe in support of my international lifestyle. To my dad and stepmom, Karsten Wehage and Pernille Henriksen, thanks for always showing me that I have a home no matter how long I've been away. To my brothers, Anders Wehage, Andreas Børme Larsen, and Peter Henriksen, despite our blended family backgrounds, I deeply value and appreciate how we come together through thick and thin and show each other what brotherhood really means. To my grandmother Herta Julia Børme, thanks for showing me what true kindness means through your empathy and passion toward helping others.

To bookend this acknowledgment, I'd like to thank my beautiful wife's family. To my mother-in-law, Yu-wen Szeto, and father-in-law, Chin Szeto, thanks for not only embracing me into this family but also teaching me about a new beautiful culture that I now get to be a part of. To my wife, Jessica Szeto Wehage, whose strength, love, and compassion continue to amaze me every day. Thank you, Jess, for being our family's foundation and for setting an example for our two beautiful boys, Cayden and Austin.

• • •

Of the more than three hundred leaders we interviewed, we would like to thank the following people, in particular, who were so generous with their time and insights in our journey to develop *Global Class*. These *Interpreneurs* are the reason why the concept of the Global Class (and the comprehensive playbook for building a global company herein) came to be:

Belal Aftab
Chukwuemeka Agbata
Luis Almanza
Joaquin Alonso Flores Oviedo
Tiffany Apczynski
Javiera Araneda
Casey Armstrong
Marcio Arnecke
Dhruv Arora
Peter Arvai
Arnaud Auger
William Bao Bean
Gonzalo Begazo
Mohan Belani
Josh Bersin
Israel Bimpe
Cindy Blanco
Steve Blank
Jeffrey Bleich
Jivko Bojinov
Whitney Bouck
Giulia Braghieri
John Brandon

Urban Brecko
Karim Bugglé
Victoria Bull
Maria Carolina Lacombe
Eddy Chan
Sokjin Chang
Lai Changwen
Jose Chapa
Federico Chester
Richard Choi
Christian Claus
Antoine Colaco
Scott Coleman
Jennifer Cornelius
Giancarlo Cozzi
Robin Daniel
Rodolfo Dañino Ruiz
Alfonso De los Rios
Glenn DeVore
Kristen Durham
Luca Eisenstecken
Ernest Eng
Gabriel Engel

Jerry Engel

Anya Eskildsen

Batara Eto

Ethan Evans

Alex Farcet

Mads Faurholt

Don Freda

Ishita Ganotra

Amit Garg

Keith Gatto

Sam Gellman

Roy Geva

Steve Goldberg

Olaf Groth

Claudio Guarcello

Jason Guesman

Ankit Gupta

Bader Hamdan

Budi Handoko

Esben Hansen

Larry Harding

Lori Harmon

David Helgason

Imre Hild

Dan Himelstein

Mikkel Hippe Brun

Klaus Holse

Shinichiro Hori

Rich Hua

Kathryn Hymes

Kang Hyunbin

Sean Jacobsohn

Prasun Jain

Thomas Jensen

Scott Jordon

Mike Jozwik

Tomas Kandl

Amira Karim

Aakash Katdare

Nataly Kelly

Scott Keyes

Jongkap Kim

Tim Kitchin

Zach Kitschke

Shawna Knauff

Kurt Kober

Karsten Koustrup Petersen

Abhishek Krishna Lahoti

Jimmy Ku

Nimit Kumar

Janice Lam

Rob Lamb

Denis Lambert

Ronen Lamdan

Doug Landis

Robyn Larsen

Casey Lau

Brad Layous

Christina Lee

John Lee

Stan Lewandowski

Marvin Liao

Cheryl Lim

Andrew Lindquist

Jerry Luk

Niklas Lundberg

Steven Lurie

Jorn Lyseggen

Alex Mackenzie-Torres

Manas Mainrai

Claudia Makadristo

Troy Malone

Piyush Malviya

Gabriel Manjarrez

Maya Manusci

Raul Marana

Bianca Martinelli

Giovander Masaglia

Seichu Masatada Kobayashi

Frederic Mazzela

Eduardo Medeiros

Carolina Mello

Thiago Miashiro

Emil Michael

Mårten Mickos

David Miltner

Gaurav Mittal

Tak Miyata

Andreas Moellmann

Chris Murphy

Thomas Myrup Kristensen

Patricia Ndikumana

Elise Ngobi

Nyssa Noyola

Alex Osterwalder

Marcus Paiva

Mark Parry

Nayan Patel

Ryan Petersen

Ase Petterson Bailey

Gadi Ponte

Ramsey Pryor

Steven Puig

Eric Quan Lee

Gautam Raj Singh

Vijay Rajendran

Karthik Rampalli

Federico Ranero

Brian Requarth

Eric Ries

Daniel Rodic

David Rodriguez

Hiro Rodriguez

Rishi Roongta

Elise Rubin

Ezequiel Rubin

Roberto Ruiz

Brieanne Runsten

Nicole Sahin

Matthew Salloway

Paula Salomaa

Marcelo Schermer

Alvaro Schocair

Philipp Schwengel

Koshambi Shah

Dawn Sharifan

Mike Shaw

Kristine Sheik

James Sherret

Francesco Simoneschi

Karan Singh

Abe Smith

Ana Sofia Guzman

Jaekwon Son

Ozan Sonmez

Guilherme Spinace

Leore Spira

Tiffany Stevenson

Daniel Sullivan

Polly Sumner

Arun Sundar

Kamlesh Talreja

Cecilia Tang

Enrique Topolansky

Daniel Valentini

Jan van Casteren

Sven Van Stichel

Scott Van Vliet

Freddy Vega

Sankar Venkatraman

Sean Wagner

Liza Wang

Mina Wasfi

Jonathan Whitmore

Paul Williamson

Jaideep Yadav

Takanari Yamashita

Chris Yeh

Muhammed Yildirim

Jennifer Yuen

Heini Zachariassen

Tania Zapata

Kelvin Zin

Adam Zoucha

• GLOSSARY/FREQUENTLY USED TERMS •

Autonomy Curve—The framework that outlines the varying amount of autonomy to grant local teams at each stage of market expansion.

Business Model Localization Canvas (BMLC)—The framework used during part one of the global agile methodology that helps companies transform their validated model in an existing market into hypotheses of how to operate their business in a new market, by filtering their current model through government regulation and culture filters.

Community Culture—An emerging type of culture that connects people with similar interests and beliefs, transcending national borders.

Company Culture—The shared beliefs, behaviors, and norms of an organization that guide how employees communicate, make decisions, and create and implement strategy..

Company-Market Fit—The right go-to-market, operational, organizational, and culture model needed to satisfy the requirements of a local market. Companies achieve company-market fit by localizing these aspects of their business while successfully managing the complexities that come along with these changes.

Decision Rights—The process by which teams divide decision-making authority between HQ and local teams.

Familiarity Bias—When a team assumes that a market geographically adjacent to the initial market, or one that speaks the same language or has a similar culture, will be a good market to launch in and will require very little adaptation to find company-market fit.

Feedback Loops—Established lines of communication that allow for a transparent, multi-directional exchange of ideas and information helping organizations move faster and gain momentum. They can exist between teams (between HQ and local markets) and within teams.

Four Commitments for Successful Global Growth—A set of commitments that companies who are successful at market entry, market growth, and reaching global scale uphold. They include: Resource Alignment, Trust and Autonomy, Communication and Clarity, and Global Agile Methodology.

Global Agile Methodology—The process of localizing a business for a new international market in an iterative manner while managing the complexities that go along with implementing these changes, with the ultimate goal of achieving company-market fit in new markets.

Global Class Company—An organization that strives for, and achieves, global scale by balancing localization and complexity, building a culturally conscious agile team, establishing the structures and management model to support a distributed organization, and balancing company and local cultures.

Global Class Management Model (GCM Model)—A management model that allows HQ and local teams to connect and collaborate to reach company-market fit. Through a combination of consistent company culture, established trust points, effective feedback loops and two-way innovation, established processes/structures, and a foundation of global agile, companies can successfully localize for new markets and manage the complexity that comes along with reaching global scale.

Global Class Mindset—The mindset adopted by Global Class Companies having the vision to *think* global from day one, leveraging a decentralized talent strategy, positioning HQ to be an enabler and supporter of local markets, and implementing a strategy that finds the local way of running a business. This is in direct opposition to the Legacy Mindset.

Global Class Team Building Framework—A hiring and team-building model Global Class Companies use to ensure they have the right team to succeed in entering and scaling in new markets. The skill-set categories include: the interpreneurial mindset, local market knowledge, company knowledge, and leadership skills for distributed organizations.

Global Growth Playbook—A resource that maps out all the steps required for successful launch and growth in new markets, capturing best practices for market entry and market growth.

Go-to-Market Strategy—The customer-facing elements of a company's business model that may need to be adapted to find traction and scale in a local market (Sales, Product, and Marketing Premiums fall under this category).

Headquarters (HQ)—The distributed enablement and support mechanisms and teams whose purpose is to enable the company's presence in local markets as the stewards of the company goals and culture and facilitators of decision-making.

Initial Market—The first market where a company validates its operational strategy, go-to-market strategy, and scalability. This may or may not be the "home" country where the company was originally founded.

Internationalization—The process whereby teams design centralized processes/ elements of the company's model that can be customized (or localized) to fit individual markets, instead of separate elements for each individual market.

Interpreneur—Someone who has the global mindset to interpret culture, the agile mindset to resiliently overcome obstacles with creative solutions, and the company mindset to sustain support and buy-in to get things done, taking a vision (theirs or someone else's) and bringing it to the world.

Job Function Pendulum—The shifting nature of functional responsibilities within an organization that is expanding to international markets whereby responsibilities shift between being localized, regionalized, or centralized, depending on the business function, available financial resources, human resources, and product or industry type.

Linked Markets—When an operational or go-to-market strategy change made to gain traction in one market can be reused when entering another market, thereby limiting the additional complexity incurred in the new market, building momentum and scale.

Local Business Culture—The shared beliefs, behaviors, and norms of a specific country or region that affect how business is conducted and how the local team operates in a professional environment. Local business culture is one of a number of subsets within local market culture.

Local Market—An international market outside of a company's initial market that they expand to and seek to scale in.

Local Market Culture—The shared beliefs, behaviors, and norms of the local population in a specific target country or region.

Local Market Team—The team that manages operations and go-to-market activities within an international market, often in-country.

Localization—The process of adapting an element of a company's operations or go-to-market strategies with the purpose of achieving company-market fit in a new market.

Localization Discovery—A process undertaken during step one of the global agile process where teams are focused on uncovering the nuances of the market by visiting in-person and speaking with key stakeholders, scoping out the likely localizations needed to gain traction.

Localization Premium—The amount of complexity incurred in the process of localizing a company's operating and go-to-market strategies to achieve company-market fit in a new market. These premiums fall into six categories: Sales, Marketing, Product, Infrastructure, Administrative, and Organizational Premiums.

Localization Premium Analysis (LPA)—The main tool Global Class Companies use to complete step two of the global agile process, which maps out, tracks, and manages the complexities (localization premiums) that come along with entering and scaling within new global markets and is the main facilitator to reach company-market fit.

Localization Resource Team (LRT)—A cross-functional team, ideally with representation from various job functions and departments, that creates momentum by removing obstacles for local teams, sharing/implementing best practices, serving as a conduit between local teams to HQ, and actively managing the complexities that come from localization.

Market Entry—The first stage of global expansion, which includes discovery and preparation, in the new market up until product-market fit is achieved where the team validates the localized go-to-market and operational strategies in-country, proving the business model is profitable and scalable.

Market Growth—The second stage of global expansion that is focused on building momentum and scale to build a global footprint and operate the business without creating too much complexity. During this stage, companies strive for and achieve company-market fit.

Market Maturity—The third stage of global expansion where companies focus on further penetrating an existing local market. Often during the Market Entry and Market Growth phases, the company isn't getting deep penetration or capturing the full market potential. The goal is to get a more dominant market share through further localization.

Momentum Builders—Structures and processes that support localization and scaling efforts, enabling communication, resource allocation, and complexity management. HQ creates processes and structures to facilitate localization through strategy development, implementation support, and tracking.

Operational Strategy—The back-end elements of a company's business model that may need to be adapted to properly operate the business in a local market (Administrative, Infrastructure, and Organizational Premiums fall under this category).

Product-Market Fit—The process of identifying a customer need and confirming your product or service meets that need in a scalable and profitable way.

Structures (& Processes)—The processes and organizational programs created to support growth and enabling an organization to reach global scale.

Three Pillars for Achieving Global Scale—The organizational capabilities that are the key facilitators of achieving company-market fit in individual local markets and across a global footprint. They include building the right team, managing the organization, and balancing different cultures to support global scale.

Trust Points—Relationships within a distributed organization where trust has been built, facilitating multi-directional communication and innovation.

· INDEX ·

• ABOUT THE AUTHORS •

AARON MCDANIEL is a corporate leader, entrepreneur, professional speaker, start-up advisor, and author. He is a member of the faculty at UC Berkeley's Haas School of Business, his alma mater. Aaron is a serial entrepreneur who co-founded global innovation ecosystem builder 10X Innovation Lab as well as three other ventures that were acquired. An alumnus of AT&T's flagship Leadership Development Program (LDP), he was also an AT&T Diamond Club award winner (top 1 percent of sales managers worldwide). He is the author of The Young Professional's Guide book series and has been featured in *Forbes, Inc., Entrepreneur,* and *Bloomberg Businessweek.* Aaron is a sought-after speaker whose client list includes The Ritz-Carlton, Deloitte Consulting, Wells Fargo, UnitedHealth Group, and many more.

KLAUS WEHAGE is an entrepreneur, start-up advisor, professional speaker, and author. He is commonly referred to as the "Silicon Valley Ambassador," coaching corporate executives, entrepreneurs, and government leaders. Currently, he holds advisory positions with three reputable Asian ministries. Through his former role as the Head of International Relations at Silicon Valley Forum and now as the co-founder & CEO of 10X Innovation Lab, Klaus has trained more than two thousand business leaders from more than fifty countries. Originally from Denmark, he has lived on four continents, speaks five languages, and holds degrees from Hult International Business School (MBA) and Copenhagen Business School (BSC). Klaus is a sought-after speaker and has worked strategically with the top echelon of the Silicon Valley business community, including Google, Salesforce, LinkedIn, IBM, HP, and more.

Also by Aaron McDaniel

The Young Professional's Guide to the Working World

The Young Professional's Guide to Managing